D0794603

| CISM | DATE DUE | c.4 |
|------|----------|-----|
| APR 1 3 2018 | | |
| | | |
| | | |
| | | |
| | | |
| | | |
| | | |
| | | |
| | | |
| | | |
| | | |
| | | |

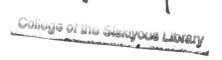
College of the Siskiyous Library

# Nature's
# Beloved Son

Bradley & Rulofson
S. F.

College of the Siskiyous Library

# Nature's Beloved Son

## REDISCOVERING
## JOHN MUIR'S
## BOTANICAL LEGACY

BONNIE J. GISEL

WITH IMAGES BY STEPHEN J. JOSEPH

FOREWORD BY DAVID RAINS WALLACE

Heyday Books ▪ Berkeley, California

College of the Siskiyous Library

Plant photography ©2008 by Stephen J. Joseph

Text ©2008 by Bonnie J. Gisel

All rights reserved. No portion of this work may be reproduced or transmitted in any form or by any means, electronic or mechanical, including photocopying and recording, or by any information storage or retrieval system, without permission in writing from Heyday Books.

Library of Congress Cataloging-in-Publication DataGisel, Bonnie Johanna, 1948-

 Nature's beloved son : rediscovering John Muir's botanical legacy / Bonnie J. Gisel and Stephen J. Joseph.

 p. cm.

 Includes bibliographical references and index.

 ISBN 978-1-59714-106-2 (hardcover : alk. paper)

 1. Muir, John, 1838-1914. 2. Naturalists—United States—Biography. 3. Conservationists—United States—Biography. 4. Botanical specimens—United States. I. Joseph, Stephen J. II. Title.

 QH31.M78.G57 2008

 580.92--dc22

2008017755

Cover: *Cypripedium montanum* Dougl., Mountain Lady's Slipper.

Frontispiece: John Muir in San Francisco, 1872. Photograph by William H. Rulofson. Courtesy of the Bancroft Library, University of California, Berkeley.

Page xi: *Epilobium obcordatum* Gray, Rock Fringe

Opposite table of contents: *Tecoma radicans* (L.) Juss, Trumpet Flower

Back cover: *Anemone narcissiflora*, Narcissus-flowered Anemone

Book Design: Jamison Design/ J. Spittler

Printed in China by Global Interprint

ORDERS, INQUIRIES, AND CORRESPONDENCE SHOULD BE ADDRESSED TO:

Heyday Books

P. O. Box 9145, Berkeley, CA 94709

(510) 549-3564, Fax (510) 549-1889

www.heydaybooks.com

FOR MORE INFORMATION ABOUT PRINTS BY STEPHEN J. JOSEPH:

www.johnmuirsbotany.com

10 9 8 7 6 5 4 3 2 1

# 2246308123
10/09

333.72092
m85gi
2008
c.4

FOR AUGUSTA & ATWOOD

AND

THE JOSEPH FAMILY

THIS PROJECT WAS MADE POSSIBLE IN PART BY
GENEROUS CONTRIBUTIONS FROM:

S. D. Bechtel, Jr. Foundation

Columbia Foundation

The Skirball Foundation

Dean Witter Foundation

THANKS ALSO TO THE FOLLOWING INDIVIDUALS:

Anonymous

Joanne Blokker

Patricia & Bob Boesch

Marilyn & Dix Boring

Robert Bransten

Janet Cobb and the California Oak Foundation

Hartley Cravens and the Malcolm Cravens Foundation

Christine & Brooks Crawford

Suzanne & David Donlon

David Elliott

Jane & David Hartley

Charlene C. Harvey

Sheila & Michael Humphreys

Guy Lampard and Aperio Group

Michael McCone

Nini McCone

Willinda & Peter McCrea

Thomas McLaughlin

Mary Louise Myers

Rosemary & Robert G. Patton

Tom White and the Harold and Alma White Memorial Fund

One impulse from a vernal wood
May teach you more than man
Of moral evil and of good
Than all the sages can.

— Wordsworth

Consider the lilies of the field how they grow
they neither toil nor spin
yet I tell you
even Solomon in all his glory
was not arrayed like one of these.

— Matthew 6:28–29

# Contents

# Foreword

## MUIR'S PLANTS
### David Rains Wallace

JOHN MUIR IS BEST KNOWN today as a wilderness advocate and mountaineer. But Muir was much too involved with the living world to be summed up in that somewhat abstract way. "He was many things: a geologist, a geographer, and a zoologist," commented Willis Linn Jepson, a scientist friend, "but he liked best to be thought a botanist." What is more basic to the living world than plants? When I first read Muir over three decades ago, it was his evocations of trees and wildflowers that most excited me, although that excitement faded through years of reading about him as a pioneer environmentalist.

This book brings the excitement back. It is a fascinating combination of the new and old. Stephen Joseph's brilliantly enhanced images of the plant specimens that Muir collected and studied would have been impossible before the digital age. Yet botany began some twenty-three hundred years ago when Theophrastus, a colleague of Aristotle, started to regard plants not only as sources of food, medicine, and magic but as interesting in themselves. He was the first western writer to ask what plants are, how they function as living beings and interact with their environment.

Those questions were central to Muir, as Bonnie Gisel shows in her eloquent account of his botanical vocation and its nineteenth-century milieu. Collecting the plants he encountered helped him to know them—to learn their names, their relationship with other plants, and their place in the wilderness ecosystems he loved. It also served as a concrete, permanent record of the places he had explored. That is why he took the trouble to carry a plant press, a bulky device for drying and preserving specimens, on his epically strenuous explorations.

*Calypso borealis* Salisb., Lady's Slipper, Hider of the North

Muir pictured his press several times in the journal of his "thousand-mile walk" to Florida in 1867. He carries it on his back as he fords a stream, and keeps it near to hand as he rests and camps. It seems a rudimentary piece of technology, two wooden grids strapped around a stack of blotting paper. In fact, as far as we know, it took almost two thousand years to develop.

Theophrastus may have had a plant collection aside from his garden at Aristotle's Athens Lyceum, but nothing remains of it. His botanical writings, *De causis plantarum* and *Historia plantarum*, lacked pictures to help readers identify the plants he described. Plant picture books, herbals, appeared in the Roman period when scribes began to write on papyrus sheets instead of scrolls, but—garbling Theophrastus with lesser writers and folklore—early herbals did little for botany. Physicians used them not to study the plants but to identify medicinal species bought from peasants. In medieval Europe, cloistered monks copied old herbals instead of drawing local plants.

Printing changed all that in the early Renaissance. Widely disseminated books resurrected Theophrastus from ancient manuscripts, encouraging scholars to venture out and study plants on their own. As they learned about living species, they commissioned artists and engravers to illustrate printed herbals, which allowed many others to learn the plants. At the same time, paper manufactured from rags and other common materials replaced parchment laboriously processed from animal skin. Light, affordable, and absorbent, paper became the basic material of the plant press and of the dried plant collection, the herbarium.

An Italian physician, Luca Ghini, is credited with pioneering the herbarium in the mid-sixteenth century. It is unclear exactly how this came about, but I have an idea. When I first saw the specimens, still so colorful over a century after their collection, so vibrantly illustrated in *Nature's Beloved Son* (one might almost say "illuminated"), they reminded me of the exquisitely hand-painted engravings in Renaissance herbals. Perhaps Ghini (or whoever influenced him—it's hard to trace innovations to their source), on looking through the new herbals, was inspired to do the reverse. Rather than hire an artist to draw plants, why not simply glue or stitch the dried plants to the paper? Of course, that would not replace the printed herbal in spreading knowledge, but it would add a precise new dimension to identification and classification.

Plant presses and herbaria caught on quickly. John Falconer, an Englishman who had visited Ghini in Pisa, "carried with him very many specimens ingeniously arranged and glued in a book" as he "traveled many lands for the study of plants." In the Age of Exploration, the plant press was among the most important scientific tools because botanical knowledge contributed more to civilization, intellectually and economically, than almost anything else.

Linnaeus carried a press to Lapland as he developed his ideas about the sexual function of flowers. (Many thought such ideas outlandish, even pornographic.) Darwin carried one around the world on the *Beagle* voyage as he had his first inklings that life has evolved. Today, the herbarium remains the basic scientific resource for identifying and classifying plants.

Muir was very conscious of working in this tradition. Early in his career, he emulated famous naturalists like Alexander von Humboldt, who had carried a press through the Amazon and Andes. Later, a famous naturalist himself, Muir contributed to botanical knowledge in his correspondence with Harvard's Asa Gray and other scientists. And although Muir's plant discoveries were less spectacular than his findings regarding glaciers in the Sierra Nevada, he added a dimension to the botanical tradition that is as important as scientific knowledge.

From Theophrastus on, botanists valued the beauty and diversity of plants, but few sought to preserve them in the wild. Muir's love of wilderness and his sense of plants as spiritual beings (a sense he evoked vividly in a story of encountering a *Calypso borealis* orchid in a lonely Canadian swamp) made him challenge anthropocentric, utilitarian assumptions that even plant-loving scientists like Darwin and Gray took for granted.

"Like other things not apparently useful to man, it has few friends," Muir wrote of poison oak, "and the blind question 'Why was it made?' goes on and on with never a guess that, first of all, it might be made for itself." He described the species as growing "harmoniously with other plants," often supporting a beautiful lily vine. (His admiration for *Rhus diversiloba* doesn't seem to have extended as far as collecting a specimen, however.)

Muir recoiled from the wanton destruction of forests and prairies even during his hard youth on the Wisconsin frontier. He tried to buy a tract of prairie from his family to preserve the wildflowers. Later, the uncontrolled logging and grazing rampant in the West largely drove him in his fight for parks and wilderness. The plants in this book are tokens of that struggle, the actual organisms that encouraged Muir to defy the destroyers.

To be sure, at a time when parks ask visitors to let native plants "live in your eye, not die in your hand," one might see irony in America's premier conservationist picking orchids and lilies. In the Renaissance, collecting for herbaria wiped out some plant populations. But Muir was no greedy rarity-grabber, and the end certainly justified the means in his case. Protecting native plants in the wild is integral to botany today. As this book vividly shows, few herbaria have more historic and aesthetic significance than John Muir's.

Missouri Botanical Garden
Herbarium

# Acknowledgments

STEPHEN JOSEPH AND I would like to thank the many individuals, institutions, and organizations who have contributed to this book. We owe them all a debt of gratitude and trust that they celebrate with us in the presentation of *Nature's Beloved Son: Rediscovering John Muir's Botanical Legacy*. Malcolm Margolin, publisher of Heyday Books, is at the top of this list. His dedication to this project has been unwavering and his enthusiasm delightful. Also, a special thank-you to Mike McCone, chairman of the Heyday board of directors, who along with Malcolm has championed this project.

The board and staff of Heyday have been amazing in their support as well. Special thank-yous to Guy Lampard, treasurer; Gayle Wattawa, acquisitions editor, who has been especially patient as we reshaped the book; Rebecca LeGates, art director, who assisted with the design and preparation of the exhibition of Muir's plant specimens at the John Muir National Historic Site; and Jeannine Gendar, editorial director.

We wish to thank the staff of the University of the Pacific, Holt-Atherton Department of Special Collections, repository of the John Muir Papers: Shan Sutton, director; Trish Richards, archivist; Michael Wurtz, archivist; and Janene Ford, former archivist. They have been of immeasurable assistance with retrieving photographs, letters, journals, books, and plant specimens. This book would not have been possible without their assistance, patience, and kindness. We owe the Hanna family a great debt for making the John Muir papers available to researchers.

The staff at the John Muir National Historic Site (JMNHS) has been dedicated to this project since its inception. A special thank-you to Glenn Fuller, former superintendent of the JMNHS. We are most grateful to David Blackburn, former chief of interpretation and

*Polypodium californicum* Kaulf., California Polypod

visitor services and curator at the JMNHS, who made available Muir's herbarium; Martha Lee, superintendent, who provided the opportunity for us to showcase Muir's herbarium in the exhibition that opened at the JMNHS in January 2006; Rick Smith; and the members of the John Muir Association for their role in organizing the opening for the exhibit.

Among the community of field botanists there is none finer and more jovial than Dean Taylor, who assisted in the classification of Muir's plant specimens and jumped for joy over the sheer beauty of the thought of Muir collecting in the High Sierra. Also a special thank-you to Barbara Ertter, former curator of Western North American flora, who made available the University and Jepson Herbaria and suggested that I include information connecting John Muir and John H. Redfield. To Richard G. Beidleman, botanist, naturalist, and ecologist, and the staff at the University and Jepson Herbaria at the University of California at Berkeley, including Brent D. Mishler, director; Andrew S. Doran, administrative curator; Ana Penny, collections management; and Kim Kersh, collections management, thank you for hosting the Muir plant specimens from the Missouri Botanical Garden, the Academy of Natural Sciences of Philadelphia, and the University of Alaska.

A delightful week was spent at the Missouri Botanical Garden (MBG) in November 2005. To Jim Solomon, curator of the herbarium at the MBG, and his staff, thank you for your expertise and kindness, and for lending John Muir's plant specimens. To Andrew Colligan, archivist at the MBG, thank you for locating information about the purchase of John H. Redfield's collection.

To James Macklin, director of collections and informatics; Emily W. Wood, senior collections associate; Walter T. Kittredge, curatorial assistant; and Lisa Ann DeCesare, head of public services and archives at the Harvard University Herbaria, thank you for sharing your expertise, for hosting visits to the herbaria, and for lending plant specimens, photographs, and letters. It was especially thoughtful to include me in your afternoon chocolate fests in fall 2004 and spring 2005. To Rusty Russell, collections manager, and Linda Hollenberg in the department of collections management in the Department of Botany at the Smithsonian Institution, thank you for hosting a visit to the collection. To Alina Freire-Fierro, collection manager, and the staff in the herbarium at the Academy of Natural Sciences of Philadelphia, and Steffi Ickert-Bond, assistant professor of botany and curator of the University of Alaska Museum Herbarium, Fairbanks, thank you for lending Muir's plant specimens.

To Peter Fraissinet, librarian at the L. H. Bailey Hortorium in the Department of Plant Biology, College of Agriculture and Life Science, at Cornell University, a special thanks for providing plant engravings for the exhibit at the JMNHS; and thank-yous to Robert Turgeon, director of graduate studies, and Robert Dirig, assistant curator, for access to the

L. H. Bailey Hortorium Library, and for providing a place to write the Alaska chapter in December 2004. Thanks to the staff and especially to Susan Snyder and David Kessler at the Bancroft Library at the University of California at Berkeley for their diligence in locating images and letters, and to Peter J. Blodgett, H. Russell Smith Foundation Curator of Western Historical Manuscripts, and the staff at the Huntington Library for their assistance.

Thanks to Chris Stein, chief of interpretation and education, Jonathan Bayless, chief curator, and Greg Stock, geologist, in Yosemite National Park for their enthusiasm and encouragement, and to Linda Eade, librarian, Yosemite Research Library, and Barbara Beroza, Yosemite National Park museum collection manager, for their assistance. Thanks to Pete Devine, educational programs director for the Yosemite Association, for including our presentation on John Muir and his life as a botanist at the Botanical Symposium held at Wawona in Yosemite National Park in October 2005. Thanks to William Swagerty, director of the John Muir Center for Environmental Studies at the University of the Pacific, for including our presentation on John Muir's herbarium in the Spring 2006 Muir Conference, "Muir in the Global Community." Thanks also to Stephen Edwards, garden director, for providing an opportunity to present a program on Muir and botany at the Wayne Roderick Lecture Series at the Tilden Regional Park Botanic Garden, in Berkeley, California, during the spring of 2007; to Tom Sargent and his staff at the Fort Baker Retreat Group, "Cavallo Point The Lodge at the Golden Gate"; to Lori Fogarty, executive director, and the dedicated staff of the Oakland Museum of California; and to Robert Lieber, director of retail, publications, and product development, Golden Gate National Parks Conservancy, Fort Mason, San Francisco.

We offer thanks to our families and friends for their continued support and love. Bonnie Gisel wishes to thank: my mother, Eleanor M. Gisel, who passed away before this book was completed, for her understanding and dedication to my research as she taped the broken spines of overused books and folded letters and articles into manila folders; my son, Nikolaus P. Gisel, who filled long days of writing and trips to herbaria with encouragement; and my Scottie dog, Atwood, for his enduring patience and his help in taking important breaks throughout each day for long walks. Stephen Joseph wishes to thank: my mother, Bunny, and my father, Howard Joseph, for fifty-four years of wonderful love and support with all of my life's projects. My father got me involved in photography, which has been my life's work. My very artistic mother gave me good taste and a sense of aesthetics. For reinforcing my self-confidence enough to tackle such projects as this book, I owe a great debt to my brother David and sister Leslie. In my home, patience is more than a virtue: my wife, Susan, and son, Julian, have endured my having a laptop as my constant companion for the past several years.

*Primula borealis* Duby, Northern Primrose

We would like to thank Jill Harcke for her support and for recording parts of the journey that we took to complete this book; Scott Cameron and Ron Knight, friends of John Muir from Canada, for their enthusiasm in discussing Muir in Canada, and for providing the Trout Map; Steve Pauly, curator of the Kimes Papers on behalf of the John Muir Association, for permission to publish the map of Dunbar, Scotland; Jim Gaines for his continued support; Susan Hanna Flynn, who provided the photograph of the Strentzel-Muir house; and Robert Engberg, who provided slides of ferns attributed to Muir. Thanks go to Bonnie Gisel's colleagues at LeConte Memorial Lodge (LML): Dave Simon, director of outings; LML committee members, especially George Pettit and Suzanne Sharrock; and volunteers and program presenters for their support as she balanced her devotion to LML with her passion for completing this book. Thanks also to Christa Frangiamore, former acquisitions editor at the University of Georgia Press, for her phone call in August 2003 that set this book in motion; to Catherine Soria, for her classroom at the Yosemite Elementary School in Yosemite National Park, where during the summer of 2005 Bonnie wrote the chapter on Muir's thousand-mile walk; and to Ronald H. Limbaugh, founding director of the John Muir Center for Environmental Studies at the University of the Pacific, to whom we will always owe a debt of gratitude for the insight and wisdom that encouraged the desire to bring forth this research.

Thanks also go out to a very caring extended family. This book would not have been possible without all of their support. Thanks go to Stephen's mentor Jack Ford for thirty-five years of meaningful advice and inspiration. For putting up with his obsessive work on this project day and night, thanks go to all of Stephen's friends, especially Greg, Bonnie, Rod, Jim, Missy, Jesse, and Mary Beth, with gratitude also to Seth, Bob, Tina, Roger, Carol, and Bob and Joan M. For artistic influence and lifestyle inspiration, thanks go to Jack Beal and Sondra Freckelton. Thanks also to the Bay Area Land Trusts, the East Bay Regional Park District, and local environmental groups and their dedicated staffs for their work and for including Stephen in their mission.

To the S. D. Bechtel, Jr. Foundation; the Skirball Foundation; the Columbia Foundation, and the Dean Witter Foundation, who provided financial support, we would like to extend a very special thank-you.

For those who have not been mentioned, who over the years extended their support, please forgive our oversight. For any and all mistakes or misinterpretations, we are solely responsible.

Lastly we would like to thank each and every place we have been in which we witnessed the beauty of the natural world. This book has been a journey across many landscapes. We owe the deepest debt of gratitude to John Muir for his pathless way that provided a map across which we sauntered.

Bonnie Johanna Gisel
YOSEMITE NATIONAL PARK

Stephen J. Joseph
PLEASANT HILL, CALIFORNIA

Sept 5/64 CW
dooryard near
Hamilton

# Introduction

## PURE AS A PLANT

A FONDNESS FOR PLANTS well suited John Muir, nature writer, preservationist, geologist, botanist. Muir's enthusiasm for botany, the scientific study of plants, began during the nineteenth century's flurry of amateur plant collecting, and as botany took on the mantle of a professional science. Botany was for him a means of making sense of the natural world, and it would significantly contribute to the value he placed on nature and wilderness. The theological framework that at the time underpinned the study of botany also appealed to Muir, and it was an opportunity for him to gain a deeper understanding of the works of the creator and to honor the creation.[1]

At the time Muir began his study of botany, the number of species of angiosperms (flowering plants with encased seeds) was estimated at fifty-six thousand. Muir seemed to intuit that there was something special about them, whether winged, feather-downed, hooked, spiked, or fruited. On a torn note he described his sensibility: "Seeds. Nature, one may fancy, amused at her own inventions. Nature's purposes seen strikingly in seeds and buds, plans of another year of thousands of years, wrapped up in them. Manner of travel, dispersal obvious and interesting, wet with dew or rain[,] sun shining through them as they shoot glad and blithesome into the welcoming sky in immortal health."[2]

Through field study and the study of the writings of explorers, naturalists, scientists, botanists, philosophers, and academicians, Muir became skilled at identifying plants and their habitats, and he developed an abiding respect for them. Through plants he gained an inordinate sense of the enormous interlinked complexity of life, writing during his first summer in the Sierra that in picking out "anything by itself, we find it hitched to everything

*Gleditsia triacanthos* L., Honey Locust

else in the universe." Were not, he asked, "all plants beautiful? or in some way useful? Would not the world suffer by the banishment of a single weed?"[3]

At heart Muir remained a botanist throughout his life, setting out to find plant friends "in all their perfection of purity and spirituality," to find the trees that waved and the flowers that bloomed, and to seek "every word of leaf and snowflake and particle of dew" in which

John Muir and Mrs. Mary A. Harriman, Pelican Bay, Klamath Falls, Oregon, 1908. Courtesy of the James Eastman Shone Collection of Muiriana, Holt-Atherton Department of Special Collections, University of the Pacific Library.

resided the beauty that he trusted. He collected plant specimens everywhere he went, stuffing them into his pockets and pressing others in his plant press. Plants also helped him to overcome the loneliness of which he often wrote: whether familiar or unknown, they were there to greet him. Sometimes he placed wildflowers between the pages of his journals, and he sent pressed plants in letters to his family, friends, and scientific colleagues. He found delight and comfort in connecting plants and people.[4]

Muir, the field botanist, concerned about plant distribution (the study of which would later be called plant ecology) and plants as soil producers and conservers, would advocate on their behalf through his writing. Conversant in the language of plants, the study of their habitats, their significant contribution to life itself, and their wonder and beauty, Muir identified with plants as civilizing agents. He believed that he should strive as should all individuals to be "brave, generous, clean as a flower...on every excursion going one's way clean and calm as a tree or a star...getting inspiration in the woods and plateaus and plains. Growing up out of natural all-devouring savagery into natural all-embracing sympathy, with eye ever open to God's beauty and love." It was to plants that he turned to breathe life into the human imagination. He would live, he wrote, "only to entice people to look at Nature's loveliness." Now, with the rediscovery and restoration of his herbarium, the plants that he collected are visible proof of Muir's desire to entice us to look at nature's irresistible, divine beauty.[5]

## FATE AND FLOWERS

From Muir's earliest experiences of flowering plants in the garden of his home in Dunbar, Scotland, he remembered them to be a perfect study in the created order of things. The familial ties that bound him to botany would be further nurtured in the setting of his new home in America. In Wisconsin, first as a young farmer and then as a student at the university, he waged his life in relation to the land and, beyond pure science, developed an appreciation for the inner beauty of plants. Through the abundance, diversity, and relation of plants to each other and to him, the study of botany was for Muir a lesson in sacred things, and flowers turned to seeds were proof of the triumph of life and hope.

Imagine Muir's delight as he stood beneath a locust tree at the University of Wisconsin to discover the harmony between it and a garden pea. Lessons in botany sent him flying to the woods and fields so that he might become better acquainted with God's plant world. Then in 1864 he traveled from the University of Wisconsin to botanize in Canada "in glorious freedom." After Muir had passed twenty-four months wading in dense swamps and working in Owen Sound at Trout's Mill, a factory engaged in the manufacture of rake and broom handles, a fire swept the mill during a fierce winter storm, and he returned to the United States in early 1866.[6]

Following a restless period of about thirteen months in Indianapolis and the near loss of his eyesight in an industrial accident, Muir, desperate at the thought of never being able to see the beauty of a flower again, set aside his study of the inventions of humanity. Anxious to travel, he revived an earlier plan for a walking journey, intent on gathering enough flowers and landscapes to last a lifetime. When he embarked on his thousand-mile walk from Louisville, Kentucky, to the Gulf of Mexico, Muir believed that he had been loosened from the ties that bound others to common affairs. In the flood of possibility he trudged southward, and the further south he walked, the stranger the plants became, crowding around him with scarce a familiar face among all the flowers.

"Fate and flowers" carried Muir to California, where he saw more plant glory than he had ever seen. Wading into the San Joaquin Valley, through a sea of golden and purple blooms five hundred miles long, he climbed the Sierra foothills in the spring of 1868 on his way to Yosemite Valley. Again a sense of freedom prevailed as he settled in among the forests and the poetry of

Jeanne C. Carr, 1876. Carte-de-Visite by Dunham & Lathrop, Oakland, California. Courtesy of the State Historical Society of Wisconsin.

Ezra S. Carr, 1857. Courtesy of the State Historical Society of Wisconsin.

glacial ice. Dr. Ezra Slocum Carr and his wife, Jeanne, who had befriended Muir in Madison, Wisconsin, when he was a student at the university, moved to California in the fall of 1868. Jeanne's presence, over the course of the next ten years, contributed significantly to the direction Muir's life would take in California. As well as traveling with Muir in the High Sierra north and east of Yosemite Valley, Mrs. Carr also sent prominent academicians, scientists, and artists to meet him. She encouraged his writing career and edited his letters for publication.[7]

While living in Yosemite Valley between 1870 and 1873, Muir studied the glacial formation and the living glaciers of the valley and published, beginning in 1871, his findings. This enlisted scientific support among eastern geologists as well as Joseph LeConte, professor of geology at the burgeoning University of California. Muir nourished the idea that glaciers provided the moraine that fed the plants of the High Sierra and Yosemite Valley, and he never forgot his roots in the study of botany. He was encouraged by the Harvard botanist Asa Gray, Gray's renowned teacher John Torrey, and the botanist and herbarium conservator at the Academy of Natural Sciences of Philadelphia, John H. Redfield, all three of whom visited Muir in Yosemite in 1872. As well as collecting plant specimens, in many instances Muir was the first to traverse canyons and mountains, studying the ecosystems through which he rambled, and providing descriptive written accounts of plant ecology, including habitat, climate, and geology.

During the winter of 1873 and until the fall of 1874, Muir resided in Oakland, where he worked on a series of articles on the Sierra for the *Overland Monthly*. Upon his return to Yosemite, he sensed that he was now a stranger, but though the Merced and Tuolumne chapter of his life was complete, he found it difficult to leave. Finally in October he walked northward along the old California-Oregon stage road to Mount Shasta and Brownsville, climbing to the top of a Douglas spruce during a storm and keeping his lofty perch for hours. It had never occurred to him until that day that trees were travelers in the ordinary sense, making what he called "many journeys, not extensive ones...but our own little journeys, away and back again, are only little more than tree-wavings."[8]

Muir returned to Oakland and months of writing, and then to San Francisco to board at the home of John Swett, a pioneer in California public education, to whom he had been introduced by Jeanne Carr. Swett urged Muir to adopt a narrative style, but Muir found it difficult if not impossible to transform his letters and journals into printed material for public consumption. As he struggled to fashion his thoughts into what he felt were half-dead words, he wrestled with the reality that he would remain for the rest of his life bound to his love of wilderness and his desire to saunter in the mountains, to the irresistible tug of friends and family, and to the endowed opportunity to share his experience of nature and his vision for her. His articles appeared in major magazines and newspapers on the West and East Coasts.

In 1879 Muir stored his herbarium in San Francisco, and he set out to explore Alaska, an irresistible journey—no matter that he had become engaged to Louie Wanda Strentzel the day prior to his departure. They were married the following year. Celebrating Alaska's noble glaciers, flora, and forest groves, Muir would, during his first three excursions to the far north, continue his work as a special correspondent for the *San Francisco Daily Evening Bulletin*, much as he had written about the Sierra Nevada from the Kings River Valley to Mount Whitney, Yosemite Valley, and Mount Shasta from 1874 until 1876, and Utah, the San Gabriel Valley, Lake Tahoe, and Nevada from 1877 until 1878. Muir's second trip to Alaska is notable for his discovery of what would be named Glacier Bay and for his excursion on Taylor Glacier with Stickeen, the little black dog. His trip with the *Corwin,* in 1881,

John Muir and John Burroughs, St. Matthew Island, Alaska, Harriman Alaska Expedition, 1899.
Photograph by Edward Curtis. Courtesy of the Missouri Botanical Garden Archives.

proved to be the most significant reconnaissance of plants Muir undertook in Alaska, where the extremes of the wealth of nature excited his imagination, deepened his loyalty to her, and resulted in his return on four occasions.

Following Muir's first three excursions to Alaska, he began to manage the Strentzel-Muir ranch in the Alhambra Valley near Martinez, California, transforming it into a commercial enterprise. A fortuitous visit Muir paid to Robert Underwood Johnson, associate editor of *The Century*, who was in San Francisco on an assignment for an article on "Gold-Hunters," resulted in an unexpected trip to Yosemite Valley and Tuolumne Meadows. Johnson later recalled that Muir, who loved the High Sierra and Yosemite Valley as a mother loves her

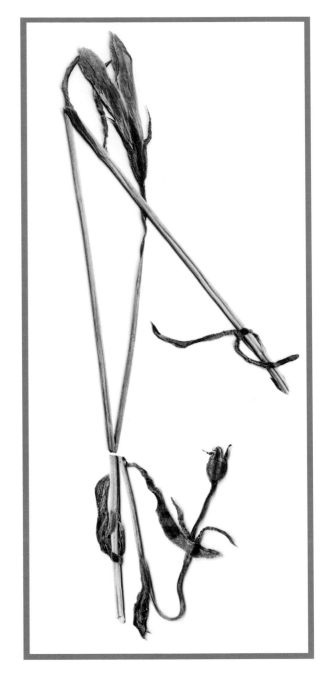

Left: *Nemophila maculata* Benth., Fivespot

Right: *Gentianopsis holopetala* (Gray) Iltis, Hiker's Gentian

child, pointed out everything living in the region, whether animal or vegetable. Their collaborative effort to create a preserve around Yosemite Valley and the Mariposa Big Tree Grove resulted in the establishment of Yosemite National Park in 1890. Muir was delighted and encouraged that the flowers would soon be back and every tree in the park would be waving its arms for joy.[9]

With the founding of the Sierra Club two years later, Muir, as its first president, became an increasingly powerful proponent for the preservation of wilderness. Later, with the inception of the Sierra Club "Outings" in 1901, intended to follow Muir's prescription to see and be in the mountains and receive their glad tidings, Muir, as often as he was able, tagged along. On a trip to Tuolumne Meadows and Hetch Hetchy, Muir, who liked best to be thought a botanist, pointed out to Willis Linn Jepson, professor of botany at

Left: *Rosa gymnocarpa* Nutt., Wood Rose

Right: John Muir (third from left), Sierra Club Outing at Porcupine Flat, Yosemite National Park, July 13, 1907. Courtesy of the John Muir Papers, Holt-Atherton Department of Special Collections, University of the Pacific Library. Copyright 1984 Muir-Hanna Trust.

the University of California at Berkeley, that there were more than two hundred Sierra Club members eagerly lined up at the commissary for dinner. While botanists, Muir assured Jepson, did not require food—and Jepson was astonished at how little Muir survived on—Muir suggested that they join the group. "The two of us took our places in line and I noticed," Jepson recalled, "that of the tasty soup and fine bread he ate as gustily as I."[10]

*The Mountains of California*, published in 1894, was the first of Muir's books to draw upon his vast knowledge of wilderness, geology, and botany. His correspondence and articles also continued to demonstrate his great concern for the preservation of wilderness. He wrote to his friend Robert Underwood Johnson that in Yosemite Valley miles of fences around hay-fields and kitchen vegetables had taken the place of wild gardens, and horses had been allowed to run loose over the unfenced portions of the valley. The trampled flora, ten times worse than when they had visited it seven years ago, required management that far exceeded what California was able to provide, and Muir called for the recession of Yosemite Valley to the federal government. The following year Muir addressed the Sierra Club public forum on National Parks and Forest Reservations. In his speech he noted that the creation of Yosemite National Park had resurrected the landscape that surrounded the valley. Flowers were once again blooming: "in all the fineness of wildness—three species of gentians, in

patches acres in extent, blue as the sky, blending their celestial color with the purple panicles of the grasses, and the daisies and bossy, rosy spikes of the varied species of orthocarpus
and bryanthus—nearly every trace of the sad sheep years of repression and destruction had
vanished."[11]

President Theodore Roosevelt's visit to Yosemite with Muir in 1903 assured that the
unification of the two parks would soon follow.

During Muir's world tour with Charles S. Sargent of the Arnold Arboretum at Harvard
in 1903 to 1904, he primarily collected plant specimens from botanical gardens. His final
voyage, in 1911 to 1912, to South America and Africa brought him face-to-face with the
giant water lily *Victoria regia*, the monkey puzzle tree, and the baobab tree. Though Muir
never lost sight of his "own special studies in geology, botany and natural history," they had
been, he thought, "seriously interrupted by the time required in the many battles necessary
to maintain and extend the reservations against the spoilers, who, with the cunning and
industry of the Devil, kept up endless war around their boundaries." For him the nation's
forests and national parks constituted a moral landscape, and there seemed to be no end to
the opposition to protect them. Though he emerged as the nation's premier preservationist, there was a personal price to pay. Muir sacrificed in part his journey into nature's wildness and the reciprocal relation he shared with the natural world. Among the fragments in
his Sierra papers there is a note that reveals Muir's true self:

> Some plants readily take on the forms and habits of society, but generally speaking soon
> return to primitive simplicity, and I too, like a weed of cultivation feel a constant tendency
> to return to primitive wildness. Well, perhaps I may yet become a proper cultivated plant,
> cease my wild wanderings, and form a so-called pillar or something in society, but if so, I
> must...learn to love what I hate and to hate what I most intensely and devoutly love.[12]

## THE IMPORTANCE OF PLANTS AND HERBARIA

Land plants are estimated to number about 300,000 species. Angiosperms, which number about 260,000 species of that total, capture the energy of sunlight primarily through
their leaves, which allows them to grow and reproduce, and provide the sustenance—the
enabling energy—for nearly all living things on Earth. Without angiosperms, life as we
know it would not exist. They have over the course of one hundred million years trans-
formed the living world.[13]

Plants, and flowering plants in particular, continue to arouse our curiosity, imagination,
and passion, and our sense of beauty. While the plants in an herbarium (or *hortus siccus,*
dried garden) have lost their color and look different from live plants, they create a beauty
all their own. Herbaria also provide a glimpse into the past, and in one location permit the

examination of flora from around the world. Making possible the simultaneous study of neighboring species and those from different localities, and species of different ages and in different stages of growth, herbaria allow us to glean from fields of wildflowers, forests of conifers, and subalpine hanging gardens a better understanding of issues as complex as biodiversity, genetics, pharmaceuticals, land management, endangered species, extinction, and climate change.[14]

The delicate nature of plant specimens requires that herbaria remain accessible to botanists and historians; however, digital photography and the creation of virtual herbaria generate opportunities to expand plant enthusiasts' access to collections. For many of us, Latin binomial plant names will always remain something of a mystery, and using keys and guides will never quite help us to identify a particular plant—still, there is nothing more beautiful than a flower, and virtual access to plant specimens tucked away in herbaria will enhance our ability to study and appreciate them. Renewed interest in plants and their habitats, botanical gardens, home gardens and landscaping, the study of botany and the science of ecology, and herbaria create opportunities for us to reevaluate the ways in which we may be engaged and assist through the lives, wonder, and beauty of plants, in preserving and conserving life on Earth. Life, after all, rests upon a petal and within a seed.[15]

John H. Redfield Herbarium Label, 1875. University and Jepson Herbaria UC87725. Courtesy of the University and Jepson Herbaria, University of California, Berkeley.

Botanist John H. Redfield, founder and conservator of the herbarium at the Academy of Natural Sciences of Philadelphia, printed labels to designate both plants and ferns—*Plantae Americae Septentrionalis* (North American Plants) and *Filices Americae Septentrionalis* (North American Ferns), the word for "north" derived from *septentriones*, the seven stars of Ursa Major. Redfield's labels support evidence that the majority of the plant specimens Muir sent to Redfield were sold by the Academy of Natural Sciences to the Missouri Botanical Garden, with some making their way to the Harvard University Herbaria and the University and Jepson Herbaria.

## AN EXCEPTIONAL SOMETHING INSPIRING

Reaching for the beauty Muir saw in plants and the joy and friendship he found among them, we must see that for him every flower was a beacon of hope—immortality rested, for Muir, in plant seeds. The grasses and wildflowers in a handpicked bouquet that made their way no further than his personal collection were as important to him as the specimens that he directed to universities, botanical gardens, and museums. There was, for Muir, within the kingdom of plants the science of beauty and the art of discovery. The plants he found in fields, meadows, mountains, and along streams and rivers revealed individual purpose, concord, and interconnectedness, woven in a web of life that glorified the work of the creator.

There was also the science of botany that spoke of the importance of discovery, collegiality, knowledge, growth, and mutability. There were family, friends, and colleagues drawn together around and by plants, no matter the distance. And faith, love, truth, and trust ignited for Muir in the lives of plants and in his relation to them. Somehow Muir found an exceptional something inspiring in plants, a glimpse of divine nature, of life expanding, and a sense of peace that lingered throughout his lifetime and still longer.

The rediscovery and exploration of John Muir's herbarium specimens engages us in what he saw, enables us to see what he touched, and revel in what he loved. Held in his hands, carried in his pockets, preserved for all time, the plants collected by Muir draw us closer to the world that he knew, where we find the purity of which he spoke and the God-given grace and sympathy in which he believed. Here, then, is Muir's gift to us, preserved in his eternal fondness for plants.

EDITOR'S NOTE: *In all cases the names Muir attributed to plant specimens have been retained in this publication. Names enclosed in brackets have been added for purposes of clarification.*

Top: *Elymus canadensis* L., Canada Wild Rye

Bottom: John Muir, August 1902. Courtesy of the John Muir Papers, Holt-Atherton Department of Special Collections, University of the Pacific Library. Copyright 1984 Muir-Hanna Trust.

# One

## FROM SCOTLAND TO WISCONSIN
### In the Fullness of Nature's Glad Wildness

Viola Canadensis
Violaceae

IN THE YARD OF THE MUIR FAMILY'S HOME on High Street in Dunbar, Scotland, stood three elm trees and a long, narrow, high-walled garden banked with flowers and boxwood hedges. According to their son John, Daniel and Ann Gilrye Muir made the garden "as much like Eden as possible." Daniel delighted in flowers as a joyful measure of God's work, and the garden was a source of family pride. For John it was a place that was sacred and priceless, and it was in the family garden that he first discovered botany. He and his siblings were each given "a little bit of ground for our very own in which we planted what we best liked, wondering how the hard dry seeds could change into soft leaves and flowers and find their way out to the light; and, to see how they were coming on, we used to dig up the larger ones, such as peas and beans, every day."[1]

The peaceful presence of plants drew kindred associations for John throughout his life: "Some of my grandfathers must have been born on a muirland, for there is heather in me, and tinctures of bog juices, that send me to *Cassiope,* and, oozing through all my veins, impel me unhaltingly through endless glacier meadows, seemingly the deeper and danker the better." This love for plants was the only nurturing ballast John received from his father, who otherwise permitted nothing of the elements of the earthly realm to penetrate the souls of his family. But he did not offer the garden as a source of unmitigated joy: wielding punishment as a physical force to keep John and his brother David focused on Bible studies, schoolwork, and away from dangerous influence, Daniel would lock them in the garden. In Muir's autobiographical notes he recalled that his "natural craving for the wilderness went on unceasingly....proof against all preaching and punishment, however solemn and serene," and he and his brother often pulled themselves over the garden wall and played along the

*Viola canadensis* L., Canadian White Violet

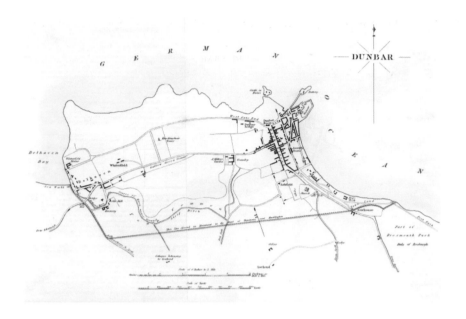

Top: Map of Dunbar, Scotland. Kimes Collection of John Muir Papers and Memorabilia. Courtesy of the John Muir Association.

Bottom: Ann G. Muir, John's mother, carried from Scotland to Wisconsin a brown leather wallet stuffed with flower seeds, and there were more wrapped in bundles and bags—reminders of the much loved garden in Dunbar—to plant along with lilacs around the pine-framed house at Fountain Lake in central southeastern Wisconsin.

rocky shore of Belhaven Bay and in the countryside's tall meadow grass out over the Lothian roads. In what he called "the fullness of Nature's glad wildness," John was free, and even at so early an age he chose to wander in the natural world.[2]

Urged on by spiritual fervor and the hope of religious freedom, Daniel Muir immigrated to America in the spring of 1849 to join the Disciples of Christ. Initially three Muir children accompanied him to south-central Wisconsin: Sarah, John, and David. Ann G. Muir and the remaining children, Margaret, Daniel, and the twins, Mary and Annie, would arrive in fall. The youngest, Joanna, was born in Wisconsin. In the township of Buffalo in Marquette County, near Portage and the Fox River, the Muir family settled to farm on one hundred and sixty acres of open woodland "overlooking a flowery glacier meadow and a lake rimmed with white waterlilies," purple swamp thistle, and cattail rush. The region was known as the District of the Sands, an unsettled landscape of wetlands, lakes, and prairies, and it was a poor place for a farm. Initially, a log shanty served as shelter, and the family built a two-story, eight-room, white pine-framed house. Eventually a group of simple farm buildings surrounded the house and another quarter-section of land to the northeast was acquired, increasing Fountain Lake Farm to three hundred and twenty acres. Daniel Muir barred domestic adornment at Fountain Lake Farm much as he had in Dunbar. The exception was the flowers that were brought as seeds from Scotland and planted along with lilacs around the house.[3]

Plashed "into pure wildness," John and his brother Daniel found everything "new and pure in the very prime of the spring when Nature's pulses were beating highest and mysteriously keeping time with our own! Young hearts, young leaves, flowers, animals, the winds and the streams and the sparkling lake, all wildly, gladly rejoicing together." In exploring the boggy mead-

"The Bur-oak Shanty. Wisconsin our first American home." Sketch by John Muir, c. 1849. Courtesy of the John Muir Papers, Holt-Atherton Department of Special Collections, University of the Pacific Library. Copyright 1984 Muir-Hanna Trust.

Muir family home at "Fountain Lake," Township of Buffalo, Marquette County, Wisconsin. Sketch by John Muir, c. 1863. Courtesy of the John Muir Papers, Holt-Atherton Department of Special Collections, University of the Pacific Library. Copyright 1984 Muir-Hanna Trust.

ows John found flowers that reminded him of Scotland, and he greeted them as friends: "Oh, you bonnie muggings! How did ye come sae far frae home?" According to Muir, every object in nature was interesting and "excited endless wonder and admiration….the great variety of soil supported a varied vegetation….fine meadows and marshes with their corresponding plants and animals." John and his mother often shared a common joy in walking in the shiny yellow marsh marigolds, the deep purple violets, and the yellow buttercups in the woods and meadows near the farm.[4]

Daniel Muir intended to see the farm pay, and the rigor of his demands and John's own sense of pride drove John to excel at farm tasks. But occasionally, in the evenings and on Sundays, John and his brothers drifted about on Fountain Lake in a boat that he built from pine boards. One of the small glacier lakes that adorned the Wisconsin landscape, Fountain Lake was surrounded by "low finely-modeled hills dotted with oak and hickory, and meadows full of grasses and sedges and many beautiful orchids and ferns":

> First there is a zone of green, shining rushes, and just beyond the rushes a zone of white and orange water-lilies fifty or sixty feet wide forming a magnificent border. On bright days, when the lake was rippled by a breeze, the lilies and sun-spangles danced together in radiant beauty…We took Christ's advice and devoutly "considered the lilies"—how they grow up in beauty out of grey lime mud, and ride gloriously among the breezy sun-spangles. On our way home we gathered grand bouquets of them…No flower was hailed with greater wonder and admiration by the European settlers…than this water-lily (*Nymphaea odorata*). It is a magnificent plant, queen of the inland waters, pure white, three or four inches in diameter, the most beautiful, sumptuous and deliciously fragrant of all our Wisconsin flowers.[5]

The oak openings, glacial lakes, springs, ponds, woods, and prairies left an indelible impression upon John. The pasque flower (*Anemone nuttalliana*) was "the very first to appear in the spring":

> A hopeful multitude of large hairy, silky buds about as thick as one's thumb came to light, pushing up…and before these buds were fairly free from the ground they opened wide and displayed purple blossoms about two inches in diameter. Instead of remaining in the ground waiting for warm weather and companions, this admirable plant seemed to be in haste to rise and cheer the desolate landscape.[6]

There was the *Cypripedium* (the lady's slipper orchid): "Several species grew in our meadow and on shady hillsides—yellow, rose-coloured and some nearly white…They caught the eye of all the European settlers and made them gaze and wonder like children." Many other plants grew in the meadow: "The beautiful Turk's turban (*Lilium superbum*) growing on stream-banks was rare…but the orange lily grew in abundance on dry ground beneath the bur-oaks...The butterfly-weed, with its brilliant scarlet flowers, attracted flocks of but-terflies and made fine masses of colour." In summer, strawberries "grew in rich beds beneath the meadow grasses and sedges." The Muirs also found, in bogs and marshes around the farm and along the Fox River, dewberries, cranberries, and huckleberries. Around the mar-gin of the meadow, ferns unfurled and fluttered their fronds—marsh fern (*Aspidium thelyp-teris*), interrupted fern (*Osmunda claytoniana*), royal fern (*O. regalis*), cinnamon fern (*O. cin-namomea*), sensitive fern (*Onoclea sensibilis*), ostrich fern [*Matteuccia struthiopteris*], and *Woodsia*. Muir remained drawn to archetypal pteridophytes throughout his life. His herbarium collec-tion included a profusion of ferns that he tucked in books or between papers pressed for personal study or sent to herbaria.[7]

For eight years the Muir family remained at Fountain Lake, and then they purchased a half-section of wild land about four miles to the southeast of the farm, more fertile than the original homestead, which had been exhausted under the intensive growing of winter wheat. John, now seventeen, walked from Fountain Lake to Hickory Hill for two growing seasons to work on the new farm until a T-shaped, two-story, framed house was built. He recalled that there was always something to do. With what little time he had to spare, he studied math-ematics, reviewed grammar, borrowed books from neighbors, and plunged into literature, poetry, history, and natural history. Young, impressionable, and an avid reader, Muir took up the study of Thomas Dick's *The Christian Philosopher*. Dick, a popular Scottish writer of scien-tific, philosophical, and theological works, intended that his book complement the revelation of the Bible. Christians, he believed, could examine the attributes of God by looking at nature and by studying science: "the works and ways of God" that "induce a spirit of piety and pro-found humility." The tenets of Dick's pragmatic theology would be important to Muir's study of botany, in which exploration, knowledge, and love of the natural world were expressions of fellowship and stewardship, and moral acts. Muir would easily have fastened his soul to the world described by Dick, the abundance of vegetable life, the predesigned relation between plant and animal, and the endless possibility of plants yet to be discovered.[8]

Muir also immersed himself in the travel narrative of Alexander von Humboldt, by far the western world's most celebrated and popular natural historian and explorer until Charles Darwin came along and in 1859, the year Humboldt died, published *On the Origin of Species by Means of Natural Selection*. That Muir's mother knew who Humboldt was is indica-tive of his fame. His name was a household word in the United Kingdom and his renown traveled across the Atlantic as well; in America his works were widely read. Humboldt wanted to know "the eternal ties which link the phenomena of life" and to study the great harmony of nature. To find the answers, he traveled constantly. Combining his love of travel, flair for danger, passion for discovery, and belief that the richness of one's life depended on what one was able to see, Humboldt slogged through unmapped jungles and over some of the tallest mountains in the world, traced the course of the Orinoco River in native canoes, climbed the volcano Chimborazo, reaching an altitude of over 9,000 feet, and collected plants. In 1804 he returned to Europe from the first extensive scientific exploration of the Andes and the Amazon with over sixty thousand plant specimens. The task of natural history, according to Humboldt, was to achieve through observation "the hidden activities of forces and powers operating in the sanctuaries of nature."[9]

Humboldt's journey to the equinoctial regions was brimming with adventure, and Muir was not alone in his desire to be like Humboldt. Natural historians and scientists including Charles Darwin, Louis Agassiz, Josiah D. Whitney, William H. Brewer, and Clarence King, as well as the artist Frederic Edwin Church, considered themselves disciples. For Muir, Humboldt was a powerful force driven by the spirit of exploration as much as by his love of nature and his ability to untangle the mysteries hidden in nature's bounty. Reverent of nature as well as courageous enough to chase his dream, Humboldt discarded doubt and convention. Though other influences would come into play as Muir formulated his ideas about the connectedness between all things in the natural world, Humboldt championed a way of seeing the natural world that cut through what appeared to be the dissimilarities among phenomena in order to focus instead on the underlying unity of all nature, what he called "la physique générale."[10]

Muir's mother encouraged the idea that he might travel like Humboldt; it was she who gave him permission to leave. His mind enthusiastically embraced the natural world and he was eager to learn about what lay beyond the farm. There would be the wealth of the natural world to study, dependent upon what he was able to see, engaged by what was quickly becoming his lifelong commitment to learn. The reflection of nature would be pressed by his senses upon his ideas and feelings.

While still at Hickory Hill, Muir often retreated to the stone-walled cellar in the early hours of the morning. Too cold to read, by candlelight he carved inventions from wood: at first a four-foot-long model of a self-setting sawmill, out of shagbark hickory, and then "water-wheels, curious doorlocks and latches, thermometers, hygrometers, pyrometers, clocks, a barometer, an automatic contrivance for feeding the horses...a lamp-lighter and fire-lighter, an early-or-late-rising machine, and so forth." He would carry the last of these, an alarm clock designed to tip his bed and set him on the floor, to the Wisconsin State Agricultural Society's Tenth Annual Fair, along with other clocks and a thermometer made from an old washboard. With towns south of Portage turning to manufacturing, he hoped to apply his art of invention to work in a machine shop, though he admitted that machines did not satisfy his hunger for knowledge and peace. On moonlit evenings he walked out under a great oak and stared up into the sky: "I roved among the planets and thought."[11]

## EYES NEVER CLOSED ON THE PLANT GLORY I HAD SEEN

In the autumn of 1860, Muir arrived at what he called a world of "new everythings," the Wisconsin State Agricultural Society's annual fair. Following the receipt of a diploma and an award of five dollars for his two clocks, Muir left Madison for Prairie du Chien in the company of fellow inventor Norman Wiard and his twenty-eight-foot steam-powered iceboat, the *Lady Franklin*. Muir remained at Prairie du Chien only three months, receiving lodging in exchange for chores at the Mondell House. It was here that he met Emily Ordelia Pelton, the niece of the proprietor, with whom he maintained a lifelong friendship. In January Muir boarded a train and returned to Madison, where, following the sale of several early-rising bedsteads and a series of odd jobs, he discovered that he could board at the university for a dollar a week and enrolled in the scientific course that began in early February of the 1860-61 academic year.[12]

From his dormitory room on the first floor of North Hall, Muir looked out upon Lake Mendota, where the thrushes whistled to him "just as they do on the black or burr oaks at Hickory," and he always kept the window open so he could hear them. He installed his early-rising machine, clocks, and a "loafer's chair" fitted with an old horse pistol loaded with a blank charge. He built a desk that would, in synch with the clock, move textbooks to the front and open them at the proper page, and he purchased a set of scientific instruments. His room took on the appearance of a showplace fitted with geological speci-

Postcard of the University of Wisconsin, Madison, c. 1861–1865. John Muir lived in North Hall, the building at the extreme right. Courtesy of the James Eastman Shone Collection of Muiriana, Holt-Atherton Department of Special Collections, University of the Pacific Library.

mens, plants, leaves, and pressed flowers, some received from his family and Emily Pelton. In a playful letter to his sisters Mary, Anna, and Joanna, he described his surroundings:

I've got a fine posy at my nose here in an old ink bottle. And I've got a peppermint plant and a young bramble in an old glass bottle and on the shelf, (the topmost one) stands my stew pan full of brambles 2 or 3 feet long and slips of gooseberry bushes and wild plum and I don't know all what, and further along you may see my tin cup in the same business, they keep fresh a long time in water.[13]

Classes in geology and botany with Dr. Ezra Slocum Carr, professor of natural science and chemistry, were offered outdoors. Possessing intellectual qualities and religious and scientific values familiar to Muir from the work of Dick and Humboldt, Carr equated the love of nature with the love of God, and he took his students to study in the fields and forests that surrounded Madison. He called them "Nature's basement rooms," where "the foundations of the earth were laid," and he instructed his students in the empirical art of observing the landscape for information about its formation. According to Muir, Carr "first laid before me the great book of Nature," teaching the processes of vegetable life, the relation between plants, and the uses of plants. It was, however, fellow student Milton S. Griswold who introduced Muir to the informal study of botany:[14]

> I was joined by Mr. Griswold, who reached up and plucked a flower from a branch of the Locust which overhung the steps, and handing it to me, he said: "Muir, do you know what family the Locust belongs to?"
>
> I said: "No, I don't know anything about botany."
> He said: "Well, what is it like?"
> "...the flower looks like the flower of the bean or pea."
> He said:... "it belongs to the bean and pea family."
> "But how can that be, when the bean and pea is usually a weak climbing herb, and this Locust is a large hard wood thorny tree?"[15]

Griswold pointed out the arrangement of the locust petals, stamens, and pistils, the seeds formed into a pod or legume like those of a pea, and the leaves composed of several leaflets that even "tasted like the leaf of the pea." He concluded:

> Now, surely you cannot imagine that all these similar characters are mere coincidences. Do they not rather go to show that the Creator in making the pea vine and locust tree had the same idea in mind, and that plants are not classified arbitrarily? Man has nothing to do with their classification. Nature has attended to all that, giving essential unity with boundless variety, so that the botanist has only to examine plants to learn the harmony of their relations.[16]

Muir's first lesson in botany "sent [him] to the woods and fields to make acquaintance with God's plant world." In less than a week he had a copy of Alphonso Wood's *Class-Book of Botany*. Published in 1845, it was the product of a graduate of Dartmouth College who taught Latin, natural history, and botany at Kimball Union Academy in Hanover, New Hampshire. Wood stimulated the study of field botany among students and amateurs by providing a means for rapid identification with analytical tables known as "keys," enabling the identification of native plants by quick, easy methods. The reasonably priced *Class-Book of Botany* was a vast pedagogical improvement over existing options and was accepted widely among

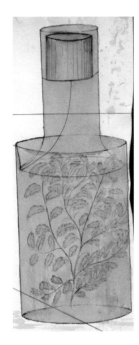

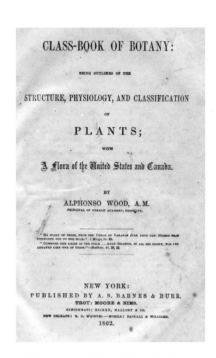

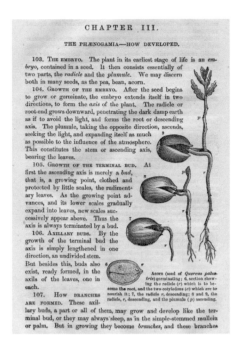

Left: "Plant in Glass, University of Wisconsin." Sketch by John Muir, c. 1861. Courtesy of the John Muir Papers, Holt-Atherton Department of Special Collections, University of the Pacific Library. Copyright 1984 Muir-Hanna Trust.

An apparatus for registering the growth of an ascending stem of a Madeira vine [*Boussingaultia*] during each of the twenty-four hours. A fine needle was threaded with a long hair and, when attached to the plant, made the record on a paper disc marked to indicate minute spaces.

Center: Title page from John Muir's copy of Alphonso Wood's *Class-Book of Botany: Being Outlines of the Structure, Physiology, and Classification of Plants; with a Flora of the United States and Canada*, published by A. S. Barnes & Burr in 1862. John Muir's Personal Library, Holt-Atherton Department of Special Collections, University of the Pacific Library.

Right: From the *Class-Book of Botany*. Courtesy of Bonnie Johanna Gisel.

teaching academies. Wood widened the scope of the text to include the growing frontier of America with each new printing, personally traveling to Ohio, the southern states, and the Pacific Coast. Remaining in print into its fiftieth edition and purchased by hundreds of thousands of students, including Griswold and Muir, Wood's *Botany* was Muir's mainstay as he reached to classify plants and understand their distribution.[17]

Armed with Wood's book, Muir and Griswold botanized around the lakes, marshes, and woods of Madison. Muir wrote that his eyes were opened to the inner beauty of plants "revealing glorious traces of the thoughts of God, and leading on and on into the infinite cosmos." He "wandered away at every opportunity, making long excursions...gathering specimens and keeping them fresh in a bucket in my room to study at night after my regular class tasks were learned; for my eyes never closed on the plant glory I had seen." Muir claimed that Griswold's lessons in botany "influenced all my after life."[18]

Jeanne Carr, the wife of Dr. Ezra Slocum Carr, was an enthusiastic plant seeker as well. She had earlier met Muir when she inspected his inventions at the Wisconsin State Agricultural Society's annual fair, and following Muir's enrollment at the university she and her children visited him at North Hall. Attracted to botany as a girl, by the age of nine she had assembled a large herbarium that included a lady's slipper orchid (*Cypripedium arietinum*). It would be lady's slipper orchids that entwined the friendship she and Muir would share over the years, and it was this friendship upon which Muir would grow to depend for encouragement, nurture, sympathy, and understanding.

*Solidago gigantea* Ait., Giant Goldenrod

As a wife and mother, Jeanne Carr was given to what she called the "petty nothings of daily life." Nonetheless she developed a network of social and intellectual connections both influential and promising. This network included Ralph Waldo Emerson, to whom she introduced Muir in 1871. While living in Madison she advanced her study of horticulture and published two articles on the cultivation of annuals and roses in *The Wisconsin Farmer*. Her love for plants was fertile ground for friendship, and her thinking, a consortium of faith and science and a nature-nourished Christianity that she freely shared with Muir, had a profound effect on his life and his writing. She was quick to invite Muir to the Carr home on Gilman Street, to tutor her four sons and study in the library and walk in the garden. She recognized him as one well principled in nature and virtuous in character—a pure mind with unsophisticated manners. The Carrs introduced Muir

Overleaf: Plant specimens, attributed to John Muir, preserved in two glassine envelopes and annexed in John Muir's copy of Alphonso Wood's *Class-Book of Botany*. John Muir's Personal Library, Holt-Atherton Department of Special Collections, University of the Pacific Library.

to the pioneer field botanist and forest preservationist Increase Allen Lapham, who served as a link between Asa Gray at Harvard and the regional botanists in Wisconsin. Lapham was famous for tramping about Wisconsin with a huge wooden collecting box hanging at his side. His selfless determination to serve as an active scientist regardless of limited financial gain would have impressed Muir, as would his understanding of forest conservation.[19]

During summers Muir left Madison and returned to Fountain Lake Farm, which was now owned by his sister Sarah and her husband, David Galloway, to help with farmwork and to collect plants. He often sat up until after midnight, analyzing and classifying the plants he kept in fresh water, and soon was familiar with the principal flowering plants of the region. The sublime beauty that Muir attributed to all plants and to the study of botany ripened his faith and provided lessons that led to the preservation ideals he would practice later in life. In his earliest extant commonplace notebook, dated 1863, Muir described the appearance of wildflowers in relation to the seasonal cycle of Wisconsin prairies and oak openings, drawing from his observation of the grasses and sedges, the variation in oak, and the effects of fire:

> We admire the hard strong oak that for ages has spoken to every wind of the hill[,] and the grand osmunda in his glory on the watered hollows[,] and the violet that does not see the sky[,] and those hardy flowers (solidago) [goldenrod] of the fall that keep up heart and continue to bloom when all beside is dying in sad autumn mornings[,] which make summers long and bloom as they can among broken fading friends and the last departing sounds and foremost frosts of winter[,] but all the great plants and the leaves and the delicate and beautiful nor all the fullest unbounded summer glory will make us forget the broad lovely flowers on the burned black naked hillsides.[20]

Upon completing what would be his final term at the university, in 1863, and after presenting a lecture on the properties of heat, Muir and two colleagues, M. M. Rice and James A. Blake, each of them carrying a plant press—a device used to press specimens between sheets of absorbent paper—departed on a botanical excursion down the Wisconsin River Valley and into Iowa. In the recess of the bluffs near MacGregor, the trio discovered "a romantic glen down which a little stream sought a path, turning the mosses to stone as it went, and watering many interesting flowers...the first specimen of Desmodium [tick clover]...and several beautiful Labiatae [mint]." Muir confessed that the miles on the map looked smoother and shorter than they actually were, and his companions, hungry and weary from suffering through nights made restless by swarms of mosquitoes, soon abandoned him. Near Madison, heavily laden with plants, Muir stopped to look back upon the university: "This was my real leave-taking of my alma mater, and the thought that those happy, eventful days were ended brought tears to my eyes. I turned away."[21]

Muir returned to Fountain Lake and remained there throughout the autumn and winter: "In my walks to and from field work and in occasional rambles I searched every inch of ground for botanical specimens." With no intention of returning to the university, "leaving the Wisconsin University for the University of the Wilderness," he carried with him not "the slightest thought of ever making myself known or writing," but simply the urge "to satisfy a hunger for natural history and geology and botany, my principal studies."[22]

# Two

## CANADA AND INDIANAPOLIS

### To Botanize in Glorious Freedom

*Calla palustris* L., Wild Calla

*Asarum canadense* L., Wild Ginger

*Dirca palustris* L., Wicopy

*Clintonia borealis* Raf., Northern Clintonia

*Botrychium virginicum* Willd., Rattlesnake Fern

*Cirsium lanceolatum* (L.) Scop., Common Thistle

Above: *Adiantum pedatum* L., Maidenhair Fern

Right: *Vicia sativa* L., Spring Vetch

*Anemone pennsylvanica* L., Pennsylvania Anemone

*Antennaria margaritacea* (L.) Sweet., Pearly Everlasting

Thimble Berry
Black Raspberry
Rubus occidentalis
Rosaceae

Aug 8th/24
Fence corner
C.R.

Above: *Fraxinus americana* L., White Ash

Left: *Rubus occidentalis* L., Black Raspberry

Twin Flower
Linnea borealis
Caprifoliaceae

*Linnaea borealis* L., Twin Flower

*Phlox subulata* L., Moss Pink

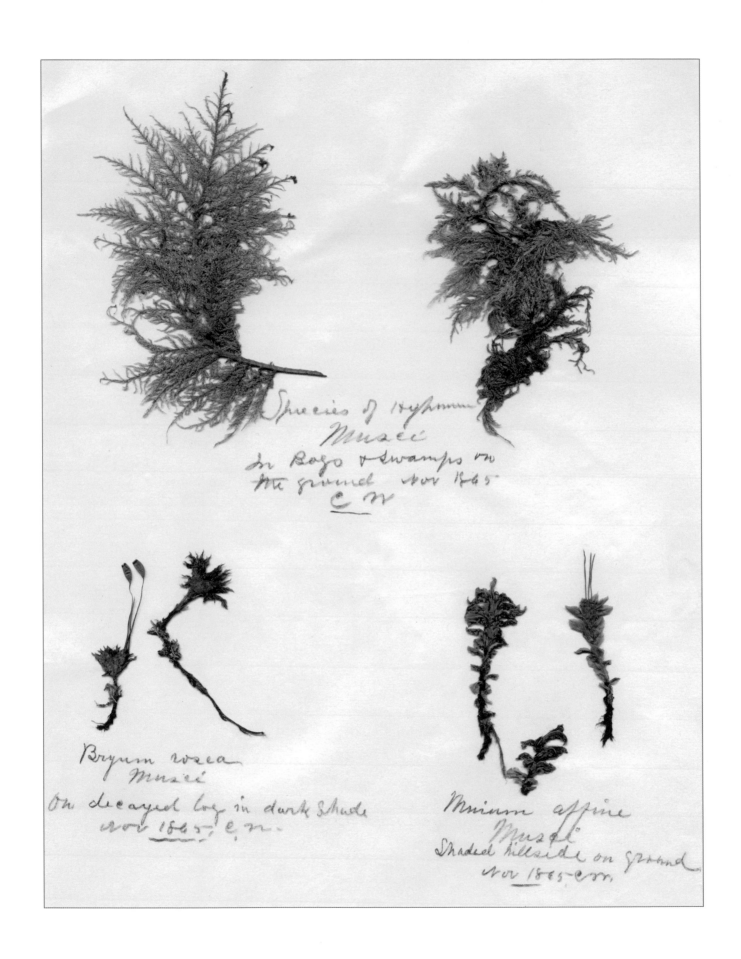

Species of Hypnum
Musci
In Bogs & swamps on
the ground Nov 1865
C. N.

Bryum roseum
Musci
On decayed log in dark Shade
Nov 1865, C. N.

Mnium affine
Musci
Shaded hillside on ground
Nov 1865, C. N.

Above: Thirteen specimens of Musci
Overleaf: [*Carex platyphylla* Carey], [Silver Sedge]

*Dicentra spectabilis* (L.) Lem., Bleeding Heart

Above: *Catalpa bignonioides* Walt., Indian Bean

Right: *Dactyloctenium egypticum* Willd., Egyptian Grass

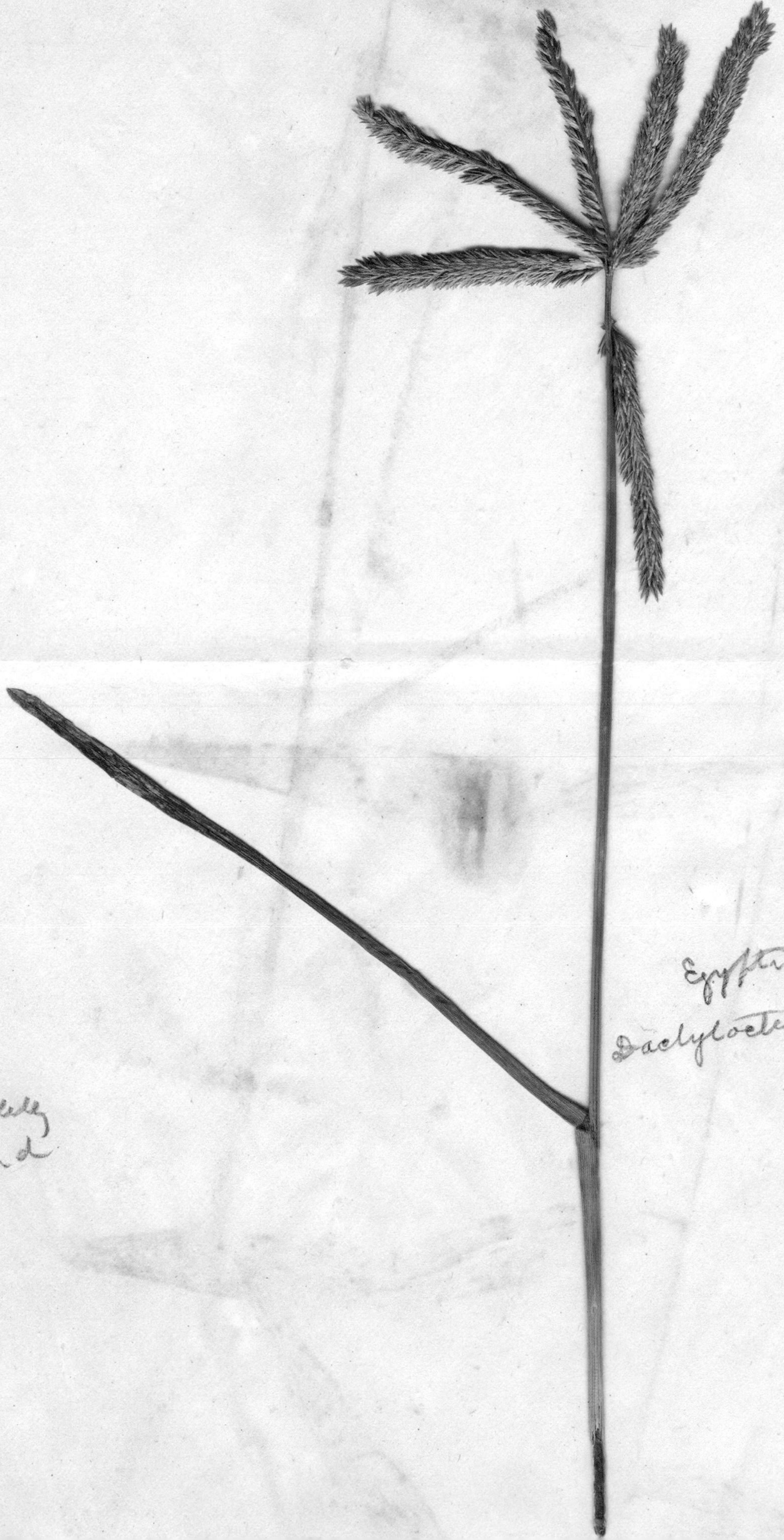

Egyptian Grass
Dactyloctenium Aegyptieum
Gram;

July 1895
gared Ind

*Roadside July 66*
*Md.*

*Solanum Carolinense*
*Solanaceae*

*Solanum carolinense* L., Horse Nettle

*Tecoma radicans* (L.) Juss., Trumpet Flower

*Tradescantia pilosa* Lehm., Spiderwort

[*Liriodendron tulipifera* L.], [Tulip Tree]

*Luzula campestris* (L.) DC., Field Rush

*Jeffersonia diphylla* (L.) Pers., Twin Leaf

WITH MANY YOUNG MEN from the township in which the Muir family resided going off to the Civil War, John Muir was certain that he would not escape his number being drawn in the draft. But the draft came and his number was not called, and in March 1864, with the first sign of spring—an anemone pushing up through the soil—he departed for Canada with a "soul-hunger of wh' we hear so much nowadays, that longing and vague unrest regarded as proof of immortality." Wandering to botanize "in glorious freedom" around the Great Lakes, he intended to meet his brother Daniel in Niagara Falls. Daniel was working in Meaford, Canada, on Georgian Bay, at the mill and factory owned by William H. Trout and his partner, Charles Jay.[1]

Muir traveled "free as a bird, independent alike of roads and people [and]...entered at once into harmonious relations with Nature like young bees making their first excursion to a flower garden." He noticed that his "vague unrest and longings" vanished and he "felt a plain, simple relationship to the Cosmos." Of his reasons for leaving Wisconsin, Muir knew only that he was seeking insight into that which orders the natural world. In a letter to his friend Emily Pelton, he noted that he felt "like Milton's Adam and Eve," for whom "the world was all before them," as he believed it was for him, and the only answer he sought was where to choose a place of rest.[2]

Information on the first six months of Muir's ramble in Canada is vague, and we are left to speculate as to whether a journal, herbarium specimens, and his copy of Wood's *Class-Book of Botany* were destroyed in the fire that in early 1866 ravaged Trout's Mill. But during the two years he was in Canada, Muir wrote letters, sketched, collected herbarium specimens, and prepared notes to accompany them. The plant specimens, with their note-billets,

*Calypso borealis* Salisb., Lady's Slipper; Hider of the North

provide a map of the landscape across which he walked. Leaving Portage, Wisconsin, Muir traveled by train to Chicago, Ann Arbor, and Detroit and then to Windsor, Ontario. In all probability at Windsor, he boarded the Great Western Railway and traveled east into south- ern Ontario. By April 1864 he was already wading in swamps, and on May 18 he started out on a "three weeks' ramble through Simcoe and Grey Counties, walking an estimated dis- tance of about three hundred miles." From within the depths of a tamarac and cedar swamp, he could see that:

> Land and water, life and death, beauty and deformity, seemed here to have disputed empire and all shared equally at last. I shall not soon forget the chaos of fallen trees in all stages of decay and the tangled branches of the white cedars through which I had to force my way; nor the feeling with which I observed the sun wheeling to the West while yet above, beneath, and around all was silence and the seemingly endless harvest of swamp.[3]

At the town of Bradford, north of Toronto, Muir lodged with a Scots family, the Campbells, devoting most of his time to collecting plants in the marshlands and tramp- ing around, covered in brown swamp mud with bits of wildflowers, mosses, grasses, and ferns sticking out from his tattered shirt and trousers. He worked enough to pay board. The Campbells nicknamed him "Botany":

> It was with no little difficulty that my object in seeking "these wilds traversed by few" was explained to the sturdy and hospitable lairds of these remote districts. "Botany" was a term they had not heard before in use. What did it mean? If told that I was collecting plants, they would desire to know whether it was cabbage plants that I sought, and if so, how could I find cabbage plants in the bush?[4]

Only once on this journey through Ontario did Muir find what he considered to be "the rarest and the most beautiful of the flowering plants," the *Calypso borealis*, or lady's slipper orchid.

> Wading bogs and swamps that seemed more and more extensive and more difficult to find one's way through, and entering one of these great tamarac swamps one morning, holding a course by compass, I began to fear that I would not be able to get out of the bog by sundown to find a dry piece of ground to lay down on, but when the way seemed most discouraging, wading the stream, on the further mossy bank I discovered this beautiful hider—this beautiful Calypso. No other bloom was near it, for the bog a short distance below the surface was still frozen and the water was ice cold, and the growth of the tamarac was so close that there was no other plant in flower near it. It seemed the most spiritual of all the flower people I had ever met—it was growing not in the ground but in a bed of yellow moss. It sprung from a small white bud, imbedded in the moss, and it had only one leaf and one flower. The flower was white and made the impression of the utmost purity and chastity—pure and chaste as

snow. I sat down opposite it and cried for joy....How long I sat beside Calypso I don't know. Hunger and weariness vanished, and only after the sun was low in the west I plashed on through the swamp, strong and exhilarated as if never more to feel any mortal care.[5]

The report of his encounter with the orchid would be published some two years later on the front page of the *Boston Recorder,* on December 21, 1866, unbeknownst to Muir, from a letter he had written to Jeanne Carr. His career as a writer began with "a plant so full of life; so perfectly spiritual, it seemed pure enough for the throne of its Creator."[6]

Walking south toward Hamilton, Muir headed for Niagara Falls, wandering "many a long wild fertile mile in the forests and bogs...gathering plants, and glorying in God's abounding inexhaustible spiritual beauty bread." He collected clover, dogbane, triangular poly-pod ferns, and eastern red cedar, and he met his brother Daniel. They returned to Meaford to work through the winter at Trout's Mill, where Muir was content to make rake and broom handles and contrivances for setting rake teeth, and he assisted in the construction of an addition to the factory. He devoted Sundays and evenings to the study of botany in an enclosing wall of verdure in Trout Hollow, and during the winter months he brought out his herbarium to show the Trouts and Jays. Touched with loneliness when Daniel returned to the United States in May 1865, Muir wrote to his friend Emily Pelton, wishing she were there to ramble and botanize with him: "Our tall tall forest trees are now all alive, and the mingled ocean of blossoms and leaves, wave and curl, and rise in rounded swells farther and farther away.... Freshness and beauty are everywhere, flowers are born every hour, living sunlight is poured over all, and everything and creation is glad,—our world is

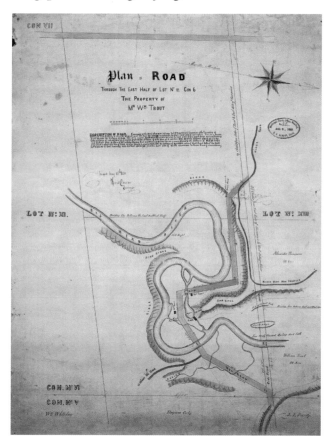

Map of the Property of William Trout, Municipal Clerk's Office, Meaford, Canada, August 8, 1893. Courtesy of the Canadian Friends of John Muir, Owen Sound and Meaford, Ontario, Canada.

indeed a beautiful one." He took a leave from the mill to botanize, retracing a portion of his previous year's route to Owen Sound, in Simcoe County, from where he sent Emily "a specimen of *Camptosorus rhizophyllus,*" the walking fern.[7]

When Muir returned to the mill he began improvements to the factory machinery, and though he felt destined for little else than inventing machinery, he remained attached to his Wisconsin friends and to the study of plants. In writing to Jeanne Carr he expressed his wish that he could "creep into that delightful kernel of your house, your library, with its portraits of scientific men, and so bountiful a store of their sheaves amid the blossom and verdure of your little kingdom of plants, luxuriant and happy as though holding their leaves to the open sky of the most flower-loving zone in the world!"[8]

Later that year Muir received a letter from his brother Daniel, who had botanized very little: "In fact I don't, and I can't, and I never did, and never will pretend to be able to go on with any study the way you have, and can, and I suppose will, as long

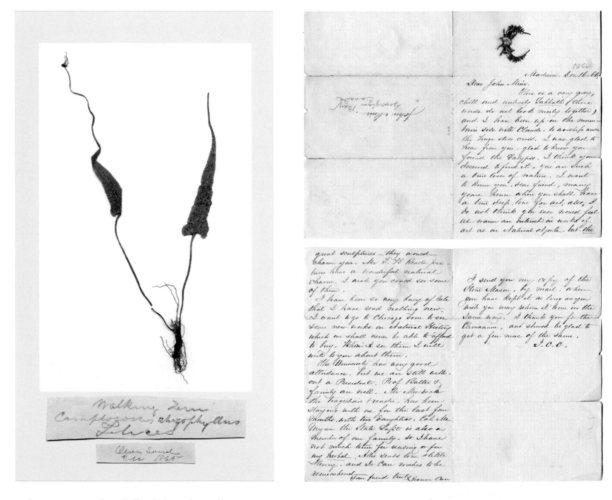

Left: *Camptosorus rhizophyllus* (L.) Link, Walking Fern

Right: Jeanne C. Carr to John Muir, Madison, Wisconsin, December 16, 1866. Courtesy of the John Muir Papers, Holt-Atherton Department of Special Collections, University of the Pacific Library. Copyright 1984 Muir-Hanna Trust.

Carr wrote to Muir that she was "Glad to hear from you—glad to know you found the Calypso. I think you deserved to find it, you are such a true lover of Nature."

as you have within your nostrils the breath of life." Daniel believed that his brother's knowledge of plants exceeded not only that of his siblings but that of everyone any of them had ever met.⁹

Not content with the limited education he had received up to that point, Muir planned to return to the United States in the summer or fall of 1866 to complete his university studies. A fateful, roaring, windy snowstorm on February 21, 1866, ignited a fire that destroyed Trout's Mill, and within a month Muir had left Canada and settled in Indianapolis, an important industrial center and the site of "one of the very richest forests of round-headed deciduous hard wood trees upon all the Continent." Muir left behind a copy of Asa Gray's *Structural*, in order that Hattie Trout might analyze plants he would send to her from Indianapolis.¹⁰

## To Study the Inventions of God

Muir's ambition—he called it an affliction—to make a useful life as an inventor was tethered incongruously to "the attractions of nature." He saw no shame in manufacturing or inventing, and in fact believed there was philanthropic value in designing machines, and expressed concern that he would become so successful as an inventor that "botanizing and geological studies might be interrupted."¹¹

In Indianapolis, he found employment with the Osgood & Smith Company, a wholesale manufacturer of hubs, spokes, and broom and rake handles. Among machines he had begun to feel that he had "some talent that way, and so I almost think, unless things change soon I shall turn my whole mind into that channel." He wrote to his sister Sarah that he was compelled to "abandon the profession of my choice, and to take up the business of an inventor." But on Sundays he walked out beyond the city in the surrounding forests to collect plants. A fortuitous letter of introduction from James D. Butler, one of his professors at the University of Wisconsin, to the prominent Merrill and Moores families noted that Solomon "could not speak more wisely" than Muir about the plant kingdom. Soon Muir was leading botanical outings organized by Catharine Merrill.¹²

Correspondence between Muir and Jeanne Carr continued and in mid-October she closed a letter to him with a tender reminder of the Carrs' recognition of his particularly insightful affection for nature. "You do not know how we hold you in our memories as one apart from all other students in your power of insight into Nature, and the simplicity of your love for her." Her encouragement was no doubt welcome in what had been a chaotic phase—by winter he had moved his belongings from boardinghouse to boardinghouse a total of five times. In January 1867, in a room with his early-rising bed and pictures he had

*Botany for Young People and Common Schools. How Plants Grow: A Simple Introduction to Structural Botany,* by Asa Gray. Courtesy of Bonnie Johanna Gisel.

John Muir had a copy of Gray's *Structural* when he was in Meaford, Canada. When he returned to the United States in 1866 he left it with Hattie Trout to assist in the identification of plants he would send to her from Indianapolis.

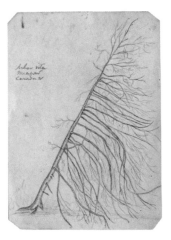

Left: "Flowers from Indiana." Note by John Muir, c. 1866. Courtesy of the John Muir National Historic Site.

Right: "Arborvitae, Meaford, Canada." Sketch by John Muir, c. 1864. Courtesy of the John Muir Papers, Holt-Atherton Department of Special Collections, University of the Pacific Library. Copyright 1984 Muir-Hanna Trust.

framed for the walls, he studied maps and planned a route for an extended botanical excursion through the southern states, the West Indies, South America, and Europe.[13]

According to Muir, the belt system in the Osgood & Smith factory, "the nerves and sinews of factory life," was compromised by atmospheric and temperature changes, bad joinings, and friction. On March 5, as he replaced a countershaft for a circular saw, the belt stretched, and as he was relacing it with a pointed file, the file slipped and pierced his right eye at the edge of the cornea. Certain that his sight was gone, he wrote to his family and friends that "not a single flower, no more of lovely scenery, not any more of beauty would ever pass the portal of my right eye...Alas, I am half-blind." Condemned to a darkened room, he

*Climacium americanum* Brid., American Climacium

scribbled notes: "The sunshine and the winds are working in all the gardens of God, but I—I am lost!" Then, assured by a specialist that he would recover most of his sight, he began to hope that soon he could "walk to the woods, where the spring's sweet first-born are waiting," and a "sweet first fern waits for me." Carr believed that Muir prized sight more than anyone she knew. She told him that God had given him:

> The eye within the eye, to see in all natural objects the realized ideas of His mind. He gave you
> pure tastes and the steady preference of whatsoever is most lovely and excellent. He has made
> you a more individualized existence than is common, and by your very nature and organization
> removed you from common temptations....He will surely place you where your work is....Dear
> friend, my recognition of you from the first was just this—"one of His beloved."

After many weeks she would receive a token of his recovery in a little package of *Climacium*, "that miniature palm among the mosses."[14]

Muir intended to return to Osgood & Smith, denying himself the study of botany, yet he was "encouraged to think that the world was still left open." He was anxious to travel and his thoughts drifted toward the plan he had devised for the walking tour, and toward Yosemite Valley, about which he had read the previous year. On an April day, with soft gray clouds filtering sunlight, walking in the woods with his eyes focused on the study of the creations of God, he wondered if, with what remained of his sight, his life should not be given "to do good and to be good?" The question for Muir was which path his life should ultimately take to accomplish that good. He bid "adieu to all thoughts of inventing machinery"; driven "to the sweet fields," he would gather enough of flowers and landscapes to last the remainder of his life. "I was," he wrote, "determined to make haste and store my mind with the Lord's beauty before another accident should deprive me of sight and seal it up in darkness." He would devote the remainder of his life "to studying the inventions of God."[15]

Leaving his mechanical inventions and botanical specimens from Canada and Indiana with the Merrill family in Indianapolis, Muir departed with Merrill Moores, the eleven-year-old nephew of Catharine Merrill, on a botanizing trip from Indianapolis through Illinois to Portage, Wisconsin. With a filmlike cloud covering his injured right eye, he crossed the northern prairie seven miles southwest of Pecatonica, Illinois, and gathered a bouquet of wildflowers, ferns, grasses, and sedges—one hundred plants gathered in walking two hundred yards in a straight line.

> I looked at my grass bouquet by chance—was startled—held it at arms length in sight of its own near and distant scenery and companion flowers—my discovery was complete and I was delighted beyond measure with the new and extreme beauty....The extremely fine and diffuse purple *Agrostis* [bent grass] contrasted most divinely with the taller, strict, taper-finished *Koeleria* [hair grass]. The long-awned single *Stipa* [needlegrass] too and *P[anicum] clandestinum* [panic grass], with their broad ovate leaves and purple muffy pistils, played an important part; so also did the cylindrical spikes of the sedges. All were just in place; every leaf had its proper taper and texture and exact measure of green. Only *P[oa] pratensis* [common meadow grass] seemed out of place, and as might be expected it proved to be an intruder, belonging to a field or bouquet in Europe.

When Muir and Moores arrived at the Carr home in Madison on their way to Portage, they were laden with pressed plants.[16]

Throughout the summer Muir remained with his sister Sarah and her husband in Wisconsin, where the flowers were, he thought, "incomparably more numerous than those of Ca[nada] or Indiana." Many of them he had not seen since leaving home:

> In company with my little friend [Merrill Moores] I visited Muir's Lake [Fountain Lake]....
> [It] came into full view all unchanged, sparkling & clear with its edging of rushes and lilies,
> and there too was the meadow with its brook, & willows, and all the well known nooks of its
> winding border, where many a moss & fern find home. I held these poor eyes to the dear dear
> scene and it washed me once more in its fullest glory with yellow pond lily, and bladderwort,
> and around to the south end columbine, bluebell, sandwort, and wild geranium.[17]

Near the end of summer Muir and Moores traveled to the Wisconsin Dells, a series of narrow rocky chasms and gorges that traverse the Wisconsin River:

> The ravines are the most perfect, the most heavenly plant conservatories I ever saw. Thousands of happy flowers are there, but ferns and mosses are the favored ones. No human language could ever describe them. We traveled two miles in eight hours and such scenery...scrambling climbing and happy hunting and happy finding of dear plant beings we never before enjoyed...The last ravine we encountered was the most beautiful and deeper and longest and narrowest. The rocks overhang and bear a perfect selection of trees which hold themselves towards one another from side to side with inimitable grace forming a flowering veil of indescribable beauty. The light is measured and mellow. For every flower springs too and pools are in their places to moisten them. The walls are fringed and painted most divinely with the bright green polypodium and asplenium and allisum and mosses and liverworts and gray lichens and here and there a clump of flowers and little bushes....Over all and above all and in all the glorious ferns tall perfect godlike, here and there amid their fronds a long cylindrical spike of the grand fringed purple orchis....who can describe a greenhouse planned and made and planted and tended by the Great Creator himself....they cut themselves keenly into our memories and remain pictured in us forever.[18]

It was a trip during which Muir gained the courage to leave behind the floral landscape with which he was familiar; it heightened his enthusiasm to study botany and inspired him to be true to himself. In mid-August he wrote to Catharine Merrill, "We have had our last communion with Muir's lake. It was glassy and calm, and full of shadows. I have said farewell to nearly all my friends too, and will soon leave home once more for I know not where." Though Muir was uncertain about the direction his life would take, he knew that in setting out to walk with nature he would find "a thousand times more of beauty than heart could wish." Bewildered and "overwhelmed in the immortal, shoreless, fathomless ocean of God's beauty," he would go south "just anywhere into the wilderness" on a thousand-mile walk to the Gulf of Mexico.[19]

Muir trusted God's active hand was always at work designing the natural world, and he believed that God meant him to use his mind and body to see and remember all things wild and beautiful. Before Muir departed to advance his education in the University of the Wilderness, he shared his sentiments with his friend Jeanne Carr.

> Can it be that a single flower or weed or grass in all these prairies occupies a chance position? Can it be that the folding or curvature of a single leaf is wrong or undetermined in these gardens that God is keeping? The most microscopic portions of plants are beautiful in themselves, and these are beautiful combined into individuals, and undoubtedly are all woven with equal care into one harmonious, beautiful whole.[20]

In that same month, Muir sent his friend Catharine Merrill a manuscript he had prepared on the *Anemone nuttalliana*: "I have had only fragments of time to work upon it, one hour one week, another hour the next, etc., besides I never sat down to describe a flower before, so I will be satisfied whether you mend it or reject it all together." Because this is the only extensive account in which Muir described in detail a particular plant, its taxonomy, and its ecology, it is included here in its entirety:[21]

## Anemone Nuttalliana

*Anemone nuttalliana* is a flower of the West. Its home is upon the open plains and breezy hillsides of the oak openings. Though not outwardly a very beautiful plant, it is admired and loved by all who know it; for it comes to us first of all, after the sleep and death of winter, blooming kindly without companions, before the spring is warm, and before its own leaves have time to grow.

The oak openings where our plant seems most at home are extremely unlike the heavily timbered portions of Michigan and Indiana, but not very unlike most of rolling prairie. Annual fires dress and keep them in such a way, that they are everywhere about as free from underbrush as the prairies themselves, and were the trees in rows they would be extremely like immense orchards, for the trees being far apart, they live in light, and are at liberty to adopt their natural apple-tree form of growth.

Myriads of strange and beautiful wild flowers are marshaled upon these wide, wide fields of our West,—the emigrant farmer makes his cabin in their midst. They look in at his door, and wait upon him far and near at every footstep, but the first that he learns to know, and to associate with garden favorites far away in the old fatherland, is *Anemone nuttalliana*.

Our plant when full grown is from eight to sixteen inches high, and has one flower, one or two inches in diameter, composed of five to seven purplish silky sepals, a circle of numerous bright yellow oval anthered stamens, and a close head of feathery pistils; the petals are wanting or represented by small inconspicuous scales.

The leaves are all radical and ternately divided and cleft into linear acute segments. It has an involucre which like the leaves is three parted, and is at first close to the flower and clothed with long silky hairs, forming a warm calyx-like cup for the tender corolla-like calyx.

The sepals seem to have been refined to the very highest point of delicacy compatible with sufficient strength for its work. Might not this anemone have been at one time the most beautiful of flowers, promoted to the leadership as reward,—its corolla all removed excepting the scales—the warm involucral calyx provided, and its harder calyx refined, and clothed, and colored for its work.

Its mode of growth is very interesting. While it is yet cold, and the gloom of winter twilight is deepest, and not a single plant whisper disturbs the sad, sad quiet, a large gray bud is seen feeling its way through ashes, or lost leaves and broken grasses. Though all seems lost, it does not stand doubting in the bud, but expands at once on reaching the light, spreading

*Anemone nuttalliana* DC, Pasque Flower

its broad flowers lovingly, low down upon the naked ground to heal its desolateness, and not until innumerable growing points have made a tinge of green, and other flowers have ventured forth to aid in the work of beauty and love, does our hero take time to rise on its stalk, and call up its leaves.

In a few weeks the glorious bands of summer stand side by side in countless multitudes—much of our anemone's work is done— its sepals fall off, the first of beauty to live, the first to die.

The involucre, now no longer required for the flower, takes a position below the middle of the stem and becomes leafy. The achenia are furnished with long plumous tails and form a head, which receives shelter very becomingly beneath the branching asters and solidagoes that keep their flowers for autumn. Before the end of June its seeds are ripe and find their places—the naked bereaved stalks are seldom seen. It had but to wait now for winter with its companions, when its stalk is broken, its leaves killed and lost, and all of its life again shut in darkness in its perennial root. It is not harmed by the loud icy winds, nor by the snows that fall upon it. Spring's earliest dawn finds it waiting, and when death has once more passed upon all, when winter and the fire have done, and all of summer is again hushed in the motionless gloom of satisfied desolation, then comes *Anemone nuttalliana*—ever the first of life, the foremost cresting of summer's wave. We will love the glossy arching sedge that cheers the silent marsh, and the grand old pine that speaks with every wind, and the tiny moss that gives itself to the fallen tree, and those noble solida-goes that keep up heart and bloom as they can when other flowers are dying in the frost and melancholy of Autumn, but no one of these treading thus nobly their golden circle of duty nor all of the full tide of summer grandeur will make us to forget our hardy pioneer—the hopeful, magnanimous *Anemone nuttalliana*.[22]

# Three

## KENTUCKY TO THE GULF OF MEXICO

### Scarce a Familiar Face among the Flowers

*Cranberry*

[*Vaccinium vitis-idaea* L.], Mountain Cranberry [Cowberry; Foxberry]

*Sassafras officinale* Nees, Sassafras

*Leiophyllum buxifolium* Elliott, Sand Myrtle

Leiophyllum buxifolium
grandfolium White

[*Viola canadensis* L.], White Violet

Catesby Oak,
Mobile,
Nov. 24.

*Quercus aquatica* (Lam.) Walter, Catesby Oak; Water Oak

Different stages of developement

ON THE FLYLEAF of his 1867 journal, encircled in a cloud, Muir wrote "John Muir, Earth-planet Universe," an address now widely recognized as the heroic start to Muir's journey of personal invention. "Doomed" by his immoderate desires to be "carried by the spirit into the wilderness," he set out for the Gulf of Mexico.[1]

Muir believed that only a "few bodies are inhabited by so satisfied a soul as to be allowed exemption from extraordinary exertion through a whole life." Seeking to comprehend what drove him, he wrote, "The sea, the sky, the rivers have their ebbs and floods, and the earth itself throbs and pulses from calms to earthquake. So also there are tides and floods in the affairs of men, which in some are slight and may be kept within bounds, but in others they overmaster everything." He saw himself fitting into the category of things and individuals who ebb and flood past all boundaries. He knew he was no ordinary man. Within him pulsed a desire to reach beyond the borders of the life he knew and stretch himself to fit the larger universe. He sought to understand who he was, who he wanted to be, and what place humanity held in relation to nature. And was not the world an open book set before him to see and enjoy and puzzle over?[2]

Muir began with what he knew from his studies at the University of Wisconsin and then in the University of the Wilderness. He was a botanist and therefore would study plants: "I have long been looking from the wild woods and gardens of the northern states to those of the warm south and at last all drawbacks overcome on the first day of September 1867 I set forth joyful and free on a thousand mile walk to the Gulf of Mexico." He would study the natural world he had never seen and rejoice "in splendid visions of pines and palms and tropic flowers in glorious array."[3]

## KENTUCKY

Reaching a wooded area on the outskirts of Louisville, Kentucky, Muir spread out his map to plan his journey. He would push on "in a general southward direction by the wildest, leafiest, least trodden way [he] could find promising the greatest extent of virgin forest." He carried a small satchel, a book of Robert Burns's poems, Milton's *Paradise Lost*, a New Testament, and a plant press. To assist in the classification of plants he may also have had Alphonso Wood's *Class-Book of Botany*—perhaps his original copy if it escaped the fire at Trout's Mill. While his belongings were few and light, Muir's mind was heavy with the

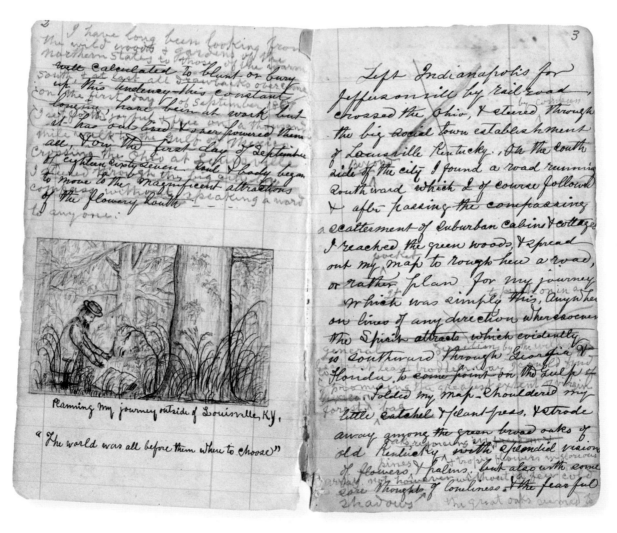

"Planning My Journey outside of Louisville, Kentucky." "Florida and Cuba Trip," September 1867–February 1868. Thousand-mile walk to the Gulf. John Muir's Journal. Courtesy of the John Muir Papers, Holt-Atherton Department of Special Collections, University of the Pacific Library. Copyright 1984 Muir-Hanna Trust.

Muir reached the outskirts of Louisville, Kentucky, and spread out his pocket map to plan his journey in a southward direction, traveling by the wild, leafy, least-trodden way: "The world was all before them where to choose."

weight of the words of natural scientists, philosophers, and friends when he embarked. As he walked south, he would sort and commingle their experiences and ideas, and the books he had read and distilled, as he shaped his own thoughts and words. The strength of Muir's vision was not so much in his independence of thought as in his ability to see more clearly than others and adapt and synthesize what appeared to be incongruous pieces into one unified whole. At the time, this vision was focused on plants.[4]

The loneliness of leaving family, friends, and familiar plants was assuaged as Muir traveled through Kentucky. Encouraged by the sight of broad-branched oaks rising to "kingly perfection in beauty and power," he surrendered any doubt that his resolve was sound. He passed the Salt River southeast of Elizabethtown and at the great caves he found ferns like those in the Wisconsin Dells and further north. With his back against a moss-clad log he spent "a long happy while, pressing specimens and printing this beauty into my mind." Writing to Jeanne Carr, he expressed his gratitude for the spark that had led him southward:

> How shall I ever tell of the miles and miles of beauty that has been flowing into me in
> such measure? These lofty curving ranks of bobbing, swelling hills, these concealed valleys
> of fathomless verdure, and these lordly trees with the nursing sunlight glancing in their
> leaves upon the outlines of the magnificent masses of shade embosomed among their wide
> branches,—these are cut into my memory to go with me forever....I am thankful...for so much.[5]

Traveling from Mammoth Cave through woods laced with mistletoe to Glasgow Junction, passing the Cumberland River and Burkesville, Muir walked in what he called "the happiest provinces of bird and flower....rapid streams flowing in beautiful flower-bordered channels embowered in dense woods." Kentucky was, he thought, the greenest, leafiest-forested state. There was beauty to be had in beholding the thick, tangled verdure, though he feared losing himself in the unfamiliar world of twisted vines, brambles, and swamps that took no pity on his human skin or soul.[6]

## TENNESSEE

Muir continued on into Tennessee through "an ocean of wooded waving swelling mountain loveliness":

> Countless forest clad hills side by side in rows and clumps seemed to enjoy the rich sunshine
> and to remain motionless only because they were so eagerly drinking the light. All were
> united by curves and slopes of inimitable softness and beauty. Oh these forest-gardens of our
> Father. What perfection, what divinity in their architecture, what simplicity, what mysterious
> complexity. Who will read the teachings of these sylvan sheets, of these flowers and all the
> glad brotherhood of rills that sing in these valleys and all the happy creatures that have homes
> here and the tender keeping of a Father's care.[7]

Inventing himself as he went along, welcoming new plants, proceeding with the grace of God, Muir read nature's scripture and experienced the pulses that beat beyond the boundaries he knew.

Muir now encountered the first mountains his feet had touched or eyes beheld: the Cumberland Mountains. As he crossed a branch of the Clinch River, strange trees began to appear and alpine flowers and shrubs met him at every step. "Every tree, every flower, every ripple and eddy...seemed solemnly to feel the presence of the Great Creator." He found a growth of shiny-leaved Ericaceae (heathworts, as he later called them) and along the roadside he saw a briar—the *Schrankia*—so sensitive that it responded to vibrations carried from one interlacing branch to another. Muir paused to think about the lives of plants. With his mental wheels turned by petaled spokes, he puzzled over "how little we know as yet of the life of plants[,] their hopes and fears, pains and enjoyments!" He doubted their inability to feel and challenged the prevailing anthropocentric view that diminished the lives and value of plants.[8]

John Muir with his plant press over his shoulder. "Florida and Cuba Trip," September 1867–February 1868. Thousand-mile walk to the Gulf. John Muir's Journal. Courtesy of the John Muir Papers, Holt-Atherton Department of Special Collections, University of the Pacific Library. Copyright 1984 Muir-Hanna Trust.

"Three kingdoms have declared war against the United States. All I have to say is America forever but I'd a heap rather they wouldn't fight." The plant press, made of two light wooden frames with leather straps, was used to tighten and compress the plant specimens that would be dried between sheets of blotting paper.

Everything that grew interested Muir, and his plan was to become acquainted with as many plants as possible. His self-employment in the study of "grasses, weeds, flowers, trees, mosses, [and] ferns" left him vulnerable to criticism. In Jamestown a blacksmith reproached him for dallying around looking for weeds and blossoms. Was not, Muir retorted, Solomon a strong-minded and wise man who "considered it was worth while to study plants; not only to go and pick them....We are told that he wrote a book about plants, not only of the great cedars of Lebanon but of little bits of things growing in the cracks of the walls." Muir continued: "Do you not remember that Christ told his disciples to 'consider the lilies how they grow'[?]...Now, whose advice am I to take, yours or Christ's?"[9]

Muir descended into the Tennessee Valley and at Kingston sent plant specimens home to his brother David. Determined to reach Savannah, he swam across the Chattahoochee

River, dragged himself up the steep bank, and spread his plants to dry. Though he had promised his mother he would not sleep on the ground unless no lodging could be found, he often slept under trees "in the one great bedroom of the open night."[10]

## GEORGIA

Walking southward through a sea of rattlesnakes and a "forest almost entirely composed of dun-green, knotty, sparsely planted pines," in Athens, Georgia, Muir found "a delicious spring in a sandstone basin overhung with shady bushes and vines." Discovering there a "fine southern fern and some new grasses," he felt that he had been directed here by providence. It is not often, he wrote, "that the joys of cool water, cool shade, and rare plants are so delightfully combined....Strange plants crowding about me now, scarce a familiar face among all the flowers of a day's walk." Having abandoned the customary for the mysterious he now found the flora with which he was acquainted supplanted by that of the strange south-land: "Known flower companions were leaving me now, not one by one as in Kentucky and Tennessee, but in whole tribes and genera, and companies of shining strangers came trooping upon me in countless ranks....Now I began to feel myself 'a stranger in a strange land.'"[11]

"Fording Chatahoochee." "Florida and Cuba Trip," September 1867–February 1868. Thousand-mile walk to the Gulf. John Muir's Journal. Courtesy of the John Muir Papers, Holt-Atherton Department of Special Collections, University of the Pacific Library. Copyright 1984 Muir Hanna Trust.

John Muir with his plant press over his shoulder, along the Chattahoochee River, where dark water oak and muscadine grape vines embroidered the banks: "May the muscadine grape vine always have a cool stream bank to hang over."

Near Augusta Muir reached the northern limit of the southern yellow pine; he saw a great number of new and beautiful grasses, and "a fruit called pomegranate"; and he marveled at the impenetrable cypress swamps that are pressed and level as if they had been constantly rolled while growing. "The branches, though spreading are careful not to pass each other and stop suddenly on reaching the general level as if they had been stopped by a ceiling."[12]

Reaching Savannah nearly penniless and waiting for money to arrive from his brother David, Muir walked out to the Bonaventure Cemetery, a sanctuary of light and plant life. He built "a small brush tent" from an armful of rushes, gathered "skeins of Tillandsia moss" for a bed, acquainted himself "with many a solitary plant creature" who, like him, "loved to hide beneath a roof of leaves," and camped in the graveyard for nearly a week.[13]

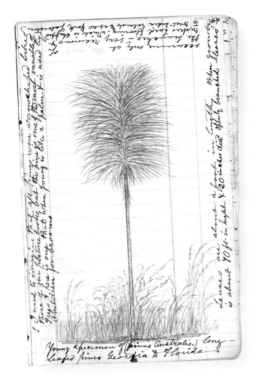

Young specimen of (Pinus Australis,) Long-
leaved pines Georgia & Florida

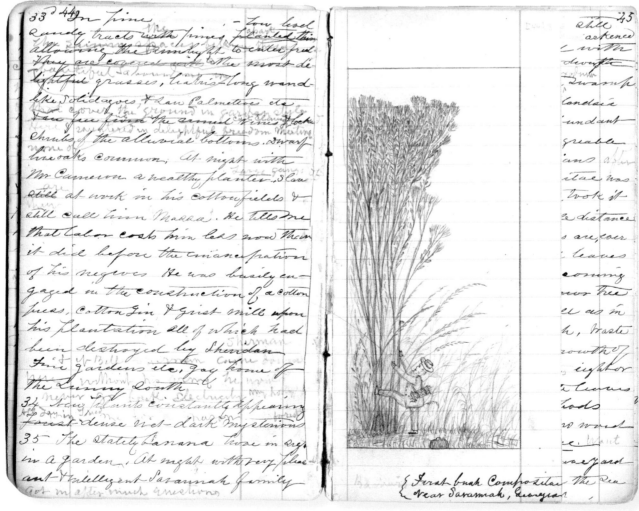

33 44 On Pine — Low level
Sandy tracts with pines, planted then
allowing the sunlight to enter first
They are covered with the most delightful grasses, liatris, long wand-
like Solidagoes, & Saw Palmettos &c
cover the ground in garden style
I am free from the armed vines & oak
chumps of the alluvial bottoms. Dwarf
live oaks common. At night with
Mr Cameron a wealthy planter. Slaves
still at work in his cottonfields &
still call him Massa. He tells me
that labor costs him less now than
it did before the emancipation
of his negroes. He was busily engaged in the construction of a cotton
press, Cotton Gin & Grist mill upon
his plantation all of which had
been destroyed by Sheridan
Fine gardens etc. Gay home of
the Sunny South
34 New Plants constantly appearing
Forest dense rich dark mysterious
35 The stately Banana rose in sight
in a garden. At night with very pleasant & intelligent Savannah family

First bush Compositae the Sea
near Savannah, Georgia

Right: "First night in Bonaventure [Cemetery]." "Florida and Cuba Trip," September 1867-February 1868. Thousand-mile walk to the Gulf. John Muir's Journal. Courtesy of the John Muir Papers, Holt-Atherton Department of Special Collections, University of the Pacific Library. Copyright 1984 Muir-Hanna Trust.

Reaching Savannah, Georgia, Muir walked to the Bonaventure Cemetery to sleep "on an old grave with owls crickets pinch-bugs & mosquitoes." The plant press is beside a tree root.

Opposite (top left): "Young specimen of (*pinus Australis*) long-leafed pine, Georgia to Florida." "Florida and Cuba Trip," September 1867–February 1868. Thousand-mile walk to the Gulf. John Muir's Journal. Courtesy of the John Muir Papers, Holt-Atherton Department of Special Collections, University of the Pacific Library. Copyright 1984 Muir-Hanna Trust.

Near Augusta, Georgia, Muir reached the northern limit of the southern yellow pine, *Pinus australis* [*P. palustris*].

Opposite (top right): "Grass." "Florida and Cuba Trip," September 1867–February 1868. Thousand-mile walk to the Gulf. John Muir's Journal. Courtesy of the John Muir Papers, Holt-Atherton Department of Special Collections, University of the Pacific Library. Copyright 1984 Muir-Hanna Trust.

Grasses became tall and cane-like the farther south Muir walked: "Some of the species are grouped in groves and thickets like trees, while others may be seen waving without any companions in sight. Some of them have wide-branching panicles like Kentucky oaks, others with a few tassels of spikelets drooping from a tall, leafless stem. But all of them are beautiful beyond the reach of language. I rejoice that God has 'so clothed the grass of the field.'" (Muir, *A Thousand-Mile Walk to the Gulf*)

Opposite (bottom): "First bush Compositae near Savannah, Georgia." "Florida and Cuba Trip," September 1867–February 1868. Thousand-mile walk to the Gulf. John Muir's Journal. Courtesy of the John Muir Papers, Holt-Atherton Department of Special Collections, University of the Pacific Library. Copyright 1984 Muir-Hanna Trust.

Muir with a plant press over his shoulder.

Left: "My Bonaventure Home." "Florida and Cuba Trip," September 1867–February 1868. Thousand-mile walk to the Gulf. John Muir's Journal. Courtesy of the John Muir Papers, Holt-Atherton Department of Special Collections, University of the Pacific Library. Copyright 1984 Muir-Hanna Trust.

"Saw Palmetto [*Serenoa repens*] & wand solidago [*Solidago altissima*], etc. Southern Georgia & Florida." Gathering *Tillandsia usneoides* (Spanish moss) and rush, Muir fashioned a tent and spent nearly a week camped in Bonaventure Cemetery.

## FLORIDA

After money from his brother arrived, Muir booked passage on the *Sylvan Shore* to make the half-day's sail to north Florida. From the town of Fernandina he sent more plant specimens to David with instructions to give them to his sister Sarah until his return: "Tell her to keep them dry and away from rats, and if you or any of you open them to look at them please be *extremely* careful to avoid mixing or misplacing them….Now do take the extremest care of my specimens."[14]

Florida would be, Muir thought, "a peculiar special home of the beings [he] was looking for….the so-called land of flowers." While visiting Florida in dreams, he arrived at "a close forest of trees every one in flower and bent down and entangled to network by luxuriant, bright-blooming vines, and over all a flood of bright sunlight." But he found the place belonged more to sea than to land, and his customary pathless wanderings were not possible—though he veered off the railroad tracks upon which he walked "when compelled by a flower of extraordinary promise" that he wanted to possess for a specimen:

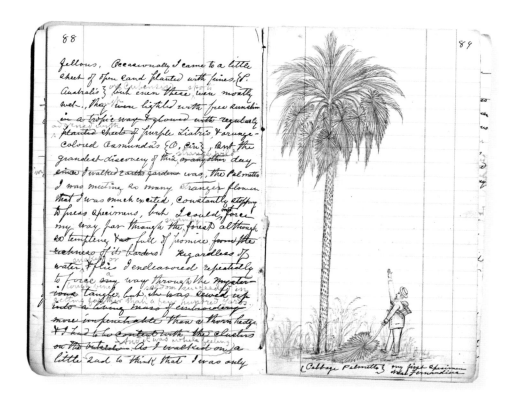

"Cabbage Palmetto [*Sabal palmetto*]. My first specimen near Fernandina, [Florida]." "Florida and Cuba Trip," September 1867–February 1868. Thousand-mile walk to the Gulf. John Muir's Journal. Courtesy of the John Muir Papers, Holt-Atherton Department of Special Collections, University of the Pacific Library. Copyright 1984 Muir-Hanna Trust.

John Muir with his plant press over his shoulder. Muir had longed to see the palmetto, from whom he said he learned far grander things than from any human priest.

A new cane-like grass, or big lily, or gorgeous flower belonging to tree or vine would catch my attention and I would throw down my satchel and press and splash through the coffee brown water for specimens, frequently sinking deeper and deeper until compelled to turn back.... sometimes tangled in a labyrinth of armed vines like a fly in a spiders web. Now climbing a tree for specimens of fruit...overwhelmed with the vastness and unapproachableness of the great guarded ocean of tropic plants.[15]

Florida flowers reached "from January to January in unbroken ranks," with the sun pouring "the sweetest rosiest light," and trees and bushes retained green leaves without any tint of autumn. On the edge of the ocean of vegetable life Muir found a palmetto that had grander things to teach than any priest. He had "longed and prayed for and had often visited [the palm] in dreams" and puzzled over the thought conceived by some "that plants are not like man immortal but are perishable—soulless creatures...this I think is something that we know exactly nothing about." Before him stood a language he had never learned, "full of influences that I never felt before," and he thanked God "with all my heart for his goodness in granting me admittance to this magnificent realm of flowery plant people."[16]

"Different Stages of Development" (of the *Sabal palmetto*). "Florida and Cuba Trip," September 1867–February 1868. Thousand-mile walk to the Gulf. John Muir's Journal. Courtesy of the John Muir Papers, Holt-Atherton Department of Special Collections, University of the Pacific Library. Copyright 1984 Muir-Hanna Trust.

Near Gainesville, Florida, Muir waded through pools and emerged from a dark forest to stand before a colony of palms, "smooth pillars rising from the grass, each capped with a sphere of leaves shining in the sun."

In late October, Muir reached the ocean, where memories of Dunbar swelled in the salt air. Breathing in the sea breeze that had not touched his thoughts or senses in many years, he wrote: "How imperishable are all the impressions that ever vibrate one's life. We cannot forget anything." Upon arriving at Cedar Keys he worked at a sawmill and waited for a ship to Cuba. The onset of malaria forced convalescence beneath live oaks draped in Spanish moss, hanging gardens of resurrection fern, and saw palmetto. He studied the dense thickets of prickly pear and yucca and crept about, "getting plants and strength."[17]

## CUBA

In mid-December Muir wrote to his brother David that he was still a prisoner of sickness and often insensible, though "hope of enjoying the glorious mountains and flower fields of South America does much to sustain me." He then gathered his plant specimens, boarded

the *Island Belle*, sailed for Cuba, and spent another month weak with fever. He had hoped to climb the central mountain range of the island and follow forests, valleys, and peaks, but instead traveled along the northern coast of interlacing vines, cacti, Compositae, and grasses and collected and pressed plant specimens: "The wild-flowers of this seaside field are a happy band closely joined in splendid array....In no section of the South is there so complicated and so gorgeously flowered vine-tangles as flourish...in the hot and humid wild gardens of Cuba." Muir wandered among coconut palms, "touching flowers at every step," gathering "about a million in my arms at once, delightfully fragrant, and in all the pomp and glory of full bloom." Each night he gathered his plant press and a handful of flowers and climbed aboard the ship.[18]

In Havana Muir boarded a schooner "crammed and covered with oranges" bound for New York, where he planned to board the *Santiago de Cuba* for Panama and

"Broken cactus [C. *opuntia*] from Lime Key, [Florida]." "Florida and Cuba Trip," September 1867–February 1868. Thousand-mile walk to the Gulf. John Muir's Journal. Courtesy of the John Muir Papers, Holt-Atherton Department of Special Collections, University of the Pacific Library. Copyright 1984 Muir-Hanna Trust.

In late October 1867, Muir reached the ocean, where he worked at a sawmill, waited for a ship to Cuba, and studied the dense thickets of prickly pear [*Cactus opuntia*].

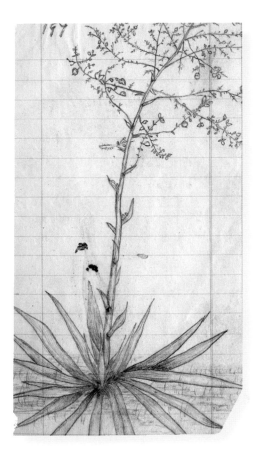

Left: "Spanish Bayonet [*Yucca*], Florida." "Florida and Cuba Trip," September 1867–February 1868. Thousand-mile walk to the Gulf. John Muir's Journal. Courtesy of the John Muir Papers, Holt-Atherton Department of Special Collections, University of the Pacific Library. Copyright 1984 Muir-Hanna Trust.

At Cedar Keys, Muir contracted malaria, convalesced beneath live oak and hanging gardens of resurrection fern (*Polypodium polypodioides*), and studied the yucca. "One of the characteristic plants of these keys is the Spanish bayonet, a species of yucca, about eight or ten feet in height, and with a trunk three or four inches in diameter when full grown. It belongs to the lily family and develops palmlike from terminal buds. The stout leaves are very rigid, sharp-pointed and bayonet-like. By one of these leaves a man might be as seriously stabbed as by an army bayonet, and woe to the luckless wanderer who dares to urge his way through these armed gardens after dark." (Muir, *A Thousand-Mile Walk to the Gulf*)

Right: "Agave." "Florida and Cuba Trip," September 1867–February 1868. Thousand-mile walk to the Gulf. John Muir's Journal. Courtesy of the John Muir Papers, Holt-Atherton Department of Special Collections, University of the Pacific Library. Copyright 1984 Muir-Hanna Trust.

"One of the most common plants of my pasture was the agave. It is sometimes used for fencing. One day, in looking back from the top of the Morro Hill, as I was returning to the *Island Belle*, I chanced to observe two poplar-like trees about twenty-five feet in height. They were growing in a dense patch of cactus and vine-knotted sunflowers. I was anxious to see anything so homelike as a poplar, and so made haste towards the two strange trees, making a way through the cactus and sunflower jungle that protected them. I was surprised to find that what I took to be poplars were agaves in flower, the first I had seen. They were almost out of flower, and fast becoming wilted at the approach of death. Bulbs were scattered about, and a good many still remained on the branches, which gave it a fruited appearance." (Muir, *A Thousand-Mile Walk to the Gulf*)

go on to California. When he arrived in New York he sent plant specimens from Cuba to his brother David: "Please give them to Sarah to keep with the others and tell her that if she opens them, to be very careful not to mix the note-billets." When he arrived in California, in March, a letter from Sarah awaited him. She had received the parcel of Florida plants and particularly admired the variety of ferns—the Cuban plants had not yet arrived. There was, she would report, a new book on photography that "explained how the dried specimens could be used as negatives, and a perfect picture produced.... You could have a large book and the picture of one of your pets on every page with their description, according as they came in order."[19]

## RETURNING TO THE PLANT PEOPLE OF THE SOUTH

Over the years, plant specimens collected by Muir were preserved in collections at the Harvard University Herbaria, the Academy of Natural Sciences of Philadelphia, the Missouri Botanical Garden, and the University and Jepson Herbaria of the University of California, Berkeley; but others slipped away unnoticed and have been lost. The plant specimens Muir collected during his thousand-mile walk did not find their way from a trunk or closet to a repository, though in 1902 Muir's sister Annie sent them to his home in Martinez, California. They are, unfortunately, missing. However, Muir made a second trip south in September 1898 with friends Charles S. Sargent, director of the Arnold Arboretum at Harvard University (to whom he was introduced by Asa Gray in 1878), and William M. Canby, a banker and amateur botanist from Wilmington, Delaware, whom Muir called "a plant-loving, plant-plucking" botanist, who "startled plants to tell their names." The previous year Muir had traveled with them on an excursion to Alaska, a trip that followed in the tradition of the Forestry Commission that had in 1896 included Muir and Sargent. Thirty-one years had passed since Muir, with a handful of knowledge about plants, headed south for the first time. He now traversed the United States, from Martinez to Boston, to meet Sargent and Canby, and together they botanized in Tennessee at Roan Mountain and then in Knoxville, where they struck the route Muir had crossed in 1867. Exploring Grandfather Mountain, in North Carolina, they made their way to Rome, Georgia, not far from where Muir had previously walked. In early October, as a result of a yellow fever quarantine, the trio retreated north to Boston from Tuscaloosa, Alabama.[20]

The troupe reconvened in Wilmington, Delaware, and skimmed through Georgia and Florida, visiting Jacksonville, Miami, St. Augustine, Key West, and Cedar Keys. Looking forward to returning to Martinez, Muir first stopped in Mobile, Alabama, to see the trees and ride in the woods with the botanist Charles T. Mohr, and then in New Orleans to meet another botanist, J. H. Mellichamp.

[*Uniola paniculata* L.], Sea Oats, and [Myrtle]

Muir's journal from the 1898 trip included descriptions of hundreds of plants that he saw. While the primary collecting was entrusted to Canby, as is apparent from the number of his plant specimens located at the Smithsonian Institution, Harvard University Herbaria, University and Jepson Herbaria, and the Missouri Botanical Garden, Muir also collected specimens—though he did not mention them in his writing. Seventeen plant specimens he collected during the excursion are annexed between the pages of his copy of S. M. Dugger's *The Balsam Groves of Grandfather Mountain* with pencil-written note-billets. [21]

Muir had hoped to continue on to Mexico, but his plans were thwarted. In late December he wrote to Sargent:

> I'm glad you're miserable about not going to Mexico, for it shows that your heartwood
> is still honest and loving towards the grand trees down there, though football games and
> Connecticut turkey momentarily got the better of you....I came pretty near making it alone—
> would certainly have done it had I not felt childishly lonesome and woebegone after you
> left me. No wonder I looked like an inland coot to friend Mellichamp. But what would that
> sharp observer have said to the Canby huckleberry party gyrating lost in the Delaware woods,
> and splashing along the edge of the marshy bay "froggin' and 'crabbin" with devout scientific
> solemnity!!!

He continued: "It will soon be dark. Soon our good botanical [l]egs will be straightened in a box and planted, and it behooves us as reasonable naturalists to keep them tramping and twinkling in the woods as long as possible."[22]

# Four

## CALIFORNIA
### The High Sierra and Yosemite

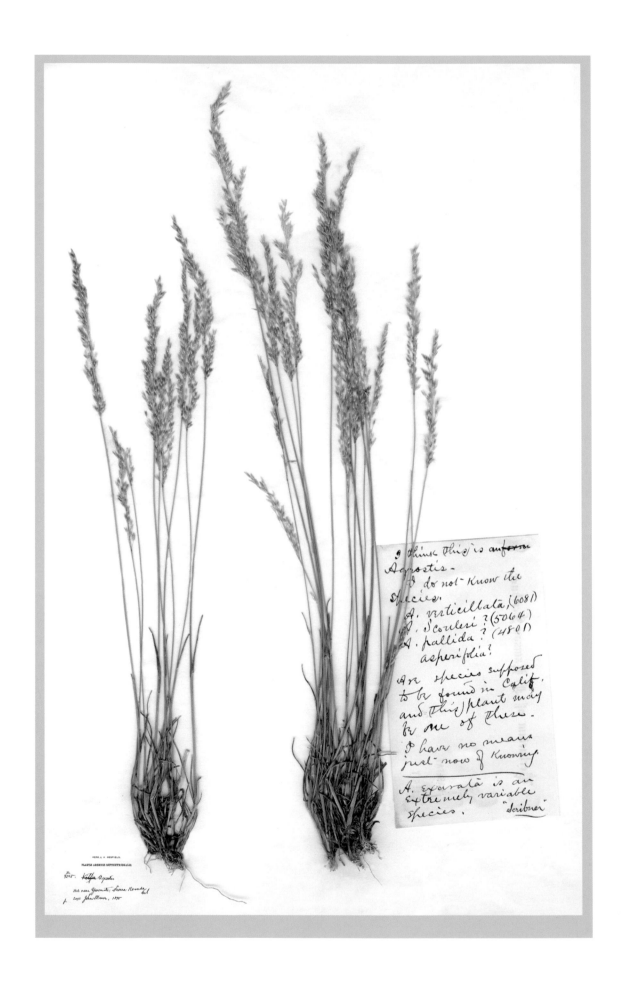

*Agrostis exarata* Trin., Bent Grass

*Cypripedium montanum* Dougl., Mountain Lady's Slipper

HERB. J. H. REDFIELD.

FILICES AMERICÆ SEPTENTRIONALIS.

No. 1701,

*Polypodium Californicum* Klf

Hab. Sierra Nevada, California

Legit John Muir, 1875

Missouri Botanical Garden Herbarium

*Polypodium californicum* Kaulf., California Polypod

Above: *Pinus ponderosa* "approaching *jeffreyi*" [P. *ponderosa* Dougl.]

[P. *jeffreyi* Murr.], Ponderosa Pine; Western Yellow Pine          Overleaf: *Pellaea densa* (Brack.) Hook., Claw Fern

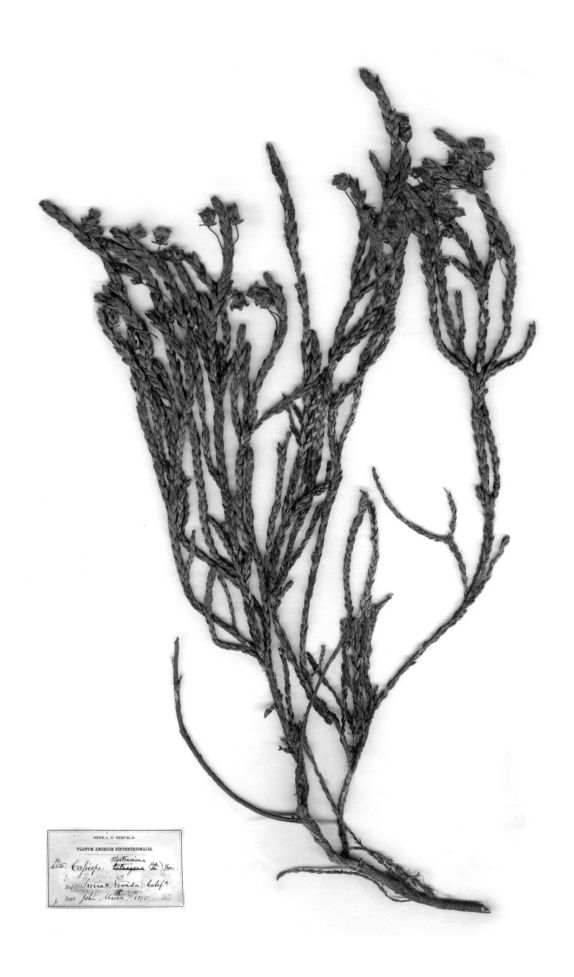

HERB. J. H. REDFIELD.

PLANTÆ AMERICÆ SEPTENTRIONALIS.

No. 4636. Cassiope Mertensiana tetragona (L.) Don.

Hab. Sierra Nevada, Calif.

Legit John Muir, 1875.

*Cassiope mertensiana* (Bong.) Don, White Heather

PH

*Epilobium obcordatum* Gray, Rock Fringe

*Milla ixioides* Baker [*Brodiaea ixioides* Wats.]

*Potentilla grayi* Wats., Gray's Cinquefoil

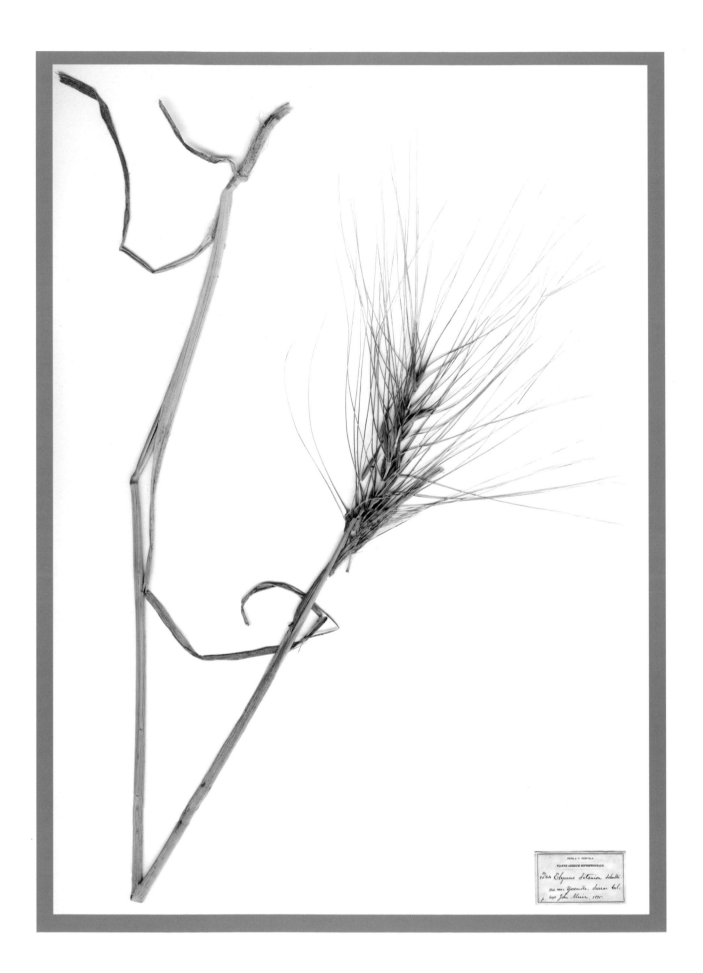

*Elymus sitanion* Schult., Wild Rye

HERB. J. H. REDFIELD.

FILICES AMERICÆ SEPTENTRIONALIS.

No.
1765.   *Woodsia scopulina* D. Eaton

Hab. Sierra Nevada, California.

Legit. John Muir, 1875.

*Woodsia scopulina* Eaton, Rocky Mountain Woodsia

*Ivesia gordonii* (Hook.) Torr. & Gray var. *lycopodioides* Wats., Gordon's Ivesia

*Woodwardia radicans* (L.) Sm. var. radicans Hook., Chain Fern

HERB. J. H. REDFIELD.

PLANTÆ AMERICÆ SEPTENTRIONALIS.

No.
8093. Lilium Washingtonianum Kell.

Hab. near Yosemite, Sierra Nevada, Cal

Legit John Muir, 1875

IF MUIR'S EXPERIENCES in Canada and during his thousand-mile walk were studies in the University of the Wilderness, then what he would encounter and learn from California, and in particular the High Sierra and Yosemite Valley, were the equivalent of graduate school. Between 1868 and 1874 Muir would travel in and out and around the Sierra and spend a total of about forty months in Yosemite. The world, he believed, was all before him there, and the fruitful years produced a wealth of ideas, amalgamated to those that had grown from past experience. His attachment to Alexander von Humboldt and his interest in the ties that linked all things in the natural world led Muir to remark during his first summer in the Sierra that "when we try to pick out anything by itself, we find it hitched to everything else in the universe." This connectedness had to do with Muir's belief that a heart beat "in every crystal and cell." He had long been aware of the "life and gentle tenderness of the rocks, and, instead of walking upon them as unfeeling surfaces, began to regard them as a transparent sky." He could see that "the winds wander, the snow and rain and dew fall, the earth whirls—all but to prosper a poor lush violet!" He often felt "like stopping to speak to the plants and animals [and rocks and glaciers] as friendly fellow mountaineers."[1]

Between the summer of 1870 and 1873, Muir would meet and become lifelong friends with a broad-ranging community of scientists, philosophers, academics, artists, and writers. Many were introduced by Jeanne Carr, who would continue to keep a close eye on him and encourage his writing career. He would also discover and enjoy a profusion of plant life from the Santa Clara Valley and the San Joaquin Valley into the foothills, the Sierra, and Yosemite. His study of botany would stretch to encompass the study of geology, which would gain him credibility within the scientific community. During his peripatetic wanderings in the Sierra

*Lilium washingtonianum* Kell., Washington Lily

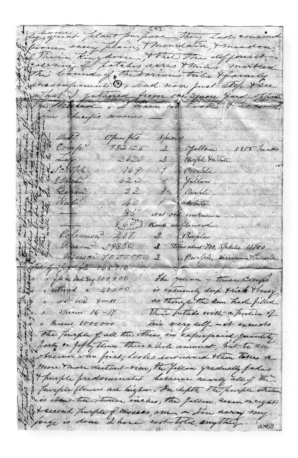

Right: John Muir to Jeanne C. Carr, Near Snelling, Merced County, California, July 26, 1868. Courtesy of the John Muir Papers, Holt-Atherton Department of Special Collections, University of the Pacific Library. Copyright 1984 Muir-Hanna Trust.

In the spring of 1868, on his first trip to Yosemite Valley, Muir wrote to Jeanne Carr describing the abundance of plant life he saw as he walked from Oakland, California, into the bloom of the San Joaquin Valley and the foothills of the Sierra. "Before studying the flowers of this valley, and their sky and all of the furniture and sounds and adornments of their home, one can scarce believe that their vast assemblies are permanent, but rather that, actuated by some plant purpose, they had convened from every plain, and mountain, and meadow of their kingdom, and that the different coloring of patches, acres, and miles marked the bounds of the various tribe and family encampments. And now just stop and see what I gathered from a square yard opposite the Merced [River]. I have no books and cannot give specific names.

Nevada, Muir would gain from the mountains that he called the "Range of Light" an enthusiasm for their beauty that would inspire him throughout the rest of his life and further kindle his desire to preserve wilderness.

## One Sea of Golden and Purple Bloom

Having sailed from Cuba to New York, in January 1868 Muir boarded a steamer en route to Panama, crossed the Isthmus, boarded the *Nebraska,* and in late March arrived in San Francisco. He and Chilwell, a young Englishman he met on the *Nebraska,* crossed the bay on the Oakland Ferry, left the train in east Oakland, and walked up the Santa Clara Valley. Passing through San Jose and the Diablo foothills to Gilroy, and over and through the Diablo Range by way of Pacheco Pass, Muir gained his first view of the Sierra. Descending into the bloom of the San Joaquin Valley, he found "the floweriest piece of the world" he had ever walked. Florida, as its name implied, had been a land of flowers, but Muir could see that in truth: "here, here is Florida!...[flowers] side by side, flower to flower, petal to petal, touching but not entwined":

All one sea of golden and purple bloom so deep and dense that in walking through it you would press more than a hundred flowers at every step. In this flower-bed, five hundred miles long…I used to camp by just lying down wherever night overtook me, and the flowers closed over me as if I had sunk beneath the waters of a lake; the radiant heads of the compositae touching each other, ray to ray, shone above me like the thickest star-clusters of the sky; and, in the morning, I sometimes found plants that were new to me looking me in the face, so that my botanical studies would begin before I got up.[2]

All the way to the Sierra foothills, the vastness of plant-wealth surpassed anything Muir had seen in the Southeast. He noted the region was "covered with bloom, making bright masses of color side by side and interblending, blue and purple and yellow." At Hill's Ferry, he and Chilwell followed the Merced River into Snelling, and from Coulterville they traveled in a general easterly direction. At Crane Flat they reached the main forest belt and began their descent into Yosemite. The "snow gradually disappeared from the pines and the sky, [and] tender leaves unfolded less and less doubtfully, lilies and violets appeared." Ten days were spent sketching, exploring the falls, and collecting plant specimens, and ended with an evening on the margin of Bridal Veil Meadow.[3]

Returning to Hopeton and Snelling by way of Clark's Station and Mariposa Grove, Muir wandered from sequoia to sequoia. "Greatest of trees, greatest of living things," he rejoiced, "their noble domes poised in unchanging repose seemed to belong to the sky." Yosemite was by far, he thought, "the grandest of all the special temples of Nature….It must be the *sanctum sanctorum* of the Sierras!"[4]

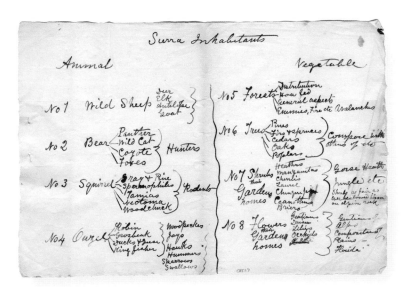 

Left: "Sierra Inhabitants." List of fauna and flora of the Sierra by John Muir, c. 1870s. Courtesy of the John Muir Papers, Holt-Atherton Department of Special Collections, University of the Pacific Library. Copyright 1984 Muir-Hanna Trust.

Right: John Muir in the Mariposa Grove, Yosemite National Park, n.d. Courtesy of the Yosemite National Park Museum.

Left: "November 18, 1868. White Oak of Sierra Foothills, 20 feet high, Q[*uercus*] *Douglasii*, Near Rock River Ranch." Sketch by John Muir, November 18, 1868. Courtesy of the John Muir Papers, Holt-Atherton Department of Special Collections, University of the Pacific Library. Copyright 1984 Muir-Hanna Trust.

Right: John Muir with *Pinus lambertiana* and *P. lambertiana* cone (sugar pine), n.d. Courtesy of the John Muir Papers, Holt-Atherton Department of Special Collections, University of the Pacific Library. Copyright 1984 Muir-Hanna Trust.

Left: Jeanne C. Carr at home at Carmelita, Pasadena, California, c. 1880s. Courtesy of the John Muir Papers, Holt-Atherton Department of Special Collections, University of the Pacific Library. Copyright 1984 Muir-Hanna Trust.

"Fate and flowers" had carried Muir to California, and he luxuriated in the wildness, once again perfectly free. There was "no human method—no law—no rule," and everything belonged to nature and nature's path where all things flowed "in indivisible, measureless currents." Hungry for a far longer reach into the Sierra, Muir determined "to get near views of the mountains in all their snowy grandeur, and study the wonderful forests."[5]

## TWENTY HILL HOLLOW: A SOFT VELVET ROBE OF LIVING GREEN

In Hopeton and Snelling on the Merced River, in French Bar (La Grange) on the Tuolumne River, and in a range centered on a small valley of twenty hemispherical hills that he called "Twenty Hill Hollow," Muir worked at a series of odd jobs and then hired on as a shepherd for Smoky Jack Connel. When he took charge of the sheep, most of the plants had already ripened their seeds and died, and June, July, August, and September were "the season of plant-rest." Then in October and until the end of November, a small unobtrusive plant, *Hemizonia virgata,* burst into bloom in patches miles long.[6]

Right: John Muir to Sarah Muir Galloway, Snelling's Ranch, March [1869], Envelope and plant specimen [unidentified]. Earliest extant California plant collected by Muir.

It was in this season of "resurrection," fall 1868, that Muir welcomed Jeanne and Ezra Carr to California. It was a new beginning with old friends. Ezra had resigned from the University of Wisconsin, and the Carrs were lured westward by what they believed were the cosmopolitan qualities of San Francisco, and by Ezra's brother Nelson Carr, a rancher in Southern California. Jeanne knew the flowers would "*never* be so dear as...*Linnaeas* and *Calypsos*," but she would find "sweet souls, pure souls" in which to see the face of God. They arrived in Oakland amidst rumors of a new university. In spring Jeanne began teaching botany at a girls' school in San Mateo, and the following summer Ezra joined the faculty at the fledgling University of California. While their move to California was not precipitated by Muir—in fact he anticipated that he would soon depart for South America to complete his original plan to travel to the Amazon—Jeanne's presence provided a wave of prosperity for him, the tone and breadth of which neither could have measured at the time.[7]

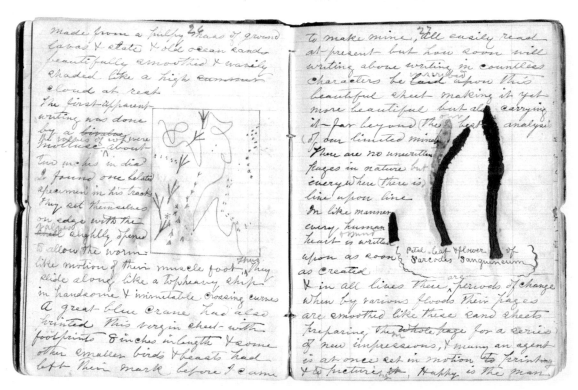

"Twenty Hill Hollow," January–May 1869. John Muir's Journal, [*Linanthus dichotomus*, Evening Snow]. Courtesy of the John Muir Papers, Holt-Atherton Department of Special Collections, University of the Pacific Library. Copyright 1984 Muir-Hanna Trust.

"Twenty Hill Hollow," January–May 1869. John Muir's Journal, "*Sarcodes sanguinea*, [Snow Plant]." Courtesy of the John Muir Papers, Holt-Atherton Department of Special Collections, University of the Pacific Library. Copyright 1984 Muir-Hanna Trust.

Muir, who claimed he had not made a single friend in California, was grateful the Carrs had arrived. He had thought about Jeanne hundreds of times in "seasons of deepest joy, amid the flower purple and gold of the plains, the fern fields in gorge and canyon, the sacred water, tree columns, and the eternal unnamable sublimities of the mountains." She was, he believed, the only one who understood his "motives and enjoyments," and it was she who often reminded Muir of the beauty of nature, of the pure and deep communion it afforded, of the glorious chart of God in nature spread out for them to see. He suggested she prepare for her Yosemite baptism and sent a flower to woo her. "Its anthers are curiously united in pairs and form stars upon its breast. The calyx seems to have been judged too plain and green to accompany the splendid corolla, and so is left behind among the leaves. I have met this plant [*Gilia tricolor* or *Leptosiphon androsaceus*] among the Sierra Nevada. There are five or six species. In beauty and simplicity they might be allowed to dwell within sight of Calypso."[8]

In January, Twenty Hill Hollow overflowed with sunlight. Muir wrote that "the ground steamed with fragrance. Light of unspeakable richness, was brooding....[and] sunshine seemed condensed into the chambers of that one glowing day." He thought of the experience as a moment of renewal for "many a plant and for me." Each day, as a plant, moss, or liverwort sprung itself loose from the ground and the "entire plain was soon covered with a soft velvet robe of living green," Muir felt inklings that he "might preach nature like an apostle."[9]

## FIRST SUMMER IN THE SIERRA

By May 1869 the scorching heat had sun-dried the landscape and again the season of plant-rest returned. Pat Delaney, whom Muir had met when he first arrived at La Grange, had noticed his "love of plants" and now urged him to accompany his sheep and shepherd Billy Simms to pasture in Tuolumne Meadows, in the High Sierra above Yosemite Valley to the east. Delaney did not suggest that Muir herd the sheep, but simply that he oversee the shepherd in his duties. This would be a practical means for Muir to explore and botanize, and though he knew nothing of the place to which he was going, he would continue with what he called "nature's doings." His journal was soon filled with vibrant notes about the abundant plant life, and he collected specimens for his herbarium, often placing the raceme of a lily or azalea in the buttonhole of his coat.[10]

Following a month in the North Fork canyon of the Merced River, Muir, Simms, and two thousand sheep headed to the Yosemite Creek Basin on Yosemite's north wall, two miles from the brink of Yosemite Valley. The charm of their camp, according to Muir, were the *Lilium pardalinum*, with flowers as big as a baby's bonnet. From here he anticipated the arrival of Jeanne Carr, whose trip to Yosemite he had been planning since November. Meanwhile, Carr disembarked from a stage at Clark's Station, near the Mariposa Grove, and fitted her eyes to what she called an "increasing grandeur of ferns, of pines, of rocks, to the deepening of the cañons and the uplifting of the mountain masses." Dressed in a divided skirt, with a garland of Washington lilies draped over her shoulder, she rode horseback from Clark's into Yosemite, "over the billows of what seemed 'a sea of mountains.'" Expecting to find Muir at Black's Hotel and finding that he was, instead, on Yosemite's north wall "entangled with sheep," she was disappointed that her letter regarding the date of her departure from Oakland had not reached him.[11]

Carr befriended James M. Hutchings, the proprietor of the Hutchings Hotel, and his wife, Elvira, and she brought to Hutchings's attention the name of John Muir. All that Carr saw during her excursion in Yosemite deepened her conviction that it was only from our "Great Mother," nature, that she learned lessons of God's love. She trod in what she believed would have been Muir's footsteps and left her thoughts for him "on the bridge between the Vernal and Nevada fall, 'the Lord bless thee & keep thee,' and this I wish always."[12]

In Tuolumne Meadows, near Soda Springs on the north bank of the Tuolumne River, Muir, Simms, and the sheep spent the summer. Muir climbed, sketched, collected and pressed plants, and explored the divide between the Tuolumne and Merced Basins, tramping down Bloody Canyon to Mono Lake. The lilies were higher than his head, and the "sunshine was warm enough for palms." The desert of Mono was "blooming in a high state of natural cultivation with the wild rose, cherry, aster, and the delicate abronia, and innumerable gilias, phloxes, poppies, and bush-compositae." He wondered how they could be so fresh and beautiful out in a volcanic desert. "They told," he found, "as happy a life as any plant-company I ever met, and seemed to enjoy even the hot sand and the wind."[13]

During this first long period of exposure to the Sierra, Muir rejoiced in what he called "a most divine piece of life among the snow peaks." He came to see how deep with beauty his "Range of Light" was overlaid. "The ground covered with crystals, the crystals with mosses and lichens and slow-spreading grasses and flowers, these with larger plants leaf over leaf with ever-changing color and form, the broad palms of the firs outspread over these, the azure dome over all like a bell-flower, and star above star."[14]

In September he returned to La Grange, working at the Delaney ranch until November. He was glad the world did not miss him: "All of my days with the Lord and his works are uncounted and unmeasured." Muir later chronicled his summer with Delaney's sheep in *My First Summer in the Sierra*.[15]

## ROCK FOOD FOR THE PINES

With Harry Randall, whom he had met at Delaney's, Muir set out for the Sierra and Yosemite in late November 1869. Muir was ready to bathe in the "spirit beams" of the mountains, lose consciousness of his own separate existence, blend with the landscape, and become "part and parcel of nature." His "love of pure unblemished Nature" seemed to "overmaster and blur out of sight all other objects and considerations." "I am," he wrote at thirty-one, "arrived at an age that requires that I should choose some definite course of life....Tomorrow I will be

Top: "Cabin in Yosemite Valley, 1869." Sketch by John Muir, 1869. Courtesy of the John Muir Papers, Holt-Atherton Department of Special Collections, University of the Pacific Library. Copyright 1984 Muir-Hanna Trust.

This was John Muir's first cabin in Yosemite Valley, to the east of Yosemite Falls on Yosemite Creek.

Bottom: "Live Oak Yosemite Valley." Sketch by John Muir, c. 1869. Courtesy of the John Muir Papers, Holt-Atherton Department of Special Collections, University of the Pacific Library. Copyright 1984 Muir-Hanna Trust.

 College of the Siskiyous Library

*"Pinus tuberculata* [Knobcone Pine], Sierra." Sketch by John Muir, c. 1870. Courtesy of the John Muir Papers, Holt-Atherton Department of Special Collections, University of the Pacific Library. Copyright 1984 Muir-Hanna Trust.

among the sublimities of Yosemite and forget that ever a thought of civilization or time-honoured proprieties [crossed my] pathless, lawless thoughts and wanderings."[16]

Approaching his studies like a leaf in a stream, Muir believed he was living without what the world would regard as a definite aim, and he enjoyed the exploration of nature in all its manifestations. He and Randall hired on to work for James M. Hutchings at Hutchings's hotel. Randall milked cows and drove oxen while Muir worked in the sawmill to the east of Yosemite Falls, cutting lumber for cottages, building partitions for the hotel rooms, and constructing a cabin for himself and Randall. Though a few flowers were blooming in summer-like nooks on the north-side rocks, Muir focused on what he called "grand glacial hieroglyphics," spending the winter and well into spring exploring the natural agencies by which Yosemite Valley had evolved. The nature of the geological formation of Yosemite had up to that point been defined by Josiah D. Whitney, director of the Geological Survey of California and professor of geology at Harvard. According to Whitney, the valley had been created by cataclysmic forces that caused the floor to sink. Muir challenged Whitney's theory with evidence of glaciation. This would bring him to the attention of the scientific community when Joseph LeConte, a friend of the Carrs and professor of geology at the University of California, arrived the following summer. Muir's empirical data attributed all the work in the valley to one single glacial period. While LeConte agreed with Muir that glaciers had been at work, he ascribed far more to pre-glacial action. While it is widely believed that there were three glacial advancements, there probably were as many as twelve, with water erosion and exfoliating granite also contributing to the formation of Yosemite Valley. Muir was more nearly correct than anyone else of his time.[17]

Muir's glacial studies were seamlessly connected to his interest in botany. The appeal and importance of the glaciers of Yosemite—and glaciers in general—was their role in the progress and perpetuity of life itself.

Glaciers *made* the mountains and ground corn for all the flowers....smoothed godlike mountain brows, and shaped lake cups for crystal waters; wove myriads of mazy canyons, and spread them out like lace....The busy snowflakes saw all the coming flowers, and the grand predestined forests. They said, "We will crack this rock for *Cassiope* where she may sway her tiny urns. Here we'll smooth a plat for green mosses, and round a bank for bryanthus bells." Thus labored the willing flake-souls linked in close congregations of ice, breaking rock food for the pines, as a bird crumbles bread for her young.[18]

Nature nurtured in equal balance rock for soil and seed for bread, "ever at work building and pulling down, creating and destroying, keeping everything whirling and flowing, allowing no rest but in rhythmical motion, chasing everything in endless song out of one beautiful form into another." Amused at her inventions, Muir was reassured that nature's purposes were "seen strikingly in seeds and buds, plans of another year[,] of thousands of years."[19]

In the spring of 1870 Muir began guiding tourists and turned his attention back to the study of botany. He sent Jeanne Carr "a moss with a globular capsule and a squinted, cowl-shaped calyptra," and to his brother David he sent a cluster of flower cups from a manzanita bush. Throughout the summer he felt he was feasting in the Lord's mountain house, and he claimed he could not escape the spell of Yosemite. "The oaks are in full leaf and have shoots long enough to bend over and move in the wind. The good old bracken is waist-high already, and almost all of the rock ferns have their outermost fronds unrolled."[20]

"What pen," Muir wrote, "may write my blessings?" But in November he and Randall returned to Delaney's. They left Yosemite Valley by way of the boulder-choked gorge of the Merced Canyon and detoured through the Merced Grove of sequoia. From the grove Muir wrote to Jeanne Carr. He hoped to render himself "more tree-wise and sequoical," and though he was leaving the Sierra, it was temporary. He surrendered his loyalty to wildness and spiritually remained in the mountains, no matter how far away he might be. "Do behold the King in his glory, King Sequoia! Behold! Behold!...I'm in the woods, woods, woods, and they are in *me-ee-ee*. The King tree and I have sworn eternal love...and I've taken the sacrament with Douglas squirrel, drank Sequoia wine, Sequoia blood, and with its rosy purple drops I am writing this woody gospel letter." His allegiance to wildness and to the mountains was not forgotten as he plowed Delaney's fields, nor was the condition of the herbarium specimens he had collected between 1868 and 1869, which he sent to Jeanne Carr for safekeeping. "A portion of my specimens collected in the last two years and left at this place [La Grange] and Hopeton are not very well cared for, and I have concluded to send them to you."[21]

## BETWEEN EVERY TWO PINE TREES THERE IS A DOOR

In January 1871 Hutchings, unable to find another sawyer of Muir's caliber, asked him to return to the mill. Muir resolved he would return to Yosemite, but not without justifying his decision to himself:

> There are eight members in our family [Muir's immediate family], all are useful members of society—save one....all exemplary, stable, anti-revolutionary. Surely then...one may be spared for so fine an experiment....I will follow my instincts, be myself for good or ill, and see what will be the upshot. As long as I live, I'll hear waterfalls and birds and winds sing. I'll interpret the rocks, learn the language of flood, storm, and the avalanche. I'll acquaint myself with the glaciers and wild gardens, and get as near the heart of the world as I can.[22]

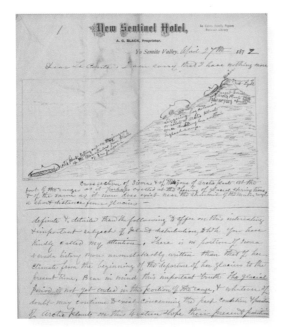

John Muir to Joseph LeConte, New Sentinel Hotel, Yosemite Valley, April 27, 1872. Courtesy of the Bancroft Library, University of California, Berkeley.

In this letter John Muir explained to Joseph LeConte his concept of plant distribution in the Sierra. "Cross section of the Sierras and of their zone of arctic plants at the foot of the ranges as it *perhaps* existed at the opening of the glacial springtime, and of the same as *it now does exist* near the summit of the main range a short distance from glaciers."

Having forfeited his handcrafted cottage to Hutchings's sister, he now slept in the sawmill, "for the sake of hearing the murmuring hush of the water," and built a small, boxlike room, where he stored his drawings and herbarium: a "hang-nest" beneath the gable at the end of the sawmill looking westward down the valley. Winter again precluded botanizing, and Muir continued to focus on his glacial studies. Nonetheless, he sent flowers, mosses, and ferns to family and friends. He sent so many sprigs of *Libocedrus* (incense cedar) out of the valley that he likened them to living postcards. "Think of the tree on which it grew, near two hundred feet in height, thirty inches in diameter, spiring up in the blue mountain air in gold and green, or waving and laving in storm." His sister Sarah's mother-in-law so prized his gift of a dried flower that she kept it in her Bible. The plants reminded his family back in Wisconsin "of rocks and mountains and of a warm enthusiastic heart very nearly allied to us wandering among and admiring their beauties."

In spring he picked violets for Sarah and asked that she send blue gentian seeds "also a few seeds of the white water lily and a few of the little blue harebells...with any little flower easily sent that I know." He welcomed the plant-friends from Wisconsin that assuaged the loneliness he often felt and somehow drew him closer to the family he knew he would not soon see.[23]

Plants and letters exchanged between Muir and his family and friends brought comfort, though Muir's literary career—shaped in large part by Jeanne Carr—ultimately required, she thought, that he cease the distraction of personal correspondence to focus on public writing. Carr's enthusiasm for Muir's career included sending friends and associates to visit him in Yosemite. J. B. McChesney, principal of the Oakland High School and later superintendent of the Oakland Public Schools, and Joseph LeConte had visited Muir the previous year, and in early May Carr orchestrated a visit from Ralph Waldo Emerson. Emerson climbed up into the hang-nest with Muir to see plant specimens and sketches he had drawn of the surrounding mountains. In later years Muir recalled that the two significant moments in his life were the discovery of the *Calypso borealis* in the Canada swamp and his meeting with Emerson.

In July Muir severed his relation with Hutchings. In Muir's opinion Hutchings had not been fair in his dealings with him and had held back wages. For his part, Hutchings resented Muir's popularity with the tourists and his lack of attentiveness to the sawmill: either he was studying wildflowers or he was called away to guide visitors in Yosemite. Muir's friendship with Hutchings's wife also aggravated the situation. Finally Muir had enough, and he spent the next six weeks exploring and studying glaciers from Mount Dana through to Bloody Canyon and Mono Lake, with his mind "untrammeled... unfrictioned, [and] unmeasured," basking in plant-glory and alpine bouquets. Drifting from rock to stream, he returned to Yosemite only to replenish his bread supply.

Asa Gray and Sir Joseph Hooker (both seated at left) and party, Western Botanical Expedition, 1877. Courtesy of the Botany Libraries, Library of the Gray Herbarium, Harvard University Herbaria, Harvard University.

> When I discovered a new plant, I sat down beside it for a minute or a day, to make its acquaintance and hear what it had to tell. When I came to moraines, or ice-scratches upon the rocks, I traced them back, learning what I could of the glacier that made them....I followed to their fountains the traces of the various soils upon which forests and meadows are planted; and when I discovered a mountain or rock of marked form and structure, I climbed about it, comparing it with its neighbors, marking its relations to living or dead glaciers, streams of water, avalanches of snow, etc., in seeking to account for its existence and character.[24]

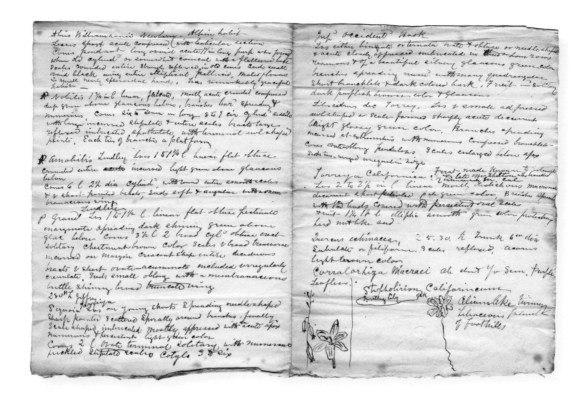

John Muir's botanical notes describing details of Sierra Nevada trees, c. 1870s. Courtesy of the John Muir National Historic Site.

In late fall Muir moved to Black's Hotel, on the south bank of the Merced River under the shadow of Sentinel Rock, where he took charge of the premises and remained over the winter, though it scarcely felt like home. While his mother questioned his ramblings—"I trust you will yet fill a more honorable and important position than you have yet attained"—he continued his botanical and glacial studies.[25]

## THE NOBLEST PLANT MOUNTAINEERS I EVER SAW

Fate kept Muir in Yosemite—there was no good reason to leave, and he had not yet learned enough of what the mountains had to teach. Revelation would require a leap of faith, and by mid-July 1872 he had made the gambol. He felt he was approaching a kind of "fruiting time." Ready to write something, he possessed, he thought, no words into which to shape his thoughts for public consumption, and he struggled. This year was by far the most intense of Muir's studies in the Sierra, and it would be, as well, the year that brought to Yosemite the renowned American botanists Asa Gray and John Torrey and the landscape painter William Keith, with whom Muir would develop a lifelong devoted friendship. A fruiting time? It was more like a harvest![26]

In spring Muir built a cabin in a clump of mountain dogwood on the bank of the Merced River, where the river approaches closest to Royal Arches and in a bold curve swings southward across Yosemite Valley. His article "Rambles of a Botanist among the Plants and Climates of California" was published in June, and in July he welcomed Gray, a colleague of Ezra Carr through mutual eastern academic and medical associations. In the morning of the day Gray arrived, Muir climbed Sentinel Rock and from the summit carried down an oak sprig that he sent to his sister Sarah, along with a letter that expressed his excitement over the Harvard botanist's visit.[27]

In December Muir had sent Gray seeds from a California nutmeg, and specimens of bird's-foot fern, lily, and *Primula.* Gray thought Muir was a splendid "plant-finder," and it was confirmed after ten days of botanizing with him in Yosemite. When Gray left by way of the Coulterville Trail, Muir returned to the valley to find John Torrey, Gray's mentor and professor of botany and chemistry at Columbia College in New York. This was, as Muir said, "a curious thing," since Gray had noted earlier that day that it was unlikely that Torrey, now a much senior scholar, would visit Yosemite. Torrey arrived with John H. Redfield, botanist and herbarium conservator at the Academy of Natural Sciences of Philadelphia. Unexpectedly, they had met in Cheyenne, Wyoming, each carrying a plant press and on his way to Yosemite to botanize. Redfield had been in Colorado botanizing with Townsend S. Brandegee, who would later become the honorary curator of the herbarium at the University of California. Redfield knew Albert Kellogg, a physician, pharma-

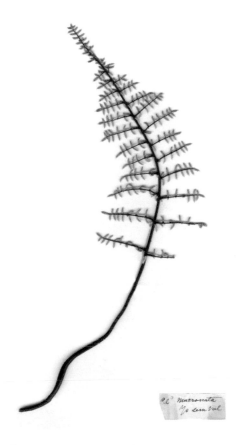

*Pellaea mucronata* Eaton, Bird's Foot Fern

cist, botanist, and founding member of the California Academy of Sciences who knew the Carrs, and as a result knew of Muir. It is likely that Kellogg introduced Redfield to Muir and his work as a botanist, and that Redfield hoped to meet Muir, though no letter of introduction preceded his visit to Yosemite. Redfield and Torrey entered Yosemite by way of the Big Oak Flat Trail and therefore did not pass Gray as he departed.[28]

The encouragement Muir received from Gray, Torrey, and Redfield rekindled his interest in the study of botany, discouraged by the absence of an authoritative botanical guide to Yosemite and High Sierra flora, which made it difficult—if not impossible—to determine species.[29]

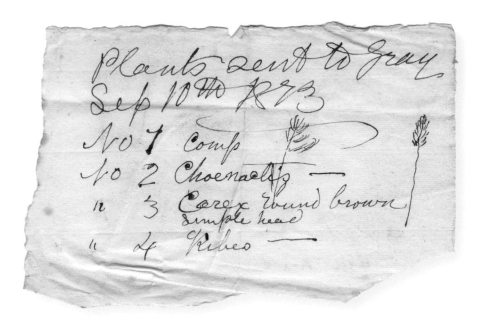

"Plants sent to Gray, September 10th, 1873." List of plant specimens John Muir sent to Asa Gray. "No. 1 Compositae[,] No. 2 Chaenactis[,] No. 3 Carex round brown simple head[,] No. 4 Ribes." Courtesy of the John Muir National Historic Site.

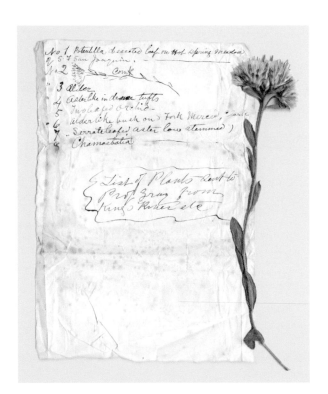 

Left: "List of plants sent by John Muir to Asa Gray from Kings River, etc.," John Muir, c. 1870s. Courtesy of the John Muir National Historic Site.

The plant specimen is No. 2, *Aster oreganus*, a member of the Asteraceae family.

Right: Note and specimen collected by John Muir and sent to Asa Gray, c. 1870s, with Gray's response. Courtesy of the John Muir National Historic Site.

Muir wrote, "From wet rock at elevation of 8,000 feet. Have seen it in Tenaya Cañon as low as 6,000 feet." Gray responded, "*Tofieldia glutinosa* not very rare."

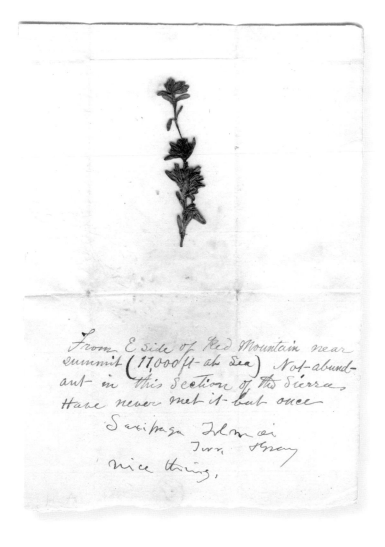

Note and specimen collected by John Muir and sent to Asa Gray, c. 1870s, with Gray's response. Courtesy of the John Muir National Historic Site.

Muir wrote, "From Mt. Lyell alt[itude] of 12,000 feet, on fissure slate rock, a few yards from the glacier." Asa Gray responded, "*Polemonium confertum* Gray. Is on very high mountains of Colorado."

Note and specimen collected by John Muir and sent to Asa Gray, c. 1870s, with Gray's response. Courtesy of the John Muir National Historic Site.

Muir wrote, "From east side of Red Mountain near summit (11,000 feet above Sea). Not abundant in this section of the Sierras. Have never met it but once." Gray responded, "*Saxifraga tolmiei* Torr. & Gray [,] nice thing."

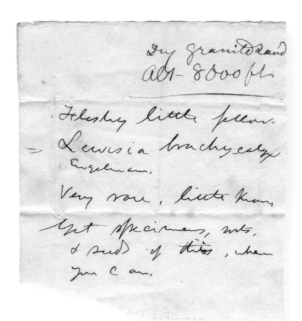

Note from John Muir that accompanied plant specimen sent to Asa Gray, c. 1872–1875, with Gray's response. Courtesy of the John Muir National Historic Site.

Muir wrote, "Dry granite sand, altitude 8,000 feet." Asa Gray's response. "Fleshy little fellow = *Lewisia brachycalyx* Engelmann. Very rare, little known. Get specimens, roots, and seeds of this, when you can."

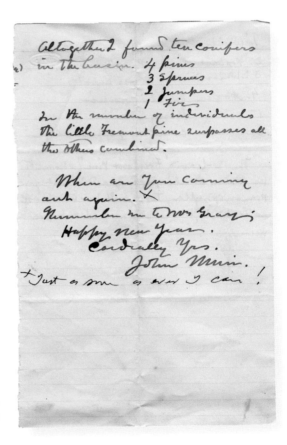

List of trees observed by John Muir with note to Asa Gray, c. 1872–1873, with Gray's response. Courtesy of the John Muir National Historic Site.

Muir wrote, "When are you coming out again. Remember me to Mrs. Gray." Gray responded regarding Pinaceae and added a personal note: "Just as soon as ever I can!"

Note from John Muir that accompanied plant specimen sent to Asa Gray, c. 1872–1875, with Gray's response. Courtesy of the John Muir National Historic Site.

Muir wrote, "Growing on sunny moraine slopes at elevation of from 7000 to 8000 feet." Gray responded, "Little Violet = *Viola nuttallii* var. *venosa* Watson."

Note from John Muir that accompanied plant specimen sent to Asa Gray, c. 1872–1875, with Gray's response. Courtesy of the John Muir National Historic Site.

Muir wrote, "From foot of Lyell Glacier, growing in fissures on rock over which ice cold water is flowing, a companion of the very bravest of the frost enduring carices." Gray responded, "*Talinum pygmaeum* Gray."

Muir sent plant specimens and field notes to Gray, who returned them to Muir (at least in part) with taxonomical notations. New specimens from the western regions began to flood the East. Muir and Kellogg sent specimens, as did John Gill Lemmon. (Lemmon, a teacher and self-taught botanist, set up a botanical establishment on Telegraph Avenue in Oakland in the 1880s and became the California State Board of Forestry's botanist in 1888.) Gray used these specimens in the preparation of a magnum opus, *A Flora of North America,* coauthored with Torrey, and in his own *Flora.* Western botanists, in general, hoping their discoveries were new to science sent specimens and field notes to Gray with considerable urgency; finding a new species and naming it or having a new plant named for the discoverer provided instant taxonomic immortality.[30]

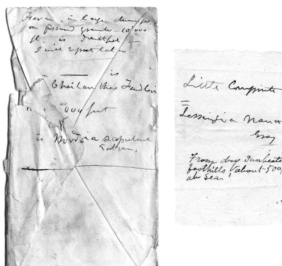

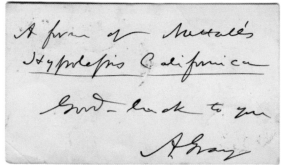

Left: Note and envelope addressed to John Muir from Asa Gray, Cambridge, Massachusetts, dated April 10, [c. 1872–1875]. Courtesy of the John Muir National Historic Site.

Gray's notation reads, "Little Compositae = *Lessingia nana* Gray. *Fendleri* in large clumps on fissured granite 10,000 feet is doubtful—I will respond later...is *Cheilanthes fendleri* and...feet is *Woodsia scopulina* Eaton." Gray was responding to Muir's plant specimen and accompanying note, "From dry sunbeaten foothills, about 500 feet above sea."

Right: Postal card from Asa Gray to John Muir, c. 1872–1873. Courtesy of the John Muir National Historic Site.

"A form of Nuttall's *Hypolepis californica.* Good luck to you."

When Gray returned to Cambridge, he sent Muir a list of plants he hoped Muir would procure for Harvard. Muir attended to Gray's request, "packing as you direct [snugly in hardy damp moss]...sections of *Pinus flexilis* and *Abies Williamsonii* from [the] foot of Lyell." Redfield, who was devoted to expanding the herbarium at the Academy of Natural Sciences of Philadelphia, in 1875 requested plant specimens from Muir to replenish the three hundred he had collected in Yosemite and the High Sierra in 1872, as well as anything new he might find. This resulted in Muir's sending him over one hundred plant specimens that year. Muir's interests were not purely philanthropic; he was eager to expand his own knowledge as well as supply the herbaria at Harvard and the Academy of Natural Sciences. Though he was willing to oblige Gray and Redfield with plant specimens, Muir refused to accommodate Gray's request that he join the faculty at Harvard. Lacking interest in what he called "all the just and proper ding dong of civilization," he chose to remain free to approach the study of botany and geology without what he perceived to be the constraints of the university and its remoteness from the subjects and objects to which he was wedded. The plain truth was that Gray had withdrawn into the laboratory, and Muir felt that Joseph LeConte had done the same. Muir would not "be caught and put in [a] professional harness."[31]

John Muir in San Francisco, during his first trip out of Yosemite Valley, to Oakland and San Francisco, following his arrival in California in 1868. Photograph by William H. Rulofson, 1872. Courtesy of the Bancroft Library, University of California, Berkeley.

In August Muir began planning a trip to Oakland to see Jeanne Carr. It would be an opportunity to discuss his writing with her, and it was a trip he would undertake at the end of the year. Meanwhile, he turned upward to Mount Lyell, McClure, and Hoffman to plant stakes in glacial ice with Merrill Moores, now sixteen, with whom he had hiked in Wisconsin, and who would spend the summer with Muir.

In October the artists William Keith and Benoni Irwin arrived in Yosemite, accompanied by a note from Jeanne Carr affirming that she had not intentionally kept "the best wine of kindred and related spirits till the last of your season's feast."[32]

Before he left for Oakland in mid-December, Muir wrote to his friend J. B. McChesney for help in identifying plants: "If I would only have access to books containing these plants I could easily name them." At a time when ten libraries in the world held all the botanical works to be found, California only had a partial collection available, at the California

Academy of Sciences. Botanists, including Muir, were apt to make mistakes in classifying plants. Earlier in September Gray had written to Muir that he was sending copies of several of his books. They arrived within days of Muir's letter to McChesney. While none of the material dealt directly with the flora of the High Sierra, it was a place to start, and Gray said as much. It is doubtful that at the time Muir even had a copy of Wood's *Class-Book of Botany*. He recognized that his ability to identify plant species was compromised without a guide or key, but overall he reached beyond these limitations—his botanical and glacial studies were empirical, and his approach to both subjects was as a methodical and systematic observer and as a vivid aesthetician in search of beauty.[33]

For little more than a week in December 1872, Muir visited Oakland and San Francisco. He described the excursion back to Yosemite by way of Turlock, Hopeton, and Coulterville in his essay "A Geologist's Winter Walk," published in the *Overland Monthly*, a retelling of a letter to Jeanne Carr. When Muir reached Yosemite Valley he was restless and tainted with what he called "the sticky sky....and town heaviness." He rolled up a pair of blankets and set out up Tenaya Canyon to make glacial measurements around the base of South Dome [Half Dome] and climb Clouds' Rest for the *Primula suffrutescens* Gray had requested:

*Primula suffrutescens* Gray, Sierra Primrose

*Ivesia muirii* Gray, Granite Mousetail

[I] ran up to Clouds' Rest for your Primulas, and as I stuffed them in big sods into a sack, I said, "Now I wonder what mouthfuls this size will accomplish for the Doctor's primrose hunger"....I ran home in the moonlight with your sack of roses slung on my shoulder...down through the junipers, down through the firs, now in black shadow, now in white light, past great South Dome white as the moon, past spirit-like Nevada, past Pywiack, through the groves of Illilouette and spiry pines of the open valley, star crystals sparkling above, frost crystals beneath, and rays of spirit beaming everywhere....I have a rare chance of getting your plants packed out of the Valley tomorrow, and so have determined to send all together with a few seeds in a box by Wells Fargo Express.[34]

Muir sent along a few plants that he asked Gray to name:

[T]wo large yellow and purple plants from the top of Mount Lyell, above all the pinched and blinking dwarfs that almost justify Darwin's mean ungodly word "struggle." They form a round expansion upon the wedge of plant life that slants up into the thin lean sky. They are the noblest plant mountaineers I ever saw, climbing above the glaciers into the frosty azure, and flowering in purple and gold, rich and abundant as ever responded to the thick, creamy sun-gold of the tropics.[35]

January brought "a block of solid sun-gold, not of the thin frosty kind, but of a quality that called forth butterflies and tingled the fern coils and filled the noontide with a dreamy hum of insect wings." Muir found "one big Phacelia [scorpion weed, probably a fiddleneck] in full bloom on the north side of the Valley....Also at the same sunny nook several bushes of *Arctostaphylos glauca* [manzanita] were in full flower, and many other plants were swelling their buds and breathing fragrance, showing that they were full of the thoughts and intentions of spring." He hoped that among the specimens he sent to Gray there would be a new genus and a half-dozen new species. Among them was an *Ivesia* he found near Mount Hoffman that Gray named *Ivesia muirii* in his honor. "If you will keep botanizing in the High Sierra," Gray wrote, "you will find curious and new things, no doubt. One such, at least, is in your present collection...the wee mouse-tail Ivesia....Get a new alpine genus, that I may make a *Muiria glacialis!*"[36]

## NEARBY A GARDEN OF LUPINES

While Muir's work on glacial studies progressed through a series of trips into the High Sierra in 1873, he remained curious about the plants he passed along the way. In early June he returned to Yosemite Valley from the Lyell Glacier in anticipation of the arrival of Jeanne Carr, William Keith, and Albert Kellogg, with whom he had planned a trip into the High Sierra. A brief interlude following their return from Tuolumne Meadows would be set aside in July for Keith, his wife, Alice Elizabeth (Lizzie), their son Charlie, and

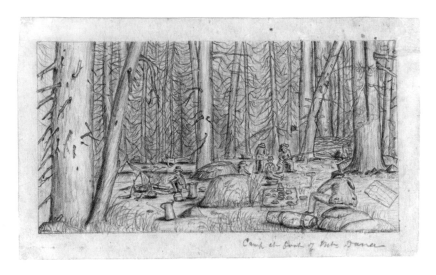

"Camp at foot of Mount Dana," Tuolumne Meadows, [Yosemite National Park]. Sketch by John Muir, c. 1873. Courtesy of the John Muir Papers, Holt-Atherton Department of Special Collections, University of the Pacific Library. Copyright 1984 Muir-Hanna Trust.

During the summer of 1873, between two trips into the High Sierra with Jeanne C. Carr and Albert Kellogg, John Muir traveled from Yosemite Valley to Tuolumne Meadows and Mount Dana with William Keith, his wife, Lizzie, their son Charlie, and Emily Pelton.

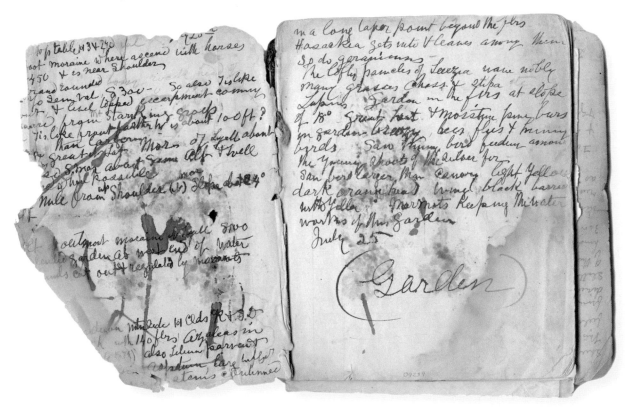

"July 25, [1873] Garden." "'Alps' and Little Yosemite," July–August 1873. John Muir's Journal, inside front cover. Courtesy of the John Muir Papers, Holt-Atherton Department of Special Collections, University of the Pacific Library. Copyright 1984 Muir-Hanna Trust.

On July 24 Muir headed from Yosemite Valley into the High Sierra with Jeanne C. Carr and Albert Kellogg on a six-week excursion to the headwaters of the Merced and San Joaquin Rivers. Little Yosemite Valley, which they would have reached the first day, was resplendent with a garden of azaleas and lupines.

Emily Pelton (Muir's friend from Prairie du Chien) and her party. A sky pilot (*Polemonium caeruleum*) Muir tucked into his pocket provided evidence that they successfully reached the summit of Mount Dana, along with other plant specimens carefully folded into a sheet of paper and preserved.[37]

Following Muir's return, he, Carr, and Kellogg headed up out of the Valley on a six-week excursion during which Carr and Kellogg made their highest camp on a "fountain summit" of the Illilouette Basin. Muir went on alone to study glaciers and botanize in the upper canyons of the middle and north forks of the San Joaquin. Crossing the Merced divide he found what he called "a meeting of lowland and alpine plants of all kinds....Perhaps it is because streams[,] descending directly from the summit mountains on both sides, bring down all higher seeds, making a kind of natural botanical garden." He was wildly delighted to meet his first California anemone (*Anemone occidentalis*), and it sent him mentally "bounding to a certain hillside in Wisconsin where the *Anemone nuttalliana* came in clouds of spring, and a dozen species of goldenrods and asters gathered and added gold to gold, and purple to purple in autumn."[38]

Plants collected by John Muir at Mount Dana and environs, 1873. Courtesy of the John Muir National Historic Site.

In mid-September Muir, Kellogg, Galen Clark, and Billy Simms set out from Yosemite to explore the headwaters of the Middle and South Forks of the San Joaquin, Kings, and Kern Rivers—a journey on horseback intended to include Jeanne Carr, who reluctantly returned to Oakland to prepare for a move to faculty housing in Berkeley. Leaving what she described to her friend Louie Wanda Strentzel as the most delightful conjunction of kindred spirits, she found that the letters she received from Muir as he traveled south only made matters worse. She regretted not continuing on with them, but as it turned out, the season was too far advanced for botanists Muir and Kellogg to accomplish much.[39]

## I CARE ONLY TO ENTICE PEOPLE TO LOOK AT NATURE'S LOVELINESS

From late 1873 until the following September, Muir lodged with the J. B. McChesney family in Oakland, where he worked on a series of articles, "Studies in the Sierra," for the *Overland*

*Monthly.* A fluent and vivid conversationalist, he found the solitary nature of writing con-
fining. There were visits from William Keith and John Swett, a pioneer California public
educator who would later offer Muir a room in his home on Taylor Street in San Francisco,
and a chance meeting the following summer with
Dr. and Mrs. John Theophile Strentzel and their
daughter Louie Wanda at the Carr home. It was
a meeting orchestrated by Jeanne Carr, who had
upon her return from Yosemite the previous year
written to Louie suggesting she meet Muir. More
than three years would elapse before Muir of his
own volition would accept the invitation he had
received from the Strentzel family to visit their
ranch in the Alhambra Valley.

*Adiantum chilense* Kaulf., Maidenhair Fern

At the McChesney home Muir found comfort
in a "wee fern leaf...here on my table trembling
in the breeze that comes sweeping across the San
Francisco bay from the ocean." He wrote to his
sister Sarah about it:

It is the maidenhair...perhaps the most graceful and
delicate of all the ferns of North America. It is found
in almost every state, but in the Sierras it is yet more
delicate and reaches higher perfection than in the
moist shadowy dells of Wisconsin. It grows in our
mountains up to an altitude of about 9000 feet....Instead of growing in soil, as in Wisconsin,
it is found only as a rock fringe where it is sheltered from storms and is abundantly supplied
with moisture...fanned by the spray of a waterfall.[40]

In September, with the Sierra series complete, Muir chanced to see a goldenrod in bloom
in a weedy spot alongside a sidewalk, packed his clothes and journals, and caught a train for
Turlock. He headed out into the familiar flower gardens of Twenty Hill Hollow, and from
there to Hopeton, on the edge of the oak fringe of the Merced River, traveling up through
the purple foothills to Coulterville, along the Merced divide, to Crane Flat, and back into
the groves and meadows of Yosemite. Not one of the rocks or any of the distant mountains
seemed to call him, and he felt as if he were a stranger. "Surely," he thought, "this Merced
and Tuolumne chapter of my life is done." He had been rereading Jeanne Carr's letters.
They formed a precious volume "whose sentences are more intimately connected with my

mountain work than any one will ever be able to appreciate." He gathered a handful of leaves for her, Keith, and Mrs. McChesney, the last of Yosemite that he would send.[41]

Muir planned to leave in a few days but a farewell was difficult to execute. The mountains seized him, and he was up the Merced Canyon "in a kind of calm, incurable ecstasy." "I am hopelessly and forever a mountaineer....I care to live only to entice people to look at Nature's loveliness. My own special self is nothing." He would preach like John the Baptist "the green brown woods."[42]

Finally, in October 1874, the Merced and Tuolumne chapter of his life drew to a close, and he walked out of Yosemite northward along the old California-Oregon stage road from Redding to Mount Shasta. In spring he moved to the home of John and Mary Swett. There was some comfort in short excursions to Mount Tamalpais and the hills across the bay, from which he returned with handfuls of flowers.

> On my way home, walked through the waterfront streets....Most every child...would cry out, "Oh, give me a flower...please give me a flower," and when I handed each of them a lily or daisy, sprig of flowering Ceanothus or azalea, it was fine to see the beautiful glow that came into the faces...as they gazed into the faces of the flowers. Their faces glowing with a beautiful enthusiasm, as if regarding each blossom as an angel from heaven.[43]

## FOR IN THE WORK OF BEAUTY NATURE NEVER STOPS

From 1874 to 1878, Muir furnished the *San Francisco Daily Evening Bulletin* with letters as a special correspondent that popularized his excursions and his study of glaciers, flora, and forests and encouraged tourists to visit Yosemite in all seasons for the health-promoting qualities and peace they would find. His columns in the *Overland Monthly* and the *Sacramento Daily Union* raised important questions about the limited value placed on wildness, professing an "inclusive right relationship" among all parts and pieces of the natural world—equal justice. Muir utilized his credibility as a naturalist to write on behalf of wilderness protection, drawing attention to public protest over the destruction of forests, and by the late 1870s he called for an end to the corporate destruction of California's natural resources, urging federal control of forests. In the early 1890s he collaborated with the associate editor of *The Century Magazine,* Robert Underwood Johnson, in promoting the establishment of Yosemite

John Muir in Scribble Den at home in Martinez, California, c. 1890s. Courtesy of the James Eastman Shone Collection of Muiriana, Holt-Atherton Department of Special Collections, University of the Pacific.

National Park to protect and preserve Yosemite Valley, and he guided the formation of the Sierra Club, which would advocate for the enjoyment, exploration, and preservation of the Sierra Nevada. Elected president of the club at its inception in 1892, he held the office until his death. In 1894 Muir's first book, *The Mountains of California,* was published, drawing from selected articles published between 1874 and 1882.[44]

A man "so fond of flowers," Muir forever believed that his "garden and herbarium and woods [were]...all in their places as they grow." What he meant was that plants belong in their native environment, and that is where they are best enjoyed and studied. This was the consummate lesson he learned from the High Sierra and Yosemite Valley. "I know them there," he said, and "[I] can find them when I will." If a bit of salvation existed on Earth, it remained for Muir always in wildness, and always in the Range of Light, among the *Cassiope,* sequoia, and sugar pine. While some would go the distance with him into the wilderness, Muir recognized that others would only survey the borders—the sense of calling or desire or ability to climb the mountains belonged to far too few. Muir would, as best as he was able, with faith and hope, balance human relations, civilized places, and the

John Muir beside a *Sequoia sempervirens* in Muir Woods, c. 1910. Courtesy of the James Eastman Shone Collection of Muiriana, Holt-Atherton Department of Special Collections, University of the Pacific.

practical issues of money with the wild gardens that remained for him the constant, to be formal if he chose, with what censorship he imposed upon himself, and without scientific purvey—if inclined. Muir's urge to entice people to see nature's beauty, grew—essentially blossomed—from his abiding love and respect for the wilderness of California.[45]

# Five

## ALASKA
### Nature's Own Reserve

*Mertensia paniculata* (Ait.) Don, Tall Bluebells

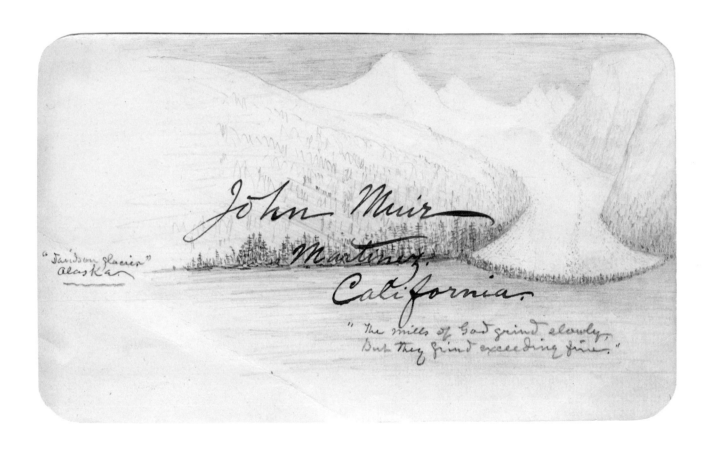

Above: Sketch by John Muir, c. 1900. Courtesy of the John Muir Papers, Holt-Atherton Department of Special Collections, University of the Pacific Library. Copyright 1984 Muir-Hanna Trust.

"John Muir[,] Martinez[,] California. 'Davidson Glacier,' Alaska. The mills of God grind slowly. But they grind exceedingly fine."

Overleaf: *Stellaria longipes* var. *edwardsii* Goldie, Long-Stalked Starwort

193

St. Mich

J. M

l's, Alaska

ir, 1891

GRAY HERBARIUM
HARVARD
UNIVERSITY

*Lloydia serotina* (L.) Salisb. ex Rchb., Snowdon Lily

*Luzula hyperborea* R. Br., Northern Woodrush

*Geum glaciale* Adams. ex Fisch. & C. A. Mey., Glacier Avens

GRAY HERBARIUM
HARVARD
UNIVERSITY

*Saxifraga davurica* Willd.

*Eritrichium nanum* L. var. *aretioides* Herder [E. *nanum* (L.) Schrad. ex Gaudin], Alpine Forget-Me-Not

*Primula borealis* Duby, Northern Primrose

GRAY HERBARIUM
HARVARD
UNIVERSITY

*Anemone parviflora* Michx., Northern Anemone

*Anemone narcissiflora* L., Narcissus-flowered Anemone

208.

Ranunc. pygmæus, Wahl.
Cape Markham, Sib.
J. Murir, 1881.

*Ranunculus pygmaeus* Wahl., Pygmy Buttercup

123.

Cassiope tetragona, Don.

Cape Thompson, Alaska

J. Muir, 1881.

MUIR WOULD BEGIN his exploration of the pure wilderness of Alaska in 1879, turning toward the regions of the far north on seven occasions over a period of twenty years and concluding his travels as a member of the Harriman Alaska Expedition in 1899. He would spend a total of twenty-two months in Alaska and probably wished he could spend more time there. While each excursion deepened Muir's loyalty, the most memorable of his experiences, the ones that excited his enthusiasm for the abundance of glaciers and profusion of plant life, occurred during his trips in 1879, 1880, and 1881. The challenges he faced were daunting by today's standards of exploration, and he managed his deliberate studies with simple tools and a reliance on immediate experience.

For Muir Alaska was a continuation of the divine spark in a world always making itself anew, growing from ice, and producing a crop of possibility, fruitful and true. Alaska's glaciers were, he said, "manifest scriptures," life-giving fountains that birthed harmonic beauty and produced food for the verdant landscape. While Muir's travels in Alaska were an opportunity for a close study of glacial history, he would not forget the plants he saw, many of them friends from the High Sierra.[1]

## A MUCKLE OF TRUE BOG BEAUTIES

During the winter of 1878 and the spring of 1879, Muir resided in San Francisco at the home of his friend Isaac Upham, a publisher and bookseller. In June he accepted an invitation to speak on the geological history of Yosemite Valley glaciers at a Sunday School convention in Yosemite. Sheldon Jackson, who also spoke at the convention, was a persuasive promoter and voluminous letter writer who filled his correspondence with urgings to see Alaska. He

*Cassiope tetragona* (L.) D. Don, White Arctic Mountain Heather

had assisted in the establishment of a Presbyterian missionary in the vicinity of Fort Wrangel (later "Wrangell"), and his presentation was an irresistible lure for Muir, fueling his desire to travel to the region. Muir's friends viewed his departure on June 20 as an indication of his restlessness. In a letter to Jeanne Carr he wrote that he was going home, "to my summer in the snow and ice forests of the north coast."[2]

Muir departed from San Francisco the day after his engagement to Louie Wanda Strentzel. Clearly, though now betrothed, he retained his independence. He was, he wrote, "accustomed to walk on, relying only on God and myself," and he assured himself that the world was all before him. The Strentzels would see him again in February, in time for the wedding in April. Within seven days of his departure, Louie wrote her first letter to him. She and her father had gone to Upham's residence to retrieve his herbarium, letters, and inventions:

> I grew more and more uneasy concerning your herbarium, until at last it seemed to me that there could be no safety for it except under my care....At Mr. Upham's they could not be expected to leave their own treasures to rescue just a lot of old papers and dried plants, while with me, well, you know only too well how precious in my sight must be always everything that is yours....I persuaded Papa to go with me to San Francisco Monday morning, and Mr. Upham said he was "very glad of our coming for those plants on account of the mice being troublesome in that closet."

Muir's herbarium specimens would be safe from fire in a trunk by the door of Louie's little room. She was kind in "caring so faithfully for [his] bits of things," he wrote.[3]

Louie Wanda Strentzel Muir, c. 1880. Courtesy of the State Historical Society of Wisconsin.

As a special correspondent for the *San Francisco Daily Evening Bulletin*, Muir wrote about his explorations in Alaska, much as he had written about Yosemite Valley and the High Sierra. His columns were read by his friends and widely reprinted throughout the United States to an ever growing circle of enthusiasts. Resounding with an invitation to tens of thousands of Americans to an Inside Passage vacation, the columns would have been a disappointment to Muir had the rhetorical net been any less widespread. By celebrating Alaska's noble wilderness, he acquainted his audience with the extravagance of glaciers, forests, and flora—the providence of God to combine ice and life. Among those who read his letters to the *Bulletin* was Louie: "Since reading your *Bulletin* letter last Saturday, I have not fretted much about a poor lost starving wanderer, as it would seem that he has full command over the very nicest most delicious fruit-garden ever known!!"[4]

Muir sailed north on the *Dakota* with his friend Thomas Magee, a San Francisco businessman and avid mountaineer who had visited him in Yosemite Valley in 1872. After they had explored Victoria, Puget Sound, and the Fraser and Columbia Rivers together, in Portland Magee boarded the *Oregon* to return to San Francisco and Muir boarded the *California* for Alaska. He would not soon forget the grand poem of God set before him during the first leg of his first trip to the far north. The dark green forests that hugged the shores urged him on in eager excitement.[5]

Samuel Hall Young, c. 1880. Courtesy of the John Muir Papers, Holt-Atherton Department of Special Collections, University of the Pacific Library. Copyright 1984 Muir-Hanna Trust.

When John Muir first arrived in Alaska in 1879, he—the gray-tweed-overcoated naturalist "Professor Muir"—was greeted by Samuel Hall Young, the resident Presbyterian missionary.

The voyage from Victoria to Alaska through the Inside Passage followed ocean inlets and narrow channels between impressive mountains densely forested from the snow line down to the water's edge. It seemed to Muir "as if a hundred Lake Tahoes were joined end to end....Day after day we seemed to float in the very heart of true fairyland, each succeeding view seeming more and more beautiful, the one we chance to have before us the most surprisingly beautiful of all." He had never before found himself embosomed in scenery that was hopelessly beyond description: "the whole is so tender, so fine, so ethereal, any penwork upon it seems course and utterly unavailing." The scale was grand and the prosperity of nature was lavish. In forests and bogs grew his old favorite flowers of Canada: "heathworts, linnaea, cranberry, huckleberries, sedum [stonecrop], and pyrola [wintergreen]." He called them "a muckle of true bog beauties dear to the heart of every dweller of the cool North." The green, damp, mossy forests were impenetrably dense, with "one generation falling and crumbling into humus, for the next to grow upon the decaying leaves, boughs and trunks and mosses forming a mass ten to fifteen feet deep."[6]

The *California* docked at Fort Wrangel, where Muir was greeted by Samuel Hall Young, the resident Presbyterian missionary. Looking out beyond Fort Wrangel Muir could see the mountains laden with glaciers and the wooded islands that circled around the bay to seaward, and it clearly exceeded the mental images he had drawn. "Land and water combined in lines and colors beautiful beyond expression, everywhere exciting and satisfying our best aspirations....The natural love of wild beauty that forms an essential part of every human being began to declare itself. Every eye was beaming and appreciative. Gaze in any direction forward, back[,] in either hand, soul and sight were filled."[7]

From Fort Wrangel Muir traveled on board the river steamer *Cassiar* with Young; John Vanderbilt, with whom he lodged; and three Presbyterian clergymen, the members of a missionary party that included Sheldon Jackson. Out through the Wrangell Narrows and up the Stickeen River, Muir studied the tall grass that formed a waving, meadowlike margin immediately in front of the dark coniferous forest bedded with golden mosses and laced with ferns. Beneath the trees the ground was covered to a depth of two or three feet with mosses of indescribable freshness and beauty. The untamed solitudes seemed both strange and familiar. In "the wild free bosom of Alaska woods" there was an eternal familiarity: "Go where we will, all over the world, we seem to have been there before."[8]

Continuing on between glaciers and canyons, the *Cassiar* anchored in Glenora, British Columbia, on the northeastern flank of the main Coast Range. Muir and Young trekked through blooming alpine meadows, miles of wild rose, clover, honeysuckle, gentian, and goldenrod. They zigzagged over fallen timber through a maze of crevasses and up steep slopes where, beyond the timberline, mountain pastures grew with luxuriant, delicate fields of flowers. According to Young, "everything that was marvelous in form, fair in colour, or sweet in fragrance seemed to be represented," and at once Muir went wild. "From cluster to cluster of flowers he ran, falling on his knees, babbling in unknown tongues, prattling a curious mixture of scientific lingo and baby talk, worshipping his little blue-and-pink goddesses":

> "Ah! My blue-eyed darlin', little did I think to see you here. How did you stray away from Shasta?
>
> "Well, well! Who'd 'a' thought that you'd have left that niche in the Merced mountains to come here!
>
> "And who might you be, now, with your wonder look? Is it possible that you can be (two Latin polysyllables)? You're lost, my dear; you belong in Tennessee.
>
> "Ah! I thought I'd find you, my homely little sweetheart."[9]

So absorbed was Muir in his "amatory botany" that he seemed to forget Young was there. Young could see that, though Muir's technical knowledge was admirable and thorough, it was not half of what Muir was about. His inquisitiveness and passion for the natural world were guided by what Young believed was "a spiritual insight into Nature's lore which is granted only to those who love and woo her in her great outdoor palaces." Muir's faith in life in all its forms and his appreciation for nature's method exceeded Young's and, indeed, that of everyone he knew. He searched for answers to the unsolved questions that lay before him, and they rested upon his mind until settled. In later years, Young recalled that one plant followed another, "with its sand-covered roots," into Muir's pockets, into:

> his handkerchief and the *full* of his shirt, until he was bulbing and sprouting all over....He was taking them to the boat to analyze and compare at leisure. Then he began to requisition my receptacles. I stood it while he stuffed my pockets, but rebelled when he tried to poke the prickly scratchy things inside my shirt.

Young had not, he admitted, attained what he called "that sublime indifference to physical comfort, that Nirvana of passivity," that Muir had found.[10]

*Picea engelmannii* Parry ex Engelm., Engelmann Spruce

Hours passed and progress was slow on the southeastern slope of the mountain as Muir and Young headed for the summit and the sunset. Beyond the flower gardens, in a land of rocks and cliffs with patches of short grass, caribou moss, and lichens, they looked out upon the deep valley of the Stickeen River to see light green cottonwood, dark green alder, acres of crimson fireweed, and small patches of dark blue lupine. Both men reached for the thin fragments of projecting slate that guarded the summit, but as Young jumped, his weak shoulder joints—injured while breaking colts in West Virginia—dislocated. Muir worked his way down to a point below Young, seized his belt and pants, and drew him over the brink, lowering him down the thousand-foot wall and half-carrying him to the *Cassiar* the following morning.[11]

A second trip from Fort Wrangel to Glenora was launched in August. Above the Stickeen River in a slightly dimpled plateau stood a forest of pine, spruce, and aspen on a tributary of Thibert Creek that flowed into the Arctic Ocean. Narrow meadows rose here and there, and throughout the region a kind of bunchgrass often four or five feet tall grew wildly in open woods, on dry hillsides, and over the prairies above the timberline. Wading through fields of dogbane, manzanita, and bedstraw, Muir ascended Glenora Peak and then

*Juniperus communis* L., Common Juniper

ran down the flowery slopes: "The plant people seemed glad, as if rejoicing with me, the little ones as well as the trees, while every feature of the peak and its traveled boulders seemed to know what I had been about and the depth of my joy, as if they could read faces." He wrote to Louie: "I have at last been blest by the good Lord in being allowed to taste of the wild and beautiful Northland away back at the fountains of the rivers."[12]

Having traveled two hundred miles by steamer and another hundred on foot in the boundless and exuberant woods, into what Muir called "God's wilds," he felt that surely Louie would understand his reluctance to leave Alaska. She would not want him taken away from his work, he suggested, "dawdling in a weak-willed way on her lounge, dozing and drying like a castaway ship on the beach."[13]

Late in the season he continued his study of glaciers, traveling in a six-fathom red-cedar canoe with Young; an old Stickeen chief, Captain Tow-a-att; another Stickeen chief, Kadishan; an interpreter, Stickeen John; and a cook, Sitka Charley. As they paddled along, Muir could see that from the fertile soil mulched by plush moss, seedling trees grew, making luxurious hanging gardens. Old trees held "hundreds of their own children in their arms."

The absolute fecundity of nature growing from ice continued to amaze him. He thought that nature's future health was secure in the abundance in which he found himself surrounded.[14]

Freezing rain fell almost continuously on the way to Chilcat, beyond Sumner Strait, and along the western shore of Kupreanof Island, in southeastern Alaska, an area of hundreds of wooded islands that form the Alexander Archipelago and that at the time was *terra incognita*. They rowed into Sit-a-ka-day Bay and masses of floating ice. It was now late October, and the freezing of the fiords produced insurmountable obstacles. Muir could only promise that he would return. Wherever they landed, he set out to study the algae that filled the small harbors, "the limpets and lichens of the rocks, the fucus pods that snapped beneath [their] feet, the grasses of the beach, the moss and shrubbery among the trees, and more than all, the majestic forests." The frozen terrain notwithstanding, after each walk he returned with his arms filled. Young wrote:

> [Now] a bunch of ferns as high as his head; now a cluster of minute and wonderfully beautiful moss blossoms; now a curious fungus growth; now a spruce branch heavy with cones; and again he would call me into the forest to see a strange and grotesque moss formation on a dead stump....[Muir's] thorough knowledge of botany and his interest in that study made every camp just the place he wished to be.

Each plant and every forest held a moral lesson. A fine landscape or a shaft of light piercing the clouds and glorifying a mountain led Muir to exclaim, as Young heard all too often, "Praise God from whom all blessings flow!"[15]

In December Muir received a letter from Louie:

> Beloved Friend: All the week of Thanksgiving I cherished the ghost of a hope that the last day would bring to me a blessed message out from the far Northland, but now there is no more than the overwhelming vastness of that Wilderness of Ice beyond me, wherein the mountains and the seas, and the sky above, are frozen and silent.

If only for a moment, she longed to see Muir and hear his voice, and she felt "utterly powerless in aiding [him] and shielding [him] from pain." God was there with him, she knew, and "while your soul is called to hear His word, I would not have you to come away—though I long to see your face, more than words can tell. But is not God here also? Therefore I trust that some blessed day He will bid you come, and there will be no more fear nor shadow of darkness." At least once or twice she must have thought that her betrothed would never anchor long in Martinez. The rolling hills of the Alhambra Valley were bright with poppy and lupine when he finally returned in mid-February.[16]

## CREATION FINER AND FINER

In April 1880, John Muir and Louie Wanda Strentzel were married. They served fruitcake to their guests and toasted their union with hand-blown wine goblets painted with golden flowing vines gathered into small clumps of raised glass grapes. Jeanne Carr sent a congratulatory letter. She knew that Muir and Louie were perfectly matched and rejoiced in his happiness, for "above fame and far stronger than [her] wish to see his genius acknowledged by his peers, [she had] desired for him the completeness which can only come in living for others, in perfected home relations."[17]

Muir wrote to his friend Asa Gray in mid-June and enclosed the cones and wood from a yellow cedar he had collected at Fort Wrangel the previous year: "I was married last April, and now have a fixed camp where I can store burs and grass." Gray wrote back congratulating Muir on his marriage. "You mentioned the name of one party, John Muir, but you say not a word about the other. Now, who is she?"[18]

John Muir and Louie Wanda Strentzel Muir, "Certificate of Marriage, April 14th, 1880." Courtesy of the John Muir Papers, Holt-Atherton Department of Special Collections, University of the Pacific. Copyright 1984 Muir-Hanna Trust.

Neither the nuptials nor the Strentzels' gift to them of the original Strentzel home with twenty acres planted in orchards and vineyards would keep Muir at home with his new family for long. In July he accepted an invitation to return to southeastern Alaska to resume his explorations, search for glaciers, and study plants. The only event that marred his departure was leaving behind his now pregnant wife. He hoped she would not feel that he was away at all. He had been alone so much of his lifetime that separation seemed natural and absolute contact seemed too good and indulgent to be true.[19]

Muir and Thomas Magee, with whom he had traveled the previous year, arrived at Fort Wrangel in mid-August to be greeted by Young and his wife's little black dog, Stickeen, and a waiting canoe. Muir was delighted to be back in Alaska, welcomed in its wildness, with its "fiords glowing with sun spangles, and its life-giving air without dust or taint scented only by the pitch and gum of the woods and kelp and dulse of the sea." Magee now went back on his bargain to accompany Muir on the canoe trip and returned to California. The adventure may have been more than he was willing to tackle: whereas Muir felt that hearty contact with Alaska could be best gained from a long, crooked voyage in a canoe, Magee was willing to forgo the experience.[20]

On his last trip Muir had left his studies at Sum Dum Bay, and he

*Cupressus nutkatensis* Hook. [*Chamaecyparis nootkatensis*], Alaska Cedar; Yellow Cypress

now returned to see snowy falls booming into deep blue water. In gullies and on slopes, cliff gardens where even a little soil lodged were bright with plant life. Grasses were tall, with ribbony leaves and nodding purple panicles, and though ferns were less numerous in species than in California, he recognized the *Aspidium*, *Woodsia*, *Lomaria*, *Polypodium*, *Cheilanthes*, and *Pteris*.[21]

The excursion party headed out into Stephens Passage, rounded Admiralty Island, crossed the Lynn Canal, entered Icy Strait, and camped on the west end of Farewell [Pyramid] Island, where wintergreen was in bloom. In Taylor Bay, from the base of a mountain-wall in a wild storm, Muir set out to walk across Taylor Glacier with Stickeen, who was no more than a "helpless wisp of hair," and yet his "horizontal brother." Growing in the garden of ice he found salmonberry, ginseng, heather, and huckleberry. From Taylor Bay they returned to what would soon be named Glacier Bay by Captain L. A. Beardslee, the local military commander. Muir and Young furnished Beardslee with a hand-drawn map that would for several years remain the only authoritative sailing chart of the region. To honor Muir's exploration, Beardslee named the largest glacier in Glacier Bay for him. Out

Strentzel-Muir house on Alhambra Valley Road, Martinez, California, c. late 1890s or early 1900s. Courtesy of the Susan Hanna Flynn Collection.

Dr. John T. Strentzel built this northward-facing house with a long, low porch across the front, on what is now Alhambra Valley Road, in the 1850s. The Strentzels presented it to Louie Wanda Strentzel Muir and John Muir as a wedding gift in April 1880. John planted a red toyon berry bush (*Heteromeles arbutifolia*) on the south side the day Wanda was born and a madrona tree (*Arbutus menziesii*) on the north side the day Helen was born. Muir sold the house to his brother David following the death of Dr. Strentzel in October 1890, after he, Louie, Wanda, and Helen moved to the Victorian house on the hill near the Adobe (now Alhambra Avenue and the John Muir National Historic Site), in order to care for Mrs. Louisiana Strentzel.

on Muir Glacier, upon the lower summit, the pale, pink-belled *Cassiope* grew in foot-thick carpets over several acres. It was, Muir thought, a garden never meant to be trampled by human feet; it was set aside upon the summits for only the wind to chime:

> Though the storm-beaten ground it is growing on is nearly half a mile high, the glacier centuries ago flowed over it as a river flows over a boulder; but out of all the cold darkness and glacial crushing and grinding comes this warm, abounding beauty and life to teach us that what we in our faithless ignorance and fear call destruction is creation finer and finer.[22]

From Sitka Muir sailed home on the monthly mail steamer. Having traveled seven hundred miles, he arrived back in the Alhambra Valley in time for Thanksgiving. Dr. John and Mrs. Louisiana Strentzel and Louie and John spent the holiday together in a happy sacred circle of four. Louisiana wore a black silk dress with a bunch of flowers in her bosom. Louie had rosebuds in her hair. The table was decorated with flowers and ferns. Turkey and pie were served. Into the evening hours logs kindled in the fireplace, under the new mantel Muir had built, behind the fenders he brought from San Francisco. The day was worth a whole lifetime, and perhaps the Strentzel family thought they had won Muir from the icy muse for good. But Alaska, his new Yosemite, would beckon his return sooner then even he knew on that Thanksgiving day.[23]

## CRUISE OF THE *CORWIN*: SEEING SO MUCH AND GOING SO FAR

Annie Wanda was, according to Muir, a "bloom baby," arriving on March 25 "in the warm sundays of the springtime with the full bloom of the fields and orchards, and the singing of the birds." Muir wrote to his friends John and Mary L. Swett: "Never since the Glacial Period began on earth were happier people." His engagement to Louie in 1879 and their wedding in 1880 had not kept Muir from Alaska, but as a result of the birth of Annie Wanda he was reluctant to accept the invitation to join Captain Calvin L. Hooper, a friend who lived in Oakland, on an expedition on the *Corwin* in search of the lost steamer *Jeannette*. It was Louie who convinced Muir that she was strong enough for him to return to Alaska, and her encouragement was all he needed to agree to go. He clearly recognized that joining Hooper was an opportunity to explore regions of Alaska he had not seen. They would cruise the Aleutian Islands and northeastern Siberia. Muir would study the extent of glaciation and the flora of the Arctic and Subarctic regions. Both he and Louie knew that he might not return for two years—this could be a long separation. But Louie believed that he was ever present, no matter how far away he was. Neither time nor space separated them as long as her soul was faithful to his, and again the booming glacial-ice drew Muir far north.[24]

Voyages of John Muir and Samuel Hall Young in 1879 and 1880 in Southeastern Alaska. Reprinted from S. Hall Young's *Alaska Days with John Muir* (New York: Fleming H. Revell, Co., 1915).

On the afternoon of May 4, the *Corwin* steamed out of San Francisco Bay, and on May 18 advanced through mountain-high waves into the harbor of Unalaska. On the windswept ridges near the sea Muir walked among willows beginning to show their silky catkins, tall grass whose purple panicles waved in the wind, broad patches of heathwort with their multitude of pink bells, anemone, bearberry, and tall lupine and fern. He seemed to take in the flora in one swoop of sight, never missing the thinnest blade of grass, the smallest bell of a flower, or the finest wisp of a fern frond. He counted over fifty species of flowering plants, the most abundant the fruitful *Vaccinium*. Heading north, they anchored at the northwest end of St. Lawrence Island and then pushed through to Norton Sound. Throughout the month it had snowed every day, but when they arrived in Norton Sound, the sun appeared through the snow-clouds and Muir wrote to Louie:

Sunshine, dear Louie, Sunshine all the day, ripe and mellow sunshine, like that which feeds
the fruits and vines!...How sweet and kindly and reviving it is after so long and deep a burial
beneath dark sleety storm-clouds! For a whole month it snowed everyday, some days only for
an hour or two, some days all day, but never one in all the month in which more or less snow
did not fall, either in wet, sleety blasts in thick gloom, or in dry crystals blowing off the deck
as fast as it fell, or sticking on the rigging and making sloppy sludge on the deck and then
freezing fast....and when we came here we seemed to have come out of a cave into the living,
exhilarating light.[25]

For days Muir had seen nothing but limitless ice. Confined within the narrow prison of
the ship, he had been disappointed—no mountains or glaciers to climb, no trees, and few
flowers. Now, in St. Michael, a village on the east coast of St. Michael Island, he walked out
on the broad boggy tundra to find spongy tussocks of grass, sedge, and moss intermingled
with asplenium, larkspur, primula, bleeding heart, alder, and willow that grew upon a stratum of solid ice. The Arctic's wild variation, islands thick with moss and *Linnaea*, shorelines
extended and expanded by sheets of ice, days that never ended and a month that was an
eternal day lay witness to Alaska's extremes. It seemed to Muir
that he had been gone a long time, and yet, he wrote to Louie,
"according to the almanac it will not be two months until the
day after tomorrow! I have seen so much and gone so far, and
the nightless days are so strangely joined, it seems more than
a year."[26]

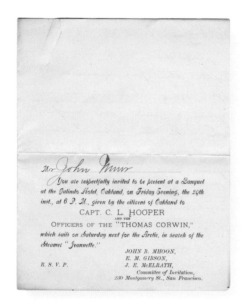

John Muir's invitation to attend a banquet in
Oakland, California, in honor of his friend
Captain C. L. Hooper and the officers of
the *Thomas Corwin*, prior to the *Corwin's*
setting sail, in May 1881, in search of the
lost steamer *Jeannette*. Courtesy of the John
Muir Papers, Holt-Atherton Department of
Special Collections, University of the Pacific
Library. Copyright 1984 Muir-Hanna Trust.

From Norton Sound the ship plunged toward East Cape, on
St. Lawrence Island, and continued on through the Bering Strait
and into the Arctic Ocean. Near Cape Thompson barren slopes
alternated with fertile valleys where Arctic plant gardens formed
brilliant masses of color. At Cape Thompson in July, Muir found
a new species of *Erigeron*, a member of the daisy family. Asa Gray
would name the plant *Erigeron muirii*, redeeming for a second
time a promise made ten years earlier when he wrote to Muir:
"Pray, find a new genus, or at least a new species, that I may have
the satisfaction of embalming your name, not in glacier-ice, but
in spicy wild perfume."[27]

On July 30 the *Corwin* rounded Point Barrow, the region
where the *Jeannette* was reported to have been lost in the ice in
1879. Continuing on to Herald Island, they hoped to find a cairn

left by the crew of the *Jeannette* but found nothing. Muir stayed out on the highest point of the island well into the night:

> The deepest silence seemed to press down on all the vast, immeasurable virgin landscape. The sun near the horizon reddened the edges of belted cloud-bars, near the base of the sky, and the jagged ice boulders crowded together over the frozen ocean, stretching indefinitely northward while more than a hundred miles of that mysterious Wrangel Land [now Wrangell Island] was seen blue, in the northwest a wavering line of hill and dale over the white and blue ice-prairie, and pale gray mountains beyond, well calculated to fix the eye of a mountaineer.

He made a hasty collection of plants as he returned to the ship, among them one of the many poppies that tinted the sloping uplands, several species of saxifrage, two sedges, one grass, and a speedwell.[28]

Though the summer of 1881 had been favorable for Arctic exploration, thick polar ice initially prevented an approach to Wrangel Land. After repeated failed attempts, the *Corwin* finally made its way through. A landing party searched for traces of the *Jeannette* and concluded there were none. Shifting drift ice prevented them from remaining on the island.

*Erigeron muirii*, Muir's Fleabane. Drawing by John Muir, c. 1881. John Muir, *The Cruise of the* Corwin: *Journal of the Arctic Expedition of 1881 in search of DeLong and the* Jeannette, edited by William Badè (Boston: Houghton Mifflin, 1917).

*Erigeron muirii* Gray, Muir's Fleabane

Abandoning hope of further exploration, the *Corwin* headed south. The visit had been far too short for Muir to make any full collection of plants. Judging from what he saw, in general the flora did not differ greatly from that of adjacent shores of Siberia and Alaska. He collected over twenty species of dwarfed plants, most in bloom, growing in small tufts at intervals of a yard or so, with bare ground between.[29]

Fourteen thousand miles of Alaskan waters were traversed during the *Corwin's* five months at sea. According to Muir, the two recuperative weeks spent at Unalaska were "foodful." He wrote to Louie that "the dangers, great as they were, while groping and grinding among the vast immeasurable ice-fields...would have seemed as nothing," had she not been his wife. Louie changed everything. At night he dreamt he heard Annie Wanda crying. He missed holding them and often thought about his warm, sunny home and the cherry trees down the hill.[30]

The cruise of the *Corwin* had proved to be, according to Muir, an "icy time." He had gathered facts concerning the formation of the Bering Sea and the Arctic Ocean, the configuration of the shores of Siberia and Alaska, and the forests that once grew there. Though he felt he had not had enough time for definitive botanical work, of his seven trips to Alaska, the cruise of the *Corwin* remained the most significant source of botanical reconnaissance and plant ecology he undertook in the far north."[31]

"First Landing on Wrangel Land by a party from the Steamer *Corwin* while searching for the *Jeannette* Expedition." Sketch by John Muir, c. August 1881. Courtesy of the John Muir Papers, Holt-Atherton Department of Special Collections, University of the Pacific Library. Copyright 1984 Muir-Hanna Trust.

## A RESERVATION OF BEAUTY

About his travels in Alaska in 1879, 1880, and 1881, Muir published thirty-nine columns as a special correspondent for the *San Francisco Daily Evening Bulletin.* Supplemented by his journals and letters, in toto they provide a wealth of information about his botanical studies as well as his knowledge of the geography of the regions he explored. Compiling his articles, journals, and letters to family and friends, Muir anticipated publishing as many as five books about Alaska. *Travels in Alaska* lay in manuscript form on his bed when he died on December 24, 1914. William Frederic Badè, Muir's literary executor, agreed to prepare the manuscript for publication in 1915. He also, at the request of Muir's daughters, Wanda Muir Hanna and Helen Muir Funk, published *The Cruise of the* Corwin in 1917. A compendium of articles and journal entries, it also drew heavily from Muir's "Botanical Notes on Alaska," published in *Cruise of the Revenue-Steamer* Corwin *in Alaska and the N.W. Arctic Ocean in 1881,* and from his report "On the Glaciation of the Arctic and Subarctic Regions Visited by the United States Steamer *Corwin* in the Year 1881," published in 1884 in the *Report of the U.S. Steamer* Thomas Corwin *in the Arctic Ocean, 1881.* Muir's publications on Alaska were extensive, second only to those he wrote about Yosemite and the High Sierra.

Muir regarded Alaska as "Nature's own reservation." His allegiance to her resulted from his deep love, respect, and sympathy, and he recognized that the beauty of the pristine wilderness must take precedence over demand for resources. Development involved the destruction of the scenic beauty with which Alaska was indelibly identified, and Muir believed that the destruction of nature was the destruction of life itself.[32]

# Epilogue

## THE VIEW FROM MUIR'S PLANTS

THE WORLD, FOR JOHN MUIR, was made more beautiful by flowering plants, and their beauty, he believed, was irresistible, contagious, and civilizing. The intimacy we see in his relationship with the plants he collected draws us to be retrospective about his life and introspective about our own. We gaze upon Muir's plants with the same hope that he saw, and of which he spoke and wrote. His herbarium is an enduring reminder to us to seek to more fully recognize, understand, celebrate, and value the world in which we live, and to appreciate the meaning of "friend" as defined by Muir—for Muir, plants were people too!

As a child growing up in western New York, I spent weekends with my family in the country, along streams, and in forests and fields. During summers we vacationed in the Adirondack Mountains. I have always been more grounded in nature and wilderness and more comfortable there than anywhere else. It is no surprise that I have spent the past seven years as the curator of LeConte Memorial Lodge in Yosemite National Park, where I met Stephen J. Joseph. Together we undertook a project to photograph wildflowers in Yosemite National Park. I called it a "living herbarium."

In October 2003 I began research on Muir's herbarium, and although I had examined Muir's plant specimens and botanical notes at the John Muir National Historic Site, I was uncertain as to how they might be incorporated into a book. A book, however, finds its own course, and as a fellow at the University of California at Berkeley, I was drawn to the University and Jepson Herbaria, where my colleague Dr. Barbara Ertter introduced me to the plant specimens Muir collected in California. It was then that I called upon Stephen to begin scanning Muir's herbarium, as I began a more extensive search for his plants. Between spring 2004 and fall 2005, I traveled to the Harvard University Herbaria, the Academy of

Left: John Muir, c. 1905. Courtesy of the John Muir Papers, Holt-Atherton Department of Special Collections, University of the Pacific Library. Copyright 1984 Muir-Hanna Trust.

Natural Sciences of Philadelphia, and the Missouri Botanical Garden. Research was also undertaken at the American Museum of Natural History and the Smithsonian Institution, and in Savannah, Georgia, I visited the Bonaventure Cemetery.

Throughout the collaborative process Stephen's enthusiasm and dedication have been a beacon. His knowledge, skill, and creative talent as a landscape photographer and print-maker have brought to life beautiful and awe-inspiring images of Muir's plants. It has been a joy to find that from the seedbed of Yosemite Valley and the High Sierra an opportunity germinated to celebrate Muir's fondness for plants and his faith in the purity of a flower.

*Nemophila menziesii* Hook. & Arn., Baby Blue Eyes

*Thalictrum anemonoídes* Michx. [*Anemonella thalictroides* L.], Meadow Rue; Rue Anemone

# Appendix

## SEARCHING FOR
## MUIR'S PLANT FRIENDS

TO BEGIN THE SEARCH for John Muir's North American herbarium required creating lists of plants derived from Muir's published articles and books, and from a composite of holographic materials that comprised his journals, letters, manuscripts, and scraps of paper, and notes to the Harvard botanist Asa Gray. Lists were constructed based on the dates of Muir's excursions and the geographical regions and specific locations through which he traveled, with as much detailed information as could be gathered from his records, including Latin and common names. Finding Muir's plant specimens also required determining the currency of the names he gave to plants about which he wrote. Instrumental in appraising Muir's taxonomy were Alphonso Wood's *Class-Book of Botany*, published in 1861; Asa Gray's *Manual of the Botany of the Northern United States*, the fifth edition, published in 1868; the Geological Survey of California publication *Botany*, volumes one and two, prepared by W. H. Brewer, Sereno Watson, and Asa Gray in, respectively, 1876 and 1880, and Mark Griffith's *Index of Garden Plants*, published in 1992. In addition, the nomenclatural database maintained by the Missouri Botanical Garden (w3TROPICOS) and the International Plant Name Index (IPNI) of the Harvard University Herbaria; the Royal Botanic Garden, Kew; and the Australian National Herbarium were consulted.

With the exception of the plant specimens preserved at the John Muir National Historic Site; the University and Jepson Herbaria at the University of California at Berkeley, with a database of California plant specimens that cross-references plants and collectors; and the hundreds of unclassified plant specimens attributed to Muir at the Holt-Atherton Special Collections at the University of the Pacific, locating Muir's herbarium required the utilization of the prepared lists in the search for each specimen. Staff at the Harvard University

Left: *Quercus lobata* Née, California White Oak; Valley Oak

Herbaria, the Academy of Natural Sciences of Philadelphia, and the Missouri Botanical Garden recalled having seen plants collected by Muir. There are, however, within a given species anywhere from a few specimens to hundreds, and they are not organized according to their collectors' names. The process is likened to finding a needle in a haystack.

Once located, each plant specimen was evaluated to determine, within the complex of Muir's collecting, its taxonomical importance (family, genus, species), the location and date (where Muir found the plant and when), and the physical condition and aesthetic quality. In 2003 the search for Muir's herbarium began at the John Muir National Historic Site (JMNHS) with the examination of the earliest extant plants he collected in Canada and Indiana between 1864 and 1867—among them the *Calypso borealis,* ubiquitous in Muir's writing (*Calypso* meaning "concealer" and *borealis* meaning "northern," as in "aurora borealis"). The JMNHS collection includes over five hundred and fifty North American plants, among them specimens collected in California during trips to Yosemite and the High Sierra in 1868, 1872, and 1873, and later in 1901 and 1907, and a trip in 1898 to the southern United States with the director of the Harvard Arnold Arboretum, Charles S. Sargent, and the botanist William Canby, from Wilmington, Delaware. It also includes plants that Muir collected during his world trip in 1903 to 1904. In addition, there is holographic material determined to be a body of correspondence and notes on plant identification written by Muir and the Harvard botanist Asa Gray. Plants collected in California in the 1870s and several collected in the early 1880s and in Alaska in 1879, 1880, and 1881 are in the University and Jepson Herbaria, the Harvard University Herbaria, the Academy of Natural Sciences of Philadelphia, and the Missouri Botanical Garden. (Additional plant specimens collected in California are located in the herbaria at the New York Botanical Garden and the Rancho Santa Ana Botanic Garden.) The unclassified plant specimens attributed to Muir located in the Holt-Atherton Special Collections at the University of the Pacific appear to represent his collecting in California, and the seventeen plants collected in 1898 are from the trip with Sargent and Canby.

## THE MIGRATION AND LOSS OF JOHN MUIR'S PLANT SPECIMENS

### Canada and Indiana

When Muir began his thousand-mile walk in 1867, he deposited his herbarium specimens, collected between 1864 and 1867, in Indiana with Julia Merrill Moores, the sister of Catharine Merrill. They were never returned to Muir. More than a half-century later, Muir's literary executor, William Frederic Badè, in the process of editing *The Life and Letters of John*

*Muir*, discovered correspondence that mentioned the plants Muir collected while in Canada and Indiana that he requested be left at the Moores's home in Indianapolis. He approached Moores's son Charles W. Moores, who found the plants in the attic of the Moores's home. Badè returned them to the Wanda Muir Hanna family, with whom they remained until donated to the John Muir National Historic Site in the 1970s. The archival conservation of the collection was completed in 1977 by Sara F. Hammett, a graduate student in Museum Studies at Texas Tech University.[1]

## Thousand-Mile Walk to the Gulf of Mexico

The plant specimens Muir collected during his thousand-mile walk have not been located. At several intervals during his trip through the south, Muir sent his plants to his brother Daniel to give to his sister Sarah for safekeeping. In 1902, Muir's sister Annie found them in the loft of the family barn in Portage, Wisconsin, and returned them to Muir in Martinez.[2]

## California

The whereabouts of Muir's plant specimens collected between 1868 and 1871 remains a mystery, with the exception of one plant Muir sent to his sister Sarah, which he had collected in 1868 in the area near Snelling or Twenty Hill Hollow, that is in the collection at the John Muir National Historic Site. In January 1871 he sent some of the plants he had collected during his first two years in California to Jeanne Carr. Muir probably retrieved them from her when he resided in Oakland or San Francisco. Following his engagement to Louie Wanda Strentzel in 1879 and his departure for Alaska, she went to the San Francisco home of Isaac Upham, where Muir had been staying, to collect his plant specimens. These may have included, at least in part, the plants Muir had sent to Carr.[3]

"In the Trunk." "Plants To be left at J. Moores Mrs if she has room." Daniel H. Muir, Jr., list of trunk contents belonging to John Muir, c. 1867. Courtesy of the Huntington Library.

According to Wanda Muir Hanna, following Muir's death in 1914, the plant specimens he had kept at his home in Martinez (and in all likelihood this entire collection consisted of plants collected during his thousand-mile walk and those that post-date his arrival in California in 1868) were in the possession of Wanda and her sister, Helen Muir Funk. Muir had made no disposition of his herbarium; some would be kept by the family, while others would be donated to an institution. There is no evidence that Muir's plant specimens, at the time of his death or shortly thereafter, were placed in an herbarium or any other repository.[4]

Plant specimens Muir collected in Yosemite Valley and the High Sierra in 1872, 1873, 1901, and 1907 are in the archives at the John Muir National Historic Site. Several are annexed with the taxonomical notes exchanged between Muir and Gray in 1872 and 1873. In July 1873 Muir traveled with William Keith, Keith's wife, Lizzie, their son Charlie, and Emily Pelton from Yosemite Valley to Tuolumne Meadows and Mount Dana. Muir picked a small bouquet of about ten plants and preserved them in a folded paper envelope. Among them are a *Vaccinium caespitosum,* a *Phlox caespitosa,* and a *Polemonium caeruleum*—the blue sky pilot that only grows two hundred feet from the summit of Mount Dana. Later, in June 1901, Muir traveled with his daughters to Sequoia National Park and Giant Forest. At Round Meadow he placed specimens of *Ceanothus integerrimus* and *Linanthus dichotomus* [*L. androsaceus*] between the pages of his journal. In 1907 Muir joined the month-long Sierra Club "Outing" to Yosemite, the High Sierra, and Hetch Hetchy, and between the pages of his journal he placed specimens of *Nemophila maculata* and *Rosa gymnocarpa.*[5]

Specimens in the collection at Harvard represent requests Gray sent to Muir in 1872 and

*Linanthus dichotomus* Benth., Evening Snow

1873 for specific plants he had either seen during his trip to Yosemite Valley in 1872 or that he knew of as a result of discussions with Muir. Among the plant specimens Gray received from Muir was a member of the Rosaceae family, a mouse-tail, the *Ivesia muirii*, discovered near Mount Hoffman at an elevation of 9,500 feet in 1872. Gray named it to honor Muir. That same year, on the bank of the South Fork of the Merced River, Muir found a species of myrtle, the *Myrica hartwegii*, a member of the Myricaceae family, also identified by Gray.[6]

Of the extant California plants collected in the mid-1870s—more than one hundred—Muir had sent the majority to John H. Redfield at the Academy of Natural Sciences of Philadelphia. Unable to identify one of the plants Muir had sent him, Redfield sent it to Gray, who named the species, a member of the Asteraceae family, *Raillardella muirii*. Rather than return it to Redfield, Gray kept the specimen and the letter for the collection at Harvard.[7]

When Redfield died in 1895, he requested that his herbarium be sold to create a fund to provide for conservation and acquisitions. In 1897, William Trelease, director of the Missouri Botanical Garden, purchased 4,511 plant specimens from the Redfield collection

Left: *Raillardella muirii* Gray, Muir's Raillardella; Muir's Tarweed [*Carlquistia muirii*]

Right: *Ceanothus integerrimus* Hook. & Arn., Deer Brush

Left: *Senecio fremontii* Torr. & Gray, Dwarf Mountain Ragwort

Right: *Ceanothus papillosus* Torr. & Gray, California Lilac

at a cost of $2,300. By 1900 the Missouri Botanical Garden had purchased a total of 16,447 plant specimens, among them many Muir had collected in Yosemite Valley and the High Sierra and sent to Redfield in 1875. Specimens from the Redfield collection are also in the collection at the University and Jepson Herbaria. There is no record of the transfer of specimens from Philadelphia to Berkeley. Some of the plants collected by Muir in Yosemite Valley and the High Sierra remained in the herbarium at the Academy of Natural Sciences of Philadelphia.[8]

There are two plant specimens in the collection at the University and Jepson Herbaria that represent Muir's collecting at Mount Whitney and at Wright's Station, on the Los Gatos–Santa Cruz railroad line. Respectively they are the *Senecio fremontii* var. *occidentalis*, collected in July 1876 (originally in the herbarium of John Gill Lemmon and the California Academy of Sciences), and the *Ceanothus papillosus*, collected on May 2, 1889 (originally in the herbarium of John Gill Lemmon).

## Alaska and a Few Species of Oaks from California

Three plant specimens located at the Missouri Botanical Garden represent Muir's collecting in Alaska in 1879 and 1880. They were sent by Muir to George Engelmann, a St. Louis physician and botanist who in the 1850s created the Missouri Botanical Garden with Henry Shaw, a wealthy St. Louis businessman, botanist, and philanthropist. Engelmann traveled to California in 1880 with Charles Christopher Parry, a physician who from 1849 until 1851 served there as an assistant surgeon, chief botanist, and geologist with the Mexican Boundary Survey. Parry was also a noted Colorado botanist who collected plants in California in 1878, the early 1880s, and later in 1886 and 1887. Though it is unclear if Engelmann visited Muir or his father-in-law, John Strentzel, in Martinez (Muir was in Alaska until Thanksgiving and Parry visited Muir sometime late in 1880), Engelmann knew of the specific location of two species of oak trees on the Strentzel-Muir Ranch. With a penchant for the genus *Quercus*, Engelmann wrote to Muir requesting specimens: "one is *quercus lobata* [valley oak], which grows...about the stables on the Creek; the other is *quercus Douglasii,* the blue mountain oak, on the bare hills above you." Both are in the herbarium at the Missouri Botanical Garden. One specimen, a woodchip from a *Cupressus nootkatensis* [*Chamaecyparis nootkatensis*], collected in 1879 by Muir at Fort Wrangel, Alaska, is in the herbaria at Harvard.[9]

Of Muir's seven excursions to Alaska, the most significant collection of plant specimens he undertook in the far north occurred during the cruise of the *Corwin* in 1881. Following the expedition, Muir sent the specimens directly to Harvard, where they were classified by the curator of the Gray Herbarium, Sereno Watson.[10]

### A Particular Affection for Ferns

There are numerous examples of ferns (pteridophytes) in the collections listed above, representing Muir's collecting in Canada, Indiana, the High Sierra near Yosemite, and Alaska. Ferns were easy to recognize when Muir began the study of botany, and he discovered that they

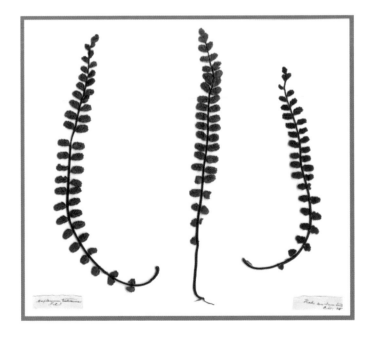

*Asplenium trichomanes* L., Maidenhair Spleenwort

were represented in nearly all ecological systems. With striking characteristics and longevity, ferns thrive in remote swamps, in dimly lit, moist, cavelike crevices, close to waterfalls,

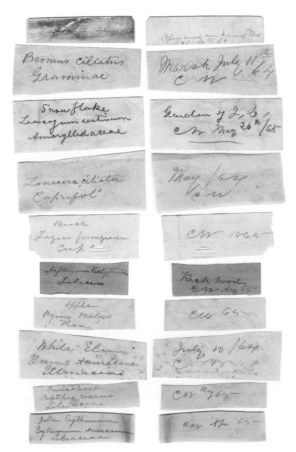

Top (left): *Cheilanthes californica* (Nutt.) Mett., California Lace Fern

Top (center): *Cystopteris fragilis* (L.) Bernh., Brittle Bladder Fern; Fragile Fern

Top (right): *Aspidium fragrans* Gray [*Dryopteris fragrans* (L.) Schott.], Shield Fern

Bottom (left): *Asplenium thelypteroides* Michx., Silvery Spleenwort

Bottom (right): John Muir plant specimen labels, c. 1864–1867. Courtesy of the John Muir National Historic Site.

and high on mountain ledges and windswept cliffs, and they form the borders of ponds and lakes. They inhabit places Muir fruitfully explored. The popularity of ferns would have had something to do with his collecting them as well. At the time, in the entire plant kingdom, nothing attracted more attention. Their subtle beauty and charm seemed to hold a peculiar power over their votaries and by far, Muir considered ferns and mosses to be the most interesting of all the natural orders.[11]

## Problems in Taxonomy and the Preservation of Plant Specimens

In classifying plants Muir depended on the names that were available to him. Following the taxonomic nomenclature practiced at the time as best he was able, he relied on familial similarities, making every effort to name a plant's genus accurately. His limited access to plant guides and the fact that, when Muir arrived in California, a plant guide for the western states did not exist, hindered his ability to recognize species in California and in Alaska. Relying on his observational skills, Wood's *Class-Book of Botany*, and later on Gray's *Manual of Botany*, it was easy to misidentify a plant. In general the rate of error was high among field botanists. In addition, Muir did not always know exactly where he was, particularly in the High Sierra and in Alaska, and geographic data was therefore compromised, limited to region or range. Following his introduction to Gray, Muir relied, as did almost everyone else in California, on his authority; Gray was passionate about raising the standard of botany in the United States and developed his herbarium at Harvard into the nation's main clearinghouse for the study, classification, and exchange of plant specimens. In all cases the names Muir attributed to plant specimens have been retained in this publication. Names enclosed in brackets have been added for purposes of clarification.[12]

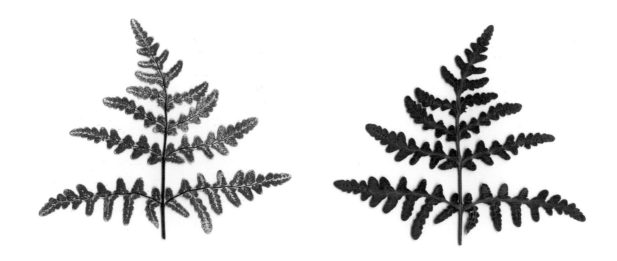

*Gymnogramma triangulare* Kaulf. [*G. triangularis*], California Gold Fern

Plant specimens should be preserved in a dry and stable environment, preferably in cabinets with an established filing system. The shuffling and poor storage options to which Muir's plant specimens were exposed compromised their care and limited his ability for comparative study. Many of Muir's specimens were preserved because they had been requested for the herbarium collections of Asa Gray and John H. Redfield. Muir's marriage to Louie Wanda Strentzel and the subsequent placement of his herbarium at their home in Martinez, California, improved the conditions in which his plants were stored.

For Muir, collecting plants had to do with more than science—or better yet, it had less to do with any interest he might have in adding to past and present accumulations of records. He was interested in expanding his own knowledge and at times he simply went for a walk and, out of the sheer joy of collecting, stuffed his pockets with plants because he was curious and they were beautiful, intending no more than to relish their beauty and, in a personal and thoughtful way, become more familiar with them.

John Muir at the home of Colonel Alfred H. Sellers, Pasadena, California, c. 1890s.
Courtesy of the James Eastman Shone Collection of Muiriana, Holt-Atherton
Department of Special Collections, University of the Pacific Library.

# PLANT GALLERY CITATIONS

Note that all specimens have been artistically enhanced.

In all cases the names Muir attributed to plant specimens have been retained in this publication. Names enclosed in brackets have been added for purposes of clarification.

## INTRODUCTION

*Gleditsia triacanthos* L.
Honey Locust
Leguminosae
Hab. near Hamilton, [Ontario], Canada
Coll. John Muir
September 5, 1864
JOMU 2028
Courtesy of the John Muir National Historic Site.

"I received my first lesson in botany from a student by the name of Griswold....I was standing on the stone steps of the north dormitory, Mr. Griswold joined me and at once began to teach. He reached up, plucked a flower from an overspreading branch of a locust tree, and, handing it to me, said, 'Muir, do you know what family this tree belongs to?'"

John Muir, *The Story of My Boyhood and Youth*; reprinted in Muir, *The Eight Wilderness Discovery Books*, 109.

*Nemophila maculata* Benth.
Fivespot
Hydrophyllaceae
Hab. above Yosemite Valley, Sierra Nevada, California
Coll. John Muir
June 29–July 24, 1907
Yosemite Trip with Sierra Club
JOMU 3561-1
Courtesy of the John Muir National Historic Site.

"*Nemophila maculata* came today. Its stigmas are small and black like spiders' eyes, and the corolla very delicate. Only the fingers of God are sufficiently gentle and tender for the folding and unfolding of petaled bundles of flowers."

John Muir, UJJM, 25

*Gentianopsis holopetala* (Gray) Iltis
Hiker's Gentian
Gentianaceae
Hab. Yosemite Valley, Sierra Nevada, California
Coll. John Muir
June 29–July 24, 1907
Yosemite Trip with Sierra Club
JOMU 3561-6
Courtesy of the John Muir National Historic Site.

"The first snow of the season that comes to the help of the streams usually falls in September or October, sometimes even in the latter part of August, in the midst of yellow Indian summer, when the goldenrods and gentians of the glacier meadows are in their prime. This...snow, however, soon melts, the chilled flowers spread their petals to the sun, and the gardens as well as the streams are refreshed as if only a warm shower had fallen."

John Muir, *The Yosemite*; reprinted in Muir, *The Eight Wilderness Discovery Books*, 630.

*Rosa gymnocarpa* Nutt.
Wood Rose
Rosaceae
Hab. Yosemite Valley, Sierra Nevada, California
Coll. John Muir
June 29–July 24, 1907
Yosemite Trip with Sierra Club
JOMU 3561-3
Courtesy of the John Muir National Historic Site.

"Miles of fences have been built around hay-fields and patches of kitchen vegetable[s] that have taken the places of the wild lily and rose gardens; and hundreds of horses have been allowed to run loose over the unfenced portion of the valley year after year until in many places it looks like a dusty, exhausted wayside pasture. The trouble seems to be not so much a lack of interest in the welfare of the valley as a want of a general, definite plan of action."

John Muir, "Yosemite Valley: Beauties of the Landscape in Early Summer. Late Changes in the Valley—Lack of Plan a Serious Impediment to Improvement—John Muir's Views. Yosemite Valley, June 21, 1889," *San Francisco Daily Evening Bulletin* (June 27, 1889): 1, cols. 5–6.

*Elymus canadensis* L.
Canada Wild Rye
Gramineae
Hab. near Indianapolis, Indiana
Coll. John Muir
July 1866
JOMU 2131
Courtesy of the John Muir National Historic Site.

"I was anxious to know the grasses and sedges of the Illinois prairies and also their comparative abundance; so I walked one hundred yards in a straight line, gathering at each step that grass or sedge nearest my foot, placing them one by one in my left hand as I walked along, without looking at them or entertaining the remotest idea of making a bouquet. At the end of this measured walk my handful, of course, consisted of one hundred plants *arranged in Nature's own way* as regards kind, comparative numbers, and size."

John Muir to Jeanne C. Carr, [Portage City, August 1867], in Bonnie Johanna Gisel, ed., *Kindred & Related Spirits: The Letters of John Muir and Jeanne C. Carr*, 54–55.

## PART ONE

*Viola canadensis* L.
Canadian White Violet
Violaceae
Hab. [Ontario], Canada
Coll. John Muir
May [1864]
JOMU 1011
Courtesy of the John Muir National Historic Site.

Ann G. Muir
Wallet, Trip from Dunbar, Scotland, to Wisconsin
1849
John Muir Papers, MS 48, Series VII, Memorabilia
Courtesy of the Holt-Atherton Department of Special Collections, University of the Pacific Library. Copyright 1984 Muir-Hanna Trust.

"My aunt had a corner assigned to her in our garden, and...it was full of tulips and lilies, and we all looked with the utmost respect and wonder and admiration at that beautiful garden, with those great lilies, and wondered whether, when we were men and women, we would be rich enough to own a garden like that....I thought them glorious."

John Muir, First Draft Autobiography, 22. John Muir Papers. Courtesy of the Holt-Atherton Department of Special Collections, University of the Pacific Library. Copyright 1984 Muir-Hanna Trust.

*Solidago gigantea* Ait.
Giant Goldenrod
Asteraceae
Hab. meadow, [Ontario], Canada
Coll. John Muir
August 9, 1864
JOMU 2038
Courtesy of the John Muir National Historic Site.

"We saw, as the stream hurried us on, that the grand harvest of Compositae would be no failure this year. It is rapidly receiving its purple and gold in generous measure from the precious light of these days."

John Muir to Jeanne C. Carr, Indianapolis, August 30, 1867, in Gisel, *Kindred & Related Spirits*, 57.

## PART TWO

*Calla palustris* L.
Wild Calla
Araceae
Hab. Devil's Half Acre, 40 miles northeast from Hamilton, Canada
Coll. John Muir
[1864]
JOMU 2117
Courtesy of the John Muir National Historic Site.

*Asarum canadense* L.
Wild Ginger
Aristolochiaceae
Hab. [Ontario], Canada
Coll. John Muir
[1864]
JOMU 2003
Courtesy of the John Muir National Historic Site.

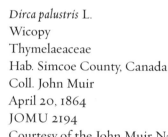

*Dirca palustris* L.
Wicopy
Thymelaeaceae
Hab. Simcoe County, Canada
Coll. John Muir
April 20, 1864
JOMU 2194
Courtesy of the John Muir National Historic Site.

"Oftentimes I had to sleep without blankets, and sometimes without supper, but usually I had no great difficulty in finding a loaf of bread here and there at the houses of the farmer settlers in the widely scattered clearings. With one of these large backwoods loaves I was able to wander many a long wild fertile mile in the forests and bogs, free as the winds, gathering plants, and glorying in God's abounding inexhaustible spiritual beauty bread."

William Frederic Badè, ed., *The Life and Letters of John Muir*; reprinted in Terry Gifford, *John Muir: His Life and Letters and Other Writings*, 71.

*Clintonia borealis* Raf.
Northern Clintonia
Lilaceae
Hab. swamp, dark woods, [Ontario], Canada
Coll. John Muir
June 4, [1864]
JOMU 2013
Courtesy of the John Muir National Historic Site.

"In the long summer days I used to get up about daylight and take a walk among the interesting plants of a broad marsh through which the Holland River flows. I had not been feeling very well and motherly Mrs.

Campbell was somewhat anxious about my health. One morning the boys, finding my bed empty and knowing that I must have gone botanising in the Holland River swamp, and knowing also the anxiety of their mother about my health, put a large bag of carpet rags, that was kept in the garret, in my bed and pulled the blankets over it."

Badè, *Life and Letters*; reprinted in Gifford, *John Muir,* 72.

*Botrychium virginicum* Willd.
Rattlesnake Fern
Ophioglossaceae
Hab. [Ontario], Canada
Coll. John Muir
July 6, 1864
JOMU 2162
Courtesy of the John Muir National Historic Site.

"When I came to the Georgian Bay of Lake Huron, whose waters are so transparent and beautiful, and the forests about its shores with their ferny, mossy dells and deposits of boulder clay, it seemed to be a most favourable place for study, and as I was also at this time out of money again I was eager to stay a considerable time. In a beautiful dell, only a mile or two from the magnificent bay, I fortunately found work in a factory where there was a sawmill and lathes for turning out rake, broom, and fork handles."

Badè, *Life and Letters*; reprinted in Gifford, *John Muir*, 74–75.

*Cirsium lanceolatum* (L.) Scop.
Common Thistle
Asteraceae
Hab. [Ontario], Canada
Coll. John Muir
July 18, 1864
JOMU 2051
Courtesy of the John Muir National Historic Site.

"I cannot understand the nature of the curse, 'Thorns and thistles shall it bring forth to thee.' Is our world indeed the worse for this 'thistly curse?' Are not all plants beautiful? or in some way useful? Would not the world suffer by the banishment of a single weed?"

John Muir, "For the *Boston Recorder.* The Calypso Borealis. Botanical Enthusiasm. From Prof. J. D. Butler," *Boston Recorder*, December 21, 1866, 1.

*Adiantum pedatum* L.
Maidenhair Fern
Adiantaceae
Hab. [Ontario], Canada
Coll. John Muir
July 18, 1864
JOMU 2129
Courtesy of the John Muir National Historic Site.

"The delicate *Adiantum* trembles upon every hillside."

John Muir to Jeanne C. Carr, "The Hollow," January 21, 1866, in Gisel, *Kindred & Related Spirits,* 35.

*Vicia sativa* L.
Spring Vetch
Leguminosae
Hab. [Ontario], Canada
Coll. John Muir
July 19, 1864
JOMU 2032
Courtesy of the John Muir National Historic Site.

*Anemone pennsylvanica* L.
Pennsylvania Anemone
Ranunculaceae
Hab. meadow, [Ontario], Canada
Coll. John Muir
July 20, 1864
JOMU 2102
Courtesy of the John Muir National Historic Site.

*Antennaria margaritacea* (L.) Sweet
Pearly Everlasting
Asteraceae
Hab. [Ontario], Canada
Coll. John Muir
July 21, 1864
JOMU 2048
Courtesy of the John Muir National Historic Site.

*Rubus occidentalis* L.
Black Raspberry
Rosaceae
Hab. [Ontario], Canada
Coll. John Muir
August 8, 1864
JOMU 2093
Courtesy of the John Muir National Historic Site.

*Fraxinus americana* L.
White Ash
Oleaceae
Hab. dry soil, [Ontario], Canada
Coll. John Muir
July 26, 1864
JOMU 2166
Courtesy of the John Muir National Historic Site.

"After earning a few dollars working on my brother-in-law's farm near Portage, I set off on the first of my long lonely excursions, botanising in glorious freedom around the Great Lakes and wandering through innumerable tamarac and arbor-vitae swamps, and forests of maple, basswood, ash, elm, balsam, fir, pine, spruce, hemlock, rejoicing in their bound wealth and strength and beauty, climbing the trees, reveling in their flowers and fruit like bees in beds of goldenrods, glorying in the fresh cool beauty and charm of the bog and meadow heathworts, grasses, carices, ferns, mosses, liverworts displayed in boundless profusion."

Badè, *Life and Letters*; reprinted in Gifford, *John Muir*, 70.

*Linnaea borealis* L.
Twin Flower
Caprifoliaceae
Hab. dry mound, tam. [tamarack] swamp, [Ontario], Canada
Coll. John Muir
August 13, 1864
JOMU 2130
Courtesy of the John Muir National Historic Site.

In September 1877 Muir, Asa Gray, and Sir Joseph Hooker of Kew Gardens, in London, were botanizing on Mount Shasta. Gray inquired why Muir had not found *Linnaea* in California. "It must," said Gray, "be here on the northern boundary of the Sierra." About noon on the following day, Muir and Hooker "came to one of the icy-cold branches of the [Sacramento] river...after we forded it we noticed a green carpet on the bank....Hooker, bestowing a keen botanic look on it, said, 'What is that?' then stooped and plucked a specimen and said, 'Isn't that *Linnaea*? It's awfully like it.'...This was the first time the blessed plant was recognized within the bounds of California; and it would seem that Gray had felt its presence the night before, on the mountain ten miles away."

John Muir, "Linnaeus," in Charles Dudley Warner, ed., *Library of the World's Best Literature* (New York: R. S. Peale and J. A. Hill, Publishers, 1896), 9082.

*Phlox subulata* L.
Moss Pink
Polemoniaceae
Hab. [Ontario], Canada
Coll. John Muir
May 25, 1865
JOMU 2318
Courtesy of the John Muir National Historic Site.

"We live in a retired and romantic hollow....Our tall, tall forest trees are now all alive, and the ocean of mingled blossoms and leaves waves and curls and rises in rounded swells farther and farther away, like the thick smoke from a factory chimney. Freshness and beauty are everywhere; flowers are born every hour; living sunlight is poured over all, and every thing and creature is glad. Our world is indeed a beautiful one!"

John Muir to Emily Pelton, May 23, 1865, BADE, 77.

[*Carex platyphylla* Carey]
[Silver Sedge]
Cyperaceae
Hab. [Ontario, Canada]
Coll. John Muir
[1865]
JOMU 1021
Courtesy of the John Muir National Historic Site.

Thirteen specimens of Musci
Hab. bogs and swamps on the ground, on decayed log in dark shade,
shaded hillside on ground, near end of stay in [Ontario], Canada
Coll. John Muir
November 1865
JOMU 2203
Courtesy of the John Muir National Historic Site.

"[I] procured ten or twelve species of moss all in fruit, also a club-moss, a fern, and some liverworts and lichens. I have also a box of thyme. I would go a long way to see your herbarium, more especially your ferns and mosses. These two are by far the most interesting of all the natural orders to me."

John Muir to Jeanne C. Carr, January 21, 1866, in Gisel, *Kindred & Related Spirits*, 35.

*Dicentra spectabilis* (L.) Lem.
Bleeding Heart
Fumariaceae
Hab. [Indiana]
Coll. John Muir
[1866]
JOMU 1043
Courtesy of the John Muir National Historic Site.

"I gathered a handful [of wildflowers] about a mile and a half from town this morning before breakfast. When I first entered the woods and stood among the beautiful flowers and trees of God's own garden, so pure and chaste and lovely, I could not help shedding tears of joy."

John Muir to Sarah Muir Galloway, Indianapolis, Indiana, May 1866. John Muir Papers, JMP A1: 00442. Copyright 1984 Muir-Hanna Trust.

*Catalpa bignonioides* Walt.
Indian Bean
Bignoniaceae
Hab. Indianapolis, Indiana
Coll. John Muir
1866
JOMU 1151
Courtesy of the John Muir National Historic Site.

*Dactyloctenium egypticum* Willd.
Egyptian Grass
Gramineae
Hab. Indiana
Coll. John Muir
July 1866
JOMU 1146
Courtesy of the John Muir National Historic Site.

"Can it be that a single flower or weed or grass in all these prairies occupies a chance position? Can it be that the folding or curvature of a single leaf is wrong or undetermined in these gardens that God is keeping?"

John Muir to Jeanne C. Carr, [August 1867], in Gisel *Kindred & Related Spirits*, 55.

*Solanum carolinense* L.
Horse Nettle
Solanaceae
Hab. road side, Indiana
Coll. John Muir
July 1866
JOMU 1092
Courtesy of the John Muir National Historic Site.

*Tecoma radicans* (L.) Juss.
Trumpet Flower
Bignoniaceae
Hab. woods, Indiana, "a magnificent vine climbing on exposed place,
Indianapolis, Indiana"
Coll. John Muir
July 8, 1866
JOMU 1097
Courtesy of the John Muir National Historic Site.

"Here with let me introduce to you Mr. John Muir, sometime a student of mine here—a worthy young man every way....If you can walk the fields with him, you will find that Solomon could speak no more wisely about plants."

James D. Butler to Catharine Merrill, Madison, Wisconsin, April 26, 1866, John Muir Papers, JMP B1:00428. Copyright 1984 Muir-Hanna Trust.

*Tradescantia pilosa* Lehm.
Spiderwort
Commelinaceae
Hab. open bank, Indianapolis, Indiana
Coll. John Muir
July 8, 1866
JOMU 1066
Courtesy of the John Muir National Historic Site.

[*Liriodendron tulipifera* L.]
[Tulip Tree]
[Magnoliaceae]
Hab. [Indiana]
Coll. John Muir
[1867]
JOMU 2282
Courtesy of the John Muir National Historic Site.

"When I received my blow I could not feel any pain or faintness because the tremendous thought glared full on me that my *right eye* was lost. I could gladly have died on the spot, because I did not feel that I could have heart to look at any flower again."

John Muir to Jeanne C. Carr, [Indianapolis], Sunday, April 6, [1867], in Gisel, *Kindred & Related Spirits*, 45.

*Luzula campestris* (L.) DC.
Field Rush
Juncaceae
Hab. woods, Indiana
Coll. John Muir
June 1867
JOMU 2228
Courtesy of the John Muir National Historic Site.

*Jeffersonia diphylla* (L.) Pers.
Twin Leaf
Berberidaceae
Hab. woods, Indiana
Coll. John Muir
June 1867
JOMU 2219
Courtesy of the John Muir National Historic Site.

*Calypso borealis* Salisb.
Lady's Slipper; Hider of the North
Orchidaceae
Hab. [Ontario], Canada
Coll. John Muir
c. 1864
JOMU 1009
Courtesy of the John Muir National Historic Site.

"I never before saw a plant so full of life, so perfectly spiritual, it seemed pure enough for the throne of its Creator. I felt as if I were in the presence of superior beings who loved me and beckoned me to come. I sat down beside them and wept for joy. Could angels in their better land show us a more beautiful plant? How good is our Heavenly Father in granting us such friends as are these plant creatures, filing us wherever we go with pleasure so deep, so pure, so endless."

Muir, "For the *Boston Recorder*. The Calypso Borealis," 1.

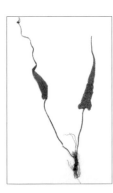

*Camptosorus rhizophyllus* (L.) Link
Walking Fern
Aspleniaceae
Hab. wet limestone, Owen Sound, [Ontario], Canada
Coll. John Muir
1865
JOMU 2349
Courtesy of the John Muir National Historic Site.

"I know many a meadow where *Calopogon* finds home. With us it is now in the plentitude of glory. *Camptosorus* is not here, but I can easily procure you a specimen from the rocks of Owen Sound, Canada. It is there very abundant, so also is *Scolopendrium*.

John Muir to Jeanne C. Carr, [August 1867], in Gisel *Kindred & Related Spirits*, 53.

*Climacium americanum* Brid.
American Climacium
Climaciaceae
Hab. [Indianapolis, Indiana]
Coll. John Muir
[1867]
JOMU 1033
Courtesy of the John Muir National Historic Site.

"I wish to try some cloudy day to walk to the woods, where I am sure some of spring's sweet fresh-born are waiting....When I can walk to where fruited specimens of *Climacium* are, I will send you as many as you wish."

John Muir to Jeanne C. Carr, Sunday, April 6, [1867], in Gisel, *Kindred & Related Spirits*, 46.

*Anemone nuttalliana* DC
Pasque Flower
Ranunculaceae
Hab. Wing-on-Wing, Garrison-on-Hudson, New York (home of Henry Fairfield Osborn, president of the American Museum of Natural History, 1908–1933)
Coll. John Muir
1898
JOMU 3561 I-3
Courtesy of the John Muir National Historic Site.

"[*Anemone nuttalliana*]...is a plant—the very first which comes up in the spring over the dry ground...before a single grass blade began to spring up...a large hairy bud was seen springing up...in countless dozens. The bud was covered with grayish hair...and as soon as it was free from the ground at the base, it immediately opened and displayed a beautiful blue blossom about two inches in diameter....it kept on growing until the plant reached a height of two or three feet."

Muir, First Draft Autobiography, 22, John Muir Papers. Copyright 1984 Muir-Hanna Trust.

## PART THREE

[*Vaccinium vitis-idaea* L.]
Mountain Cranberry [Cowberry; Foxberry]
Ericaceae
Hab. unknown
Coll. John Muir
1898
S. M. Dugger, *The Balsam Groves of Grandfather Mountain* (Banner Elk, N.C.: Shepherd M. Dugger, 1892). John Muir Personal Library.
Courtesy of the Holt-Atherton Department of Special Collections, University of the Pacific Library.

"Crossed the outlet of Champlain L[ake], a beautiful stream, good views of lake from cars, woods in fine color, vivid red hot and all shades of yellow brown and purple and red, here and there mixed with pines and hemlocks which help to show forth the burning trees and bushes, maples, ashes, elms, oaks, poplar, vaccinium, dogwood, etc."

John Muir, "Rambles thru the South," 13. John Muir Papers. Copyright 1984 Muir-Hanna Trust.

*Sassafras officinale* Nees
Sassafras
Lauraceae
Hab. unknown
Coll. John Muir
1898
S. M. Dugger, *The Balsam Groves of Grandfather Mountain* (Banner Elk N.C.: Shepherd M. Dugger, 1892). John Muir Personal Library.
Courtesy of the Holt-Atherton Department of Special Collections, University of the Pacific Library.

"October 8th....Just returned from a magnificent drive up spur of Cumberland 5 or 6 miles from Huntsville.... The woods and plants in general very interesting, many rare, as Yellowwood, here abundant and a fall-fruiting elm found here for the first time; Texas oak, chestnut, white, black and magnificent hickory 3 feet diameter, 3 species, grand Tulip, sassafras, sorrel, cherry, rhamnus, linden, ash, 3 species elm."

John Muir, "Rambles thru the South," 9. John Muir Papers. Copyright 1984 Muir-Hanna Trust.

*Leiophyllum buxifolium* Elliott
Sand Myrtle
Ericaceae
Hab. Grandfather Mountain, western North Carolina
Coll. John Muir
1898
S. M. Dugger, *The Balsam Groves of Grandfather Mountain* (Banner Elk, N.C.: Shepherd M. Dugger, 1892). John Muir Personal Library.
Courtesy of the Holt-Atherton Department of Special Collections, University of the Pacific Library.

"September 24, 1898. On Roan High Bluff, over 6200 [feet] above sea. Gray granite rock joints weathering, lovely slopes feathered with coloring trees descending in fine lines. Gray rocks on top, then a border of rich vigorous *rhododendron catawbiens[e]* with *Leiophyll[um] buxifolium*, charming shrub with white flowers and small sparkling leaves."

John Muir, "Rambles thru the South," 1898, Notebook 40, JMP MS48, Series 5A, Related Papers, Badè Transcripts of Muir Journals, Box 5, 5. Copyright 1984 Muir-Hanna Trust.

[*Viola canadensis* L.]
White Violet
Violaceae
Hab. Roan Mountain, Tennessee
Coll. John Muir
1898
S. M. Dugger, *The Balsam Groves of Grandfather Mountain* (Banner Elk, N.C.: Shepherd M. Dugger, 1892). John Muir Personal Library.
Courtesy of the Holt-Atherton Department of Special Collections, University of the Pacific Library.

*Quercus aquatica* (Lam.) Walter
Catesby Oak; Water Oak
Fagaceae
Hab. Mobile, Alabama
Coll. John Muir
November 24, 1898
S. M. Dugger, *The Balsam Groves of Grandfather Mountain* (Banner Elk, N.C.: Shepherd M. Dugger, 1892). John Muir Personal Library.
Courtesy of the Holt-Atherton Department of Special Collections, University of the Pacific Library.

Near Athens, Georgia.... "The water oak is abundant on stream banks and in damp hollows. Grasses are becoming tall and cane-like and do not cover the ground with their leaves as at the North. Strange plants are crowding about me now. Scarce a familiar face appears among all the flowers of the day's walk."

John Muir, A *Thousand Mile Walk to the Gulf*; reprinted in Muir, *The Eight Wilderness Discovery Books*, 135.

[*Uniola paniculata* L.]
Sea Oats
Gramineae
[Myrtle]
[Ericaceae]
Hab. [Florida]
Coll. John Muir
1898
JOMU 3561 1-4
Courtesy of the John Muir National Historic Site.

"The sun pours down double measure of the very sweetest rosiest light, in quality like that which fills the balmiest days of your Indiana summer. I know of but one deciduous tree or bush on these islands. All retain their green leaves without any tint of autumn, but plant green here is not so bright and pure as it is at the north....The whole green of the landscape is thus mixed and whitened....Another reason is that the grasses are coarser in leaf and stand more apart."

John Muir to Merrill Family, Cedar Keys, [Florida], January 6, 1868. John Muir Papers, JMP A1:00610. Copyright 1984 Muir-Hanna Trust.

## PART FOUR

*Agrostis exarata* Trin.
Bent Grass
Gramineae
Hab. near Yosemite, Sierra Nevada, California
Coll. John Muir
1875
Herb. J. H. Redfield #9205
Plantae Americae Septentrionalis
Missouri Botanical Garden 2871529
Courtesy of the Missouri Botanical Garden.

"Tuolumne Divide. August 21, 1872. Grass, a species of *Agrostis*, with tall, unbranched, strong stem and panicle of purple flowers, arches and waves above the low velvet sod like tropic bamboos."

John Muir, *John of the Mountains. The Unpublished Journals of John Muir*, 89.

*Cypripedium montanum* Dougl.
Mountain Lady's Slipper
Orchidaceae
Hab. near Yosemite, Sierra Nevada, California
Coll. John Muir
1875
Herb. J. H. Redfield #7891
Plantae Americae Septentrionalis
Missouri Botanical Garden 3380753
Courtesy of the Missouri Botanical Garden.

"The common orchidaceous plants are corallorhiza, goodyera, spiranthes, and habenaria. *Cypripedium monatum*, the only moccasin flower I have seen in the Park, is a handsome, thoughtful-looking plant living beside cool brooks. The large oval lip is white, delicately veined with purple; the other petals and sepals purple, strap-shaped, and elegantly curved and twisted."

John Muir, "The Wild Gardens of the Yosemite Park," *The Atlantic Monthly* 86 (August 1900): 174.

*Polypodium californicum* Kaulf.
California Polypod
Polypodiaceae
Hab. Sierra Nevada, California
Coll. John Muir
1875
Herb. J. H. Redfield #1701
Filices Americae Septentrionalis
Missouri Botanical Garden
Courtesy of the Missouri Botanical Garden.

"This is a delightful nook, or recess, running back of the foot of the fall [Lower Yosemite] about a hundred yards on the west side, its walls well fringed with maidenhair and spiraea and tufts of live-oak....The purple Leuchera with its airy panicles is abundant here, and near the fall is a ledge thickly fronded with Polypodium and Gymnogramme."

Muir, *John of the Mountains*, 63.

*Pinus ponderosa* "approaching *jeffreyi*"
[*P. ponderosa* Dougl.]
[*P. jeffreyi* Murr.]
Ponderosa Pine; Western Yellow Pine
Pinaceae
Hab. Yosemite, Sierra Nevada, California
Coll. John Muir
n.d.
Missouri Botanical Garden
Courtesy of the Missouri Botanical Garden.

"Because of its superior powers of enduring variations of climate and soil, [the Ponderosa Pine]...has a more extensive range than any other conifer growing in the Sierra....The bark is mostly arranged in massive plates....The cones are about three to four inches long, and two and a half wide, growing in close, sessile clusters among the leaves....The Jeffrey variety attains its finest development in the northern portion of the range, in the wide fountain basins of the McCloud and Pitt rivers, where it forms magnificent forests scarcely invaded by any other tree."

Muir, *The Yosemite*; reprinted in Muir, *The Eight Wilderness Discovery Books*, 652–653.

*Pellaea densa* (Brack.) Hook.
Claw Fern
Adiantaceae
Hab. Yosemite Valley, Sierra Nevada, California
Coll. John Muir
1875
Missouri Botanical Garden 876367
Courtesy of the Missouri Botanical Garden.

"*P. Bridgesii*, with blue-green, narrow, simply pinnate fronds, is about the same size as *Breweri* and ranks next to it as a mountaineer, growing in fissures and around boulders on glacier pavements. About a thousand feet lower we find the smaller and more abundant *P. densa*, on ledges and boulder-strewn fissured pavements, watered until late in summer by oozing currents from snow banks or thin outspread streams from moraines, growing in close sods, its little, bright green, triangular, tripinnate fronds, about an inch in length, as innumerable as leaves of grass."

Muir, "Wild Gardens of the Yosemite Park": 172.

*Cassiope mertensiana* (Bong.) Don
White Heather
Ericaceae
Hab. Sierra Nevada, California
Coll. John Muir
1875
Herb. J. H. Redfield #4636
Plantae Americae Septentrionalis
Missouri Botanical Garden 2541166
Courtesy of the Missouri Botanical Garden.

"Here, too, in this so-called 'land of desolation,' I met *Cassiope*, growing in fringes among the battered rocks. Her blossoms had faded long ago, but they were still clinging with happy memories to the evergreen sprays, and still so beautiful as to thrill every fiber of one's being. Winter and summer, you may hear her voice, the low, sweet melody of her purple bells. No evangel among all the mountain plants speaks Nature's love more plainly than *Cassiope*. Where she dwells, the redemption of the coldest solitude is complete. The very rocks and glaciers seem to feel her presence, and become imbued with her own fountain sweetness."

John Muir, "In the Heart of the California Alps," *Scribner's Monthly* 20 (July 1880): 348.

*Epilobium obcordatum* Gray
Rock Fringe
Onagraceae
Hab. alpine, Sierra Nevada, California
Coll. John Muir
1875
Herb. J. H. Redfield
Plantae Americae Septentrionalis
Academy of Natural Sciences of Philadelphia 912975
Courtesy of the Academy of Natural Sciences of Philadelphia. In this image the original plant specimen has been modified by Stephen J. Joseph.

"Along a narrow seam in the very warmest angle of the wall a perfectly gorgeous fringe of *Epilobium obcordatum* with flowers an inch wide, crowded together in lavish profusion, and coloured as royal a purple as ever was worn by any high-bred plant of the tropics; and best of all, and greatest of all, a noble thistle in full bloom, standing erect, head and shoulders above his companions, and thrusting out his lances in sturdy vigour as if growing on a Scottish brae."

John Muir, *The Mountains of California*; reprinted in Muir, *The Eight Wilderness Discovery Books*, 347.

*Milla ixioides* Baker [*Brodiaea ixioides* Wats.]
Golden Brodiaea
Liliaceae
Hab. near Yosemite, Sierra Nevada, California
Coll. John Muir
1875
Herb. J. H. Redfield #8940
Plantae Americae Septentrionalis
Missouri Botanical Garden 05060293
Courtesy of the Missouri Botanical Garden.

"In the midst of these tangles, and along their margins, small garden-like meadows occur where the stream has been able to make a level deposit of soil. They are planted with luxuriant *carices*, whose long, arching leaves wholly cover the ground. Out of these rise splendid larkspurs, six to eight feet high, columbines, lilies, and a few polygonums and erigerons. In these moist garden-patches, so thoroughly hidden, the bears like to wallow like hogs. I found many places that morning where the bent and squeezed sedges showed that I had disturbed them, and knew I was likely at any moment to come upon a cross mother with her cubs."

John Muir, "Explorations in the Great Tuolumne Cañon," *The Overland Monthly* 11 (August 1873): 143–144.

*Potentilla grayi* Wats.
Gray's Cinquefoil
Rosaceae
Hab. alpine, Sierra Nevada, California
Coll. John Muir
1875
Herb. J. H. Redfield
Plantae Americae Septentrionalis
University and Jepson Herbaria UC114356
Courtesy of the University and Jepson Herbaria, University of California, Berkeley.

"On the dry meadow-margin ferny leaves and flowers make a fine carpet. St. John's-wort, yellow-starred, makes the softest mats of all. *Monardella*, *Gayophytum*, musk *Mimulus*, pink *Gilia*, and blue-curls in moist shadows, with a margin of ferns and life-everlasting. *Rubus nutkanus* under the trees. *Potentilla*, snowberry, and purple *Eunanus*, purple-flowered *Malva*, and a violet like a hairy wood rush."

Muir, *John of the Mountains*, 216–217.

*Elymus sitanion* Schult.
Wild Rye
Gramineae
Hab. near Yosemite, Sierra Nevada, California
Coll. John Muir
c. 1875
Herb. J. H. Redfield #9644
Plantae Americae Septentrionalis
Missouri Botanical Garden 3053563
Courtesy of the Missouri Botanical Garden.

"Through the midst flows a stream only two or three feet wide, silently gliding as if careful not to disturb the hushed calm of the solitude, its banks embossed by the common sod bent down to the water's edge, and trimmed with mosses and violets; slender grass panicles lean over like miniature pine trees, and here and there on the driest places small mats of heathworts are neatly spread, enriching without roughening the bossy down-curling sod."

Muir, "Wild Gardens of the Yosemite Park": 177.

*Woodsia scopulina* Eaton
Rocky Mountain Woodsia
Woodsiaceae
Hab. Sierra Nevada, California
Coll. John Muir
1875
Herb. J. H. Redfield #1713
Filices Americae Septentrionalis
Missouri Botanical Garden 92041
Courtesy of the Missouri Botanical Garden.

"Many a fine, hanging-garden aloft on breezy inaccessible heights owes to it its freshness and fullness of beauty; ferneries in shady nooks, filled with adiantum, woodwardia, woodsia, aspidium, pellaea, and cheilanthes, rosetted and tufted and ranged in lines, daintly overlapping, thatching the stupendous cliffs with softest beauty, without any connection with rock or stream."

Muir, *The Yosemite*; reprinted in Muir, *The Eight Wilderness Discovery Books*, 622.

*Ivesia gordonii* (Hook.) Torr. & Gray var. *lycopodioides* Wats.
Gordon's Ivesia
Rosaceae
Hab. alpine, Sierra Nevada, California
Coll. John Muir
1875
Herb. J. H. Redfield
Plantae Americae Septentrionalis
University and Jepson Herbaria UC114514
Courtesy of the University and Jepson Herbaria, University of California, Berkeley.

"*Alpine gardens* of gentle evanescent beauty adorn the most enduring granite, closely embraced by strong rocky bosses. Many alpine plants form tufts on rock fissures or seams, short stems massed into cushions, perennial roots perhaps a century old, fed by invisible ooze from some snow-fountain above it. Many ivesias and eriogonums offer fine examples of this sort, old perhaps as the trees."

Muir, *John of the Mountains*, 163.

*Woodwardia radicans* (L.) Sm. var. *radicans* Hook.
Chain Fern
Blechnaceae
Hab. Sierra Nevada, California
Coll. John Muir
c. 1875
Herb. J. H. Redfield #1708
Filices Americae Septentrionalis
Missouri Botanical Garden 2525051
Courtesy of the Missouri Botanical Garden.

"The glory of this fall is the abundance of luxuriant groviness about it and mingling with it. Its white waters issue from a tangle of evergreen trees and shrubs and ferns and mosses and flow through a tangle into a tangle. Ferns, tall woodwardian and gentle floating maidenhairs and emerald mosses in sheltered coves ever wet with mealy spray are precious and luxuriant fringes of maidenhair and thickets of the tall *Woodwardia*."

John Muir to Jeanne C. Carr, Yosemite Valley, December 25, 1872, in Gisel, *Kindred & Related Spirits*, 202.

*Lilium washingtonianum* Kell.
Washington Lily
Liliaceae
Hab. near Yosemite Valley, Sierra Nevada, California
Coll. John Muir
1875
Herb. J. H. Redfield #8093
Plantae Americae Septentrionalis
Missouri Botanical Garden 3342702
Courtesy of the Missouri Botanical Garden.

"The Washington lily (*L. washingtonianum*) is white, deliciously fragrant, moderate in size, with three to ten flowered racemes. The largest I ever measured was eight feet high, the raceme two feet long, with fifty-two flowers, fifteen of them open; the others had faded or were still in the bud. This famous lily is distributed over the sunny portions of the sugar-pine woods, never in large garden companies like pardalinum, but widely scattered, standing up to the waist in dense ceanothus and manzanita chaparral, waving its lovely flowers above the blooming wilderness of brush, and giving their fragrance to the breeze. These stony, thorny jungles are about the last places in the mountains in which one would look for lilies. But though they toil not nor spin, like other people under adverse circumstances, they have to do the best they can."

John Muir, "Wild Gardens of the Yosemite Park": 173.

John Muir to Sarah Muir Galloway, Snelling's Ranch, March [1869]
Envelope and plant specimen [unidentified]
JOMU 3561 F-2
Courtesy of the John Muir National Historic Site.

"Splendid fields of wild oats (*Avena fatua*). The delightful *Gilia* (*G. tricolor*) was very abundant in sweeping hill-side sheets, and a *Leptosiphon* (*L. andros*[*aceus*]) and *Claytonias* were everywhere by the roadsides, and lilies and dodecatheons by the streams: no wonder the air was so good, waving and rubbing on such a firmament of flowers!"

John Muir, "Rambles of a Botanist among the Plants and Climates of California," *Old and New* 5 (June 1872): 768.

*Pellaea mucronata* Eaton
Bird's Foot Fern
Adiantaceae
Hab. Yosemite Valley, California
Coll. John Muir
1875
Missouri Botanical Garden 876359
Courtesy of the Missouri Botanical Garden.

"We found ferns in abundance all through the pass. Some far down in dark cañons, as the polypodium and rock fern, or high on sunlit braes, as *Pellaea mucronata*.

John Muir, "Rambles of a Botanist...": 769.

*Primula suffrutescens* Gray
Sierra Primrose
Primulaceae
Hab. Cloud's Rest
Coll. Asa Gray
Journey to California 1872
Missouri Botanical Garden 2571921
Courtesy of the Missouri Botanical Garden.

"I received the last of your notes two days ago, announcing the arrival of the ferns. You speak of three boxes of *Primula*. I sent seven or eight. I had some measurements to make about the throat of the South Dome, so yesterday I climbed there, and then ran up to Cloud's Rest for your *Primulas*, and as I stuffed them in big sods into a sack, I said, 'Now I wonder what mouthfuls this size will accomplish for the Doctor's primrose hunger.'"

John Muir to Asa Gray, Yosemite Valley, December 18, 1872, in Badè, *Life and Letters*; reprinted in Gifford, *John Muir*, 183–184.

*Ivesia muirii* Gray
Granite Mousetail
Rosaceae
Hab. west slope, North Peak in unglaciated granite gravel, altitude 11,600 feet, vicinity of Mt. Conness, Tuolumne County, Sierra Nevada, California
Coll. C. W. Sharsmith #2233
July 25, 1936
Herbarium of the University of California
Plants of California
University and Jepson Herbaria UC 642925
Courtesy of the University and Jepson Herbaria, University of California, Berkeley.

"If you will keep botanizing in the high Sierras you will find curious and new things, no doubt. One such, at least, is in your present collection...the wee mouse-tail *Ivesia*. And the rare sp[elling] of *Lewisia* is as good as *new*, and is so wholly to California."

Asa Gray to John Muir, Botanic Garden, Cambridge, Massachusetts, April 9, 1873. John Muir Papers, JMP A2: 01261. Copyright 1984 Muir-Hanna Trust.

(Carl W. Sharsmith, inspired by the work of John Muir, enrolled in the Yosemite School of Field Natural History in 1930. The following year he was hired by the National Park Service as a seasonal ranger-naturalist in Tuolumne Meadows, Yosemite National Park. Sharsmith received a BA from the University of California, Los Angeles, in 1933 and a PhD in botany from the University of California, Berkeley, in 1940. Said to have explored nearly every nook and cranny of Yosemite's High Sierra, he was motivated not by the search for data but by the appeal to the heart of the natural world. From 1950 until 1973, he was a professor of botany at San Jose State.)

Hab. Mount Dana and region, Sierra Nevada, California
Coll. John Muir
July 15, 1873, during an excursion with William Keith, Keith's wife, Alice Elizabeth (Lizzie), their son Charlie, and Emily Pelton (a friend from Muir's days in Prairie du Chien, Wisconsin)
JOMU 3561 B4
Courtesy of the John Muir National Historic Site.

Clockwise from upper left:
*Vaccinium caespitosum* Michx. (Dwarf Blueberry), Ericaceae
*Vaccinium caespitosum* Michx.
(upper) *Arabis lyallii* Wats. (Lyall's Rockcress), Cruciferae
(lower) *Saxifraga virginiensis* Michx. (Early Saxifrage), Saxifragaceae
(upper) *Arabis lyallii* Wats.
(lower) *Saxifraga virginiensis* Michx.
(upper) *Arabis lyallii* Wats.
(lower) *Ivesia lycopodioides* Gray, Rosaceae
*Draba stenoloba* Ledeb. (Whitlow Grass), Cruciferae
*Phlox caespitosa* Nutt. (Alpine Phlox), Polemoniaceae
*Erigeron pygmaeus* (Gray) Greene (Pygmy Fleabane), Asteraceae
*Poa alpina* L. (Blue Grass), Gramineae
*Sibbaldia procumbens* L. (Creeping Sibbaldia), Rosaceae
*Polemonium caeruleum* L. (Sky Pilot; Jacob's Ladder), Polemoniaceae

*Adiantum chilense* Kaulf.
Maidenhair Fern
Adiantaceae
Hab. Sierra Nevada, California, alt. 2,000 feet
Coll. John Muir
1875
Missouri Botanical Garden 876365
Courtesy of the Missouri Botanical Garden.

"They are the most delicate and graceful plant creatures I ever beheld, waving themselves in lines of the most refined of heaven's beauty to the music of the water. The motion of the purple dulses in pools left by the tide on the sea-coast of Scotland was the only memory that was stirred by these spiritual ferns."

John Muir to Jeanne C. Carr, Yosemite, December 6, 1869, in Gisel, *Kindred & Related Spirits*, 95.

## PART FIVE

*Mertensia paniculata* (Ait.) Don
Tall Bluebells
Boraginaceae
Hab. St. Michael, Alaska
Coll. John Muir
Cruise of the *Corwin* #167
1881
Courtesy of the Harvard University Herbaria.

"[St. Michael, Alaska]...the plants in bloom were, primula, kalmia, dicentra, mertensia, veratrum, sedum, saxifrage, cupatorium, cranberry, draba of several species, lupine, telima, silene, phlox, buckbean, bryanthus, several sedges, a liliaceous plant new to me, five species of willow, dwarf birch, alder, and a purple pedicularis, the showiest of them all."

John Muir, "Return to St. Michael's. Preparing for Another Cruise—The Busy Season at St. Michael's—San Francisco Prospectors Heard From—Fauna and Flora—Volcanic Cones. St. Michael's Alaska, July 8, 1881," *San Francisco Daily Evening Bulletin* (August 15, 1881): 3, col. 8.

*Stellaria longipes* var. *edwardsii* Goldie
Long-Stalked Starwort
Caryophyllaceae
Hab. St. Michael, Alaska
Coll. John Muir
Cruise of the *Corwin* #193
1881
Courtesy of the Harvard University Herbaria.

"St. Michael....I took a long walk of twelve or fourteen miles over the tundra to a volcanic cone and back, leaving the ship about twelve in the forenoon and getting back at half-past eight. I found a great number of flowers in full bloom, and birds of many species building their nests, and a capital view of the surrounding country from the rim of an old crater, altogether making a delightful day."

John Muir to Louie Wanda Strentzel Muir, St. Michael, Alaska, June 21, 1881, in Badè, *Life and Letters*; reprinted in Gifford, *John Muir*, 270.

*Lloydia serotina* (L.) Salisb. ex Rchb.
Snowdon Lily
Liliaceae
Hab. St. Michael, Alaska
Coll. John Muir
Cruise of the *Corwin* #165
1881
Courtesy of the Harvard University Herbaria.

"The moss mantle for the most part rests on a stratum of ice that never melts to any great extent, and the ice on a bed of rock of black vesicular lava. Ridges of the lava rise here and there above the general level in rough masses, affording ground for plants that like a drier soil. Numerous hollows and watercourses also occur on the general tundra, whose well-drained banks are decked with gay flowers in lavish abundance, and meadow patches of grasses shoulder high, suggestive of regions much father south."

John Muir, "Botanical Notes," in *Cruise of the Revenue-Steamer* Corwin *in Alaska and the N.W. Arctic Ocean in 1881. Notes and Memoranda,* 49.

*Luzula hyperborea* R. Br.
Northern Woodrush
Juncaceae
Hab. head of Kotzebue Sound
Coll. John Muir
Cruise of the *Corwin* #50
1881
Courtesy of the Harvard University Herbaria.

"The flora of the region about the head of Kotzebue Sound is hardly less luxuriant and rich in species than that of other points visited by the *Corwin* lying several degrees farther south. Fine nutritious grasses suitable for the fattening of cattle and from 2 to 6 feet high are not of rare occurrence on meadows of considerable extent and along stream banks wherever the stagnant waters of the tundra have been drained off, while in similar localities the most showy of the Arctic plants bloom in all their freshness and beauty, manifesting no sign of frost, or unfavorable conditions of any kind whatever."

Muir, "Botanical Notes," *Revenue-Steamer* Corwin, 50.

*Geum glaciale* Adams. ex Fisch. & C. A. Mey.
Glacier Avens
Rosaceae
Hab. Cape Thompson, Alaska
Coll. John Muir
Cruise of the *Corwin* #102
1881
Courtesy of the Harvard University Herbaria.

"On the 20th of May we found the showy *Geum glaciale* already in flower, also an arcto-staphylos and draba, on a slope facing the south, near the harbor of Ounalaska. The willows, too, were then beginning to put forth their catkins, while a multitude of green points were springing up in sheltered spots wherever the snow had vanished. At a height of 400 and 500 feet, however, winter was still unbroken with scarce a memory of the rich bloom of summer."

Muir, "Botanical Notes," *Revenue-Steamer* Corwin, 47.

*Saxifraga davurica* Willd.
Saxifragaceae
Hab. Cape Thompson, Alaska
Coll. John Muir
Cruise of the *Corwin* #107
1881
Courtesy of the Harvard University Herbaria.

*Eritrichium nanum* L. var. *aretioides* Herder
[*E. nanum* (L.) Schrad. ex Gaudin]
Alpine Forget-Me-Not
Boraginaceae
Hab. Cape Thompson, Alaska
Coll. John Muir
Cruise of the *Corwin* #93
1881
Courtesy of the Harvard University Herbaria.

"The Cape Thompson flora is richer in species and individuals than that of any other point on the Arctic shores we have seen, owing no doubt mainly to the better drainage of the ground through the fissured frost-cracked limestone, which hereabouts is the principal rock. Where the hill-slopes are steepest the rock frequently occurs in loose angular masses and is entirely bare of soil. But between these barren slopes there are valleys where the showiest of the Arctic plants bloom in rich profusion and variety, forming brilliant masses of color...where certain species form beds of considerable size, almost to the exclusion of others."

Muir, "Botanical Notes," *Revenue-Steamer* Corwin, 50–51.

*Primula borealis* Duby
Northern Primrose
Primulaceae
Hab. Point Hope, Alaska
Coll. attributed to John Muir
Cruise of the *Corwin*
1881
Courtesy of the Harvard University Herbaria.

"St. La[w]rence Island, Alaska, the largest in [the] Behring Sea....All the surface of the low grounds in the glacial gaps as well as the flat table-lands are covered with wet spongy tundra of mosses and lichens with patches of blooming heathworts and dwarf willows, and grasses and sedges, with larkspurs, saxifrages, daisies, primulas, anemones, ferns, etc....with a luxuriance and brightness of color, little to be hoped for in so cold and dreary looking a region."

John Muir, "St. La[w]rence Island. Arctic Volcanoes—A Land of Lava and Craters—A Ghastly Scene in an Arctic Golgotha—The Work of a Famine. Steamer *Corwin*, St. La[w]rence Island, Alaska, July 3, 1881," *San Francisco Daily Evening Bulletin* (August 15, 1881): 3, cols. 7–8.

*Anemone narcissiflora* L.
Narcissus-flowered Anemone
Ranunculaceae
Hab. Cape Thompson, Alaska
Coll. John Muir
Cruise of the *Corwin* #101
1881
Courtesy of the Harvard University Herbaria.

*Anemone parviflora* Michx.
Northern Anemone
Ranunculaceae
Hab. Cape Thompson, Alaska
Coll. John Muir
Cruise of the *Corwin* #69
1881
Courtesy of the Harvard University Herbaria.

*Ranunculus pygmaeus* Wahl.
Pygmy Buttercup
Ranunculaceae
Hab. Cape Markham, Siberia
Coll. John Muir
Cruise of the *Corwin* #208
1881
Courtesy of the Harvard University Herbaria.

"[East Cape, Siberia]...I stopped to gather the flowers that I found in bloom. The banks of a stream coming from a high basin filled with snow was quite richly flowered with anemones, buttercups, potentillas, draba, primulas and many species of dwarf willows, up to a h[e]ight of about a thousand feet above the level of the sea."

John Muir, "At East Cape. Ashore—A Siberian Village—The Arctic Hunter's Luxurious Home—Arctic Cemeteries—Botanizing on the Siberian Shore—Tracing the Ice Floods. Steamer *Corwin*, East Cape, Siberia, July 1, 1881," *San Francisco Daily Evening Bulletin* (August 16, 1881): 1, col. 2.

*Cassiope tetragona* (L.) D. Don
White Arctic Mountain Heather
Ericaceae
Hab. Cape Thompson, Alaska
Coll. John Muir
Cruise of the *Corwin* #123
1881
Courtesy of the Harvard University Herbaria.

"The plants named in the following notes were collected at many localities on the coasts of Alaska and Siberia, and on Saint Lawrence, Wrangel, and Herald Islands...in the course of short excursions, some of them less than an hour in length. Inasmuch as the flora of the arctic and subarctic regions is nearly the same everywhere, the discovery of many species new to science was not to be expected. The collection, however, will no doubt be valuable for comparison with the plants of other regions."

John Muir, "Botanical Notes," *Revenue-Steamer* Corwin, 47.

*Picea engelmannii* Parry ex Engelm.
Engelmann Spruce
Pinaceae
Hab. Dease Lake, northeast of Sitka, latitude 60 degrees, altitude 4,000 feet, British
Columbia, tree 140 feet high, very slender
Coll. John Muir
August 1879
Herb. G. Engelmann, St. Louis, Missouri
Missouri Botanical Garden 2505880
Courtesy of the Missouri Botanical Garden.

*Juniperus communis* L.
Common Juniper
Cupressaceae
Hab. Alaska
Coll. John Muir
1880
Missouri Botanical Garden 3934177
Courtesy of the Missouri Botanical Garden.

*Cupressus nutkatensis* Hook.
[*Chamaecyparis nootkatensis*]
Alaska Cedar; Yellow Cypress
Cupressaceae
Hab. Sitka, Alaska
Coll. John Muir
1879
Herb. G. Engelmann, St. Louis, Missouri
Missouri Botanical Garden 2969601
Courtesy of the Missouri Botanical Garden.

"The bulk of the forests of Southeastern Alaska is made up of three species of evergreen, all of which are of good size, and grow close together, covering almost every acre of the islands, however rocky, and the margin of the coast and the mountain slopes up to the height of about 2,000 feet. The most important of these…is the yellow cedar, or cypress (*Cupressus nutkatensis*), a truly noble tree.…The branches are pinnate, drooping, feathery…like those of the California libocedrus, but with finer foliage and more delicate plumes.…The only California wood that resembles this is the torreya, which has the same delicate yellow color and close texture, but the pleasant scent is wanting."

John Muir, "Alaska Forests. Evergreens—The Yellow Cedar and Its Various Uses. The White Spruce—Pines and Cottonwoods—Firs and Hardwoods. Extent and Commercial Value of Alaska Forests—The 'Devil's Club.' (Special Correspondence of the *Bulletin*.) Fort Wrangel, October 8, 1879," *San Francisco Daily Evening Bulletin* (October 30, 1879): 4, cols. 1–2.

*Cupressus nutkatensis* Hook.
[*Chamaecyparis nootkatensis*]
Alaska Cedar; Yellow Cypress
Cupressaceae
Hab. Fort Wrangel, Alaska
Coll. John Muir
1879
Courtesy of the Harvard University Herbaria.

"The menzies spruce is bluish green, the merten spruce and the cedar bright yellow-green, and all more or less draped and tufted with gray and yellow lichens and mosses, the whole producing a delightful effect. Our camp-fire smoke is lying motionless in the branches of the trees like a stranded cloud."

John Muir, "Alaska Land. John Muir Revisits the Scene of Last Year's Exploration. A Land of Abundance—A Canoe Voyage among the Islands and Icebergs. Magnificent Scenery—The Hoona Indians—Among the Salmon. (Special Correspondence of the *Bulletin*.) In Camp, Near Cape Fanshaw, August 18, 1880," *San Francisco Daily Evening Bulletin* (September 25, 1880): 4, cols. 6–8.

*Erigeron muirii* Gray
Muir's Fleabane
Asteraceae
Hab. Philip Smith Mountains Quad; Uyamitquaq Creek and vicinity; dry sandstone outcrop; NE area of site
Coll. D. A. Walker and N. Lederer
July 5, 1987
University of Alaska Herbarium ALAV96229
Courtesy of the University of Alaska Museum Herbarium

At Cape Thompson, Alaska, in July 1881, Muir found a new species of *Erigeron* and redeemed a promise made ten years earlier by Asa Gray: "Pray find a new genus, or at least a new species, that I may have the satisfaction of embalming your name, not in glacier-ice, but in spicy wild perfume."

Asa Gray to John Muir, Botanic Garden, Cambridge, Mass., January 4, 1872, John Muir Papers, JMP A2:01020. Copyright 1984 Muir-Hanna Trust.

## EPILOGUE

*Nemophila menziesii* Hook. & Arn.
Baby Blue Eyes
Hydrophyllaceae
Hab. [California]
Coll. attributed to John Muir
c. 1870s
David Hanna Botanical Series, Box 1 and 2. John Muir Personal Library.
Courtesy of the Holt-Atherton Department of Special Collections, University of the Pacific Library.

"In March, plant-life is more than doubled [in Twenty Hill Hollow]. The little, pioneer cress, by this time, goes to seed, wearing daintily embroidered silicles. Several *Claytonias* appear; also, a large, white *Leptosiphon* [Phlox,

Polemoniaceae], and two *Nemophilas*. A small *Plantago* becomes tall enough to wave and show silky ripples of shade. Toward the end of this month or the beginning of April, plant-life is at its greatest height."

John Muir, "Twenty Hill Hollow," *The Overland Monthly* 9 (July 1872): 85.

*Thalictrum anemonoides* Michx.
[*Anemonella thalictroides* L.]
Meadow Rue; Rue Anemone
Ranunculaceae
Hab. Indiana
Coll. John Muir
[1866]
JOMU 1041
Courtesy of the John Muir National Historic Site.

"In this first walk I found *Erigenia*, which here is ever first, and sweet little violets, and *Sanguinaria*, and *Isopyrum* too, and *Thalictrum anemonoides* were almost ready to venture their faces to the sky. The red maple was in full flower glory; the leaves below and the mosses were bright with its fallen scarlet blossoms. And the elm too was in flower and the earliest willows. All this when your fields had scarce the *memory* left in them."

John Muir to Jeanne C. Carr, Indianapolis, May 2, 1867, in Gisel, *Kindred & Related Spirits*, 52.

# APPENDIX

*Quercus lobata* Née
California White Oak; Valley Oak
Fagaceae
Hab. Martinez, California (Strentzel home)
Coll. John Muir
April 1881
Herb. G. Engelmann, St. Louis, Missouri
Missouri Botanical Garden 3532024
Courtesy of the Missouri Botanical Garden.

"As I certainly shall not (if at all) be there [in California] in season for the flowering of the oaks, I would ask you to get for me at least the two species which grow close about you. One is *quercus lobata*, which grows, as you know, about the stables on the Creek; the other is *quercus Douglasii*, the blue mountain oak, on the bare hills above you. A few specimens of each of them in flower and again a week or two later when the leaves are not yet fully grown (showing the female flowers or young acorns) would be very desirable. I would say that I found a few specimens of the *lobata* also on the hills, but *Douglasii* is readily distinguished by the smoother, white bark, the smaller and less lobar leaves, it seems to be the common tree on the arid hills."

George Engelmann to John Muir, St. Louis, Missouri, April 11, 1881. John Muir Papers, JMP A4:02214. Copyright 1984 Muir-Hanna Trust.

*Linanthus dichotomus* Benth.
Evening Snow
Polemoniaceae
Hab. Giant Forest, Sequoia National Park, California
Coll. John Muir
1901
JOMU 3561-8
Courtesy of the John Muir National Historic Site.

*Raillardella muirii* Gray
Muir's Raillardella; Muir's Tarweed
Asteraceae
Hab. vicinity of Yosemite Valley, Sierra Nevada, California
Coll. John Muir
1875
Harvard University Herbaria 11588
Courtesy of the Harvard University Herbaria and the Botany Libraries, Library of the Gray Herbarium, Harvard University Herbaria, Harvard University.

*Ceanothus integerrimus* Hook. & Arn.
Deer Brush
Rhamnaceae
Hab. Giant Forest, Sequoia National Park, California
Coll. John Muir
1901
JOMU 3561-10
Courtesy of the John Muir National Historic Site.

"In the sugar-pine woods the most beautiful species is *C. integerrimus*, often called California lilac, or deer brush. It is five or six feet high, smooth, slender, willowy, with bright foliage and abundance of blue flowers in close showy panicles. Two species, *prostratus* and *procumbens*, spread handsome blue-flowered mats and rugs on warm ridges beneath the pines, and offer delightful beds to the tired mountaineer."

Muir, "Wild Gardens of the Yosemite Park": 170.

*Senecio fremontii* Torr. & Gray
Dwarf Mountain Ragwort
Asteraceae
Hab. Mount Whitney, California
Coll. John Muir
July 1876
Lemmon Herbarium/California Academy of Sciences
University and Jepson Herbaria UC335851
Courtesy of the University and Jepson Herbaria, University of California, Berkeley.

"A garden with *Senecio* and yarrow, dense mosses, *Camassia*, and *Viola* with purple-striped lip, oval opposite petals turning back, delicate spurs seen between short stems, every hair tipped with dew. The young buds look like the bills of gorblings [Scottish name for unfledged birds], and the heart-shaped round leaves mingle with the primrose and *Mimulus*."

Muir, *John of the Mountains*, 216.

*Ceanothus papillosus* Torr. & Gray
California Lilac
Rhamnaceae
Hab. Wright's Station, [Santa Clara County], California
Coll. John Muir
May 2, 1889
Lemmon Herbarium
Herbarium of the University of California
Plants of California
University and Jepson Herbaria UC 338131
Courtesy of the University and Jepson Herbaria, University of California, Berkeley.

"Camp in a mountain garden, South Fork of Kaweah River....The river goes foaming past two thousand feet below, while the sequoia forest rises shadowy along the ridge on the north. This little garden is only about half an acre in size, full of goldenrods and Eriogona and tall vaselike tufts of waving grasses with silky panicles....The whole is fenced in by a close hedgelike growth of wild cherry, mingled with *Ceanothus* and glossy evergreen manzanita, not drawn around in strict lines, but waving in and out in a succession of bays and swelling bosses exquisitely painted with the best Indian-summer light, and making a perfect paradise of color."

Muir, *John of the Mountains*, 231.

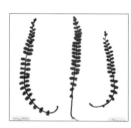

*Asplenium trichomanes* L.
Maidenhair Spleenwort
Aspleniaceae
Hab. rocks near Owen Sound, [Ontario], Canada
Coll. John Muir
1865
JOMU 2347
Courtesy of the John Muir National Historic Site.

"I would take pleasure in showing you my collection of ferns, the eyes are so few that appreciate such beauties. I send you a few mosses[.] I only began their analysis this fall and these are some of my first specimens[. M]any of them are imperfect[,] in some cases the male flower is wanting still."

John Muir to Emily Pelton, Trout's Mill, November 12, 1865, State Historical Society of Wisconsin Archives, Madison, Wisconsin.

*Cheilanthes californica* (Nutt.) Mett.
California Lace Fern
Adiantaceae
Hab. Sierra Nevada, California
Coll. John Muir
1875
Herb. J. H. Redfield #1702
Filices Americae Septentrionalis
Missouri Botanical Garden 2475165
Courtesy of the Missouri Botanical Garden.

"Three species of *Cheilanthes*, *Californica*, *gracillima*, and *myriophylla*, with beautiful two to four pinnate fronds, an inch to five inches long, adorn the stupendous walls of the cañons however dry and sheer. The exceedingly delicate and interesting *Californica* is rare, the others abundant at from three thousand to seven thousand feet elevation, and are often accompanied by the little gold fern, *Gymnogramme triangularis*, and rarely by the curious little *Botrychium simplex*, the smallest of which are less than an inch high."

Muir, "Wild Gardens of the Yosemite Park": 172.

*Cystopteris fragilis* (L.) Bernh.
Brittle Bladder Fern; Fragile Fern
Woodsiaceae
Hab. Cape Thompson, Alaska
Cruise of the *Corwin* #98
Coll. John Muir
1881
Courtesy of the Harvard University Herbaria.

*Aspidium fragrans* Gray
[*Dryopteris fragrans* (L.) Schott.]
Shield Fern
Dryopteridaceae
Hab. St. Michael, Alaska
Coll. John Muir
Cruise of the *Corwin* #171
1881
Courtesy of the Harvard University Herbaria.

"[Fort Wrangel, Alaska]...Pushing my way through a tangle of bushes well back into the forest, I found it composed almost entirely of two spruces, *abies menziesii* and *A. mertensia[na]* [*Tsuga mertensiana*], with a few specimens of yellow cypress. The ferns were developed in remarkable beauty and size—two aspidiums, one of which is about six feet high; a woodsia, comaria and polypodium."

John Muir, "Alaska Glaciers. An Ounalaska Yosemite. Glacial Theology and Sermons in Ice. The Rocks, Plants and Trees of Alaska. (Correspondence of the *Bulletin*.) Fort Wrangel, Alaska, September 5, 1879," *San Francisco Daily Evening Bulletin*, September 23, 1879: 4, col. 1.

*Asplenium thelypteroides* Michx.
Silvery Spleenwort
Aspleniaceae
Hab. [Ontario], Canada, Michigan, Indianapolis
Coll. John Muir
1866
JOMU 1124
Courtesy of the John Muir National Historic Site.

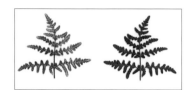

*Gymnogramma triangulare* Kaulf.
[*G. triangularis*]
California Gold Fern
Adiantaceae
[Pteridaceae]
Hab. California
Coll. attributed to John Muir
n.d.
David Hanna Botanical Series, Box 1 and 2. John Muir Personal Library.
Courtesy of the Holt-Atherton Department of Special Collections,
University of the Pacific Library.

"Some of the hills have rock ribs that are brightly coloured with red and yellow lichens, and in moist nooks there are luxuriant mosses—*Bartramia, Dicranum, Fumaria,* and several *Hypnums.* In cool, sunless coves the mosses are companioned with ferns—*Cystopteris* and the little gold-dusted rock fern, *Gymnogramme triangulare.*"

Muir, "Twenty Hill Hollow," *The Overland Monthly* 9 (July 1872): 85.

## TECHNICAL AND AESTHETIC APPLICATION

*Kalmia glauca* Ait.
Pale Laurel
Ericaceae
Hab. Sierra Nevada, California
Coll. John Muir
1875
Herb. J. H. Redfield
Plantae Americae Septentrionalis
Missouri Botanical Garden 107236
Courtesy of the Missouri Botanical Garden.

"I followed the main Yosemite rim northward, passing round the head of the second Yosemite tributary which flowed about northeast until bent southward by the main current. About noon I came to the basin of the third ice tributary of the west rim, a place of domes....First there is the pure glassy plantless water center, then a light green fringe of *Carex* which has long arching leaves that dip to the water, then a beveled border of yellow *Sphagnum* moss, coming exactly to the water's edge....The purple *Kalmia* has a place here also, and the splendidly flowered *Phyllodoce,* but these last are small, and weave into the sod, spreading low down in the grasses and living with them."

John Muir to Clinton L. Merriam, Camp-fire 8 miles north of Yosemite Falls, September 19, 1871. John Muir Papers, JMP 2:00968. Copyright 1984 Muir-Hanna Trust.

# TECHNICAL AND
# AESTHETIC APPLICATION

## STEPHEN J. JOSEPH

This is the largest single project I have undertaken, and it began with extensive computer and digital photographic experience. Three and a half years were spent working on an Apple G4 computer, scanning over six hundred Muir plant specimens, artifacts, letters, photographs, and maps, and restoring with Photoshop one hundred and seventy of them. My specialty is large-scale panoramic landscapes, and this project has been an exciting opportunity to work in a macro world where I was able to explore my interest in history, and combine it with natural science, art, and photographic work.

My process began while Bonnie Gisel was on a treasure hunt that took her to herbaria across the United States. Some plant specimens were scanned on location, while others were sent to the University and Jepson Herbaria at the University of California, Berkeley, who hosted the receipt of specimens. The scanning was completed with a 2450 or a 4870 Epson flatbed scanner using Epson software adjusted to accentuate any remaining color in the plants. Contrast was increased and the color heightened. All scans were made in sixteen bits with file sizes ranging up to 500 MB. The larger plants were scanned in sections and stitched together in Photoshop. Plant specimens are fragile and easily broken, and handling them required extreme care. I am pleased to say not a single plant was damaged in the process. Scanning, though tedious, was exciting. When I opened a folder containing a plant, I felt as if I was on a journey of discovery. I never tired of the thought that John Muir had picked and preserved each plant.

While Bonnie considered the importance of each plant specimen from perspectives of Muir's life, botany, history, chronology, and aesthetics, I determined which plants were restorable. The specimens looked very gray. Many of them had been sprayed with chemicals,

Left: *Mertensia paniculata* (Ait.) Don, Tall Bluebells

eaten by bugs, broken into multiple pieces, and glued and taped onto herbarium sheets with few aesthetic considerations. On an Apple G4 computer I created interesting layouts utilizing the plants and various artifacts—labels and letters. The first order was to remove the tape and glue, using cloning and selection techniques in Photoshop. The plant sections hidden behind tape or surrounded by glue were rebuilt and I repaired broken leaves and stems with the use of the same Photoshop techniques. The objective was to restore the plant specimens to appear closer to the way they looked to Muir. Liberating the specimens from their herbarium sheets by creating new backgrounds with the use of the color-range selection tool in Photoshop refreshed the look of the plants as well. The main Photoshop adjustments used were levels and curves; I increased the contrast and heightened the color. Though I attempted to remain true to the faded colors of the plants, the prints are my artistic interpretation. Depending on condition, restoration took from three to twenty hours for each plant.

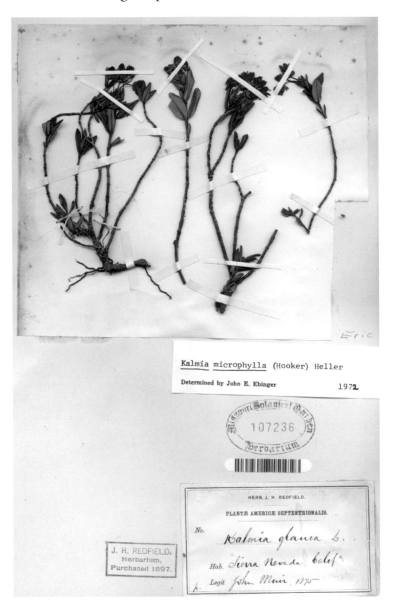

Once the plants were restored to my satisfaction, I added labels and artifacts to create the final prints. Throughout the process, overall design and composition were major factors. Selecting border colors often began with sampling colors from the plants and then mixing the color with gray for the final image. Most of the images are of very high resolution and capable of being printed as large as six or seven feet in height or width. Archival prints are made with an Epson 9800 printer on Somerset Velvet paper.

A most rewarding experience that will stay with me the rest of my life, recreating John Muir's herbarium has tremendously influenced my printmaking.

Opposite and above: *Kalmia glauca* Ait., Pale Laurel

# NOTES

The following abbreviations are used throughout the Notes section:

BADE    William Frederic Badè. *The Life and Letters of John Muir*. Boston: Houghton Mifflin, 1924; reprinted in *John Muir: His Life and Letters and Other Writings*, ed. Terry Gifford. London: Baton Wicks, 1996.

JMP     John Muir Papers. Holt-Atherton Department of Special Collections, University of the Pacific Library. Copyright 1984 Muir-Hanna Trust.

K&RS    Bonnie Johanna Gisel, ed. *Kindred & Related Spirits: The Letters of John Muir and Jeanne C. Carr*. Salt Lake City: University of Utah Press, 2001.

LJM     Linnie Marsh Wolfe. *Son of the Wilderness: The Life of John Muir*. New York: Alfred A. Knopf, 1945; reprint, Madison: University of Wisconsin Press, 1978.

LTAF    John Muir. *Letters to a Friend: Written to Mrs. Ezra Carr, 1866–1879*. Boston: Houghton Mifflin, 1915; reprint, Dunwoody, Ga.: Norman Berg, 1973.

SFDEB   *San Francisco Daily Evening Bulletin*.

SHSW    State Historical Society of Wisconsin Archives, Madison, Wisconsin.

UJJM    John Muir. *John of the Mountains. The Unpublished Journals of John Muir*. Edited by Linnie Marsh Wolfe. Boston: Houghton Mifflin, 1938; reprint, Madison: University of Wisconsin Press, 1979.


## INTRODUCTION

1.  See Elizabeth B. Keeney, *The Botanizers: Amateur Scientists in Nineteenth-Century America*; George H. Daniels, "The Process of Professionalism in American Science: The Emergent Period, 1820-1860," and *Science in American Society: A Social History*; W. G. Farlow, "The Task of American Botanists"; Robert V. Bruce, *The Launching of Modern American Science, 1846–1876*; Joseph Ewan, "San Francisco as a Mecca for Nineteenth Century Naturalists"; and Barbara Ertter, "People, Plants, and Politics: The Development of Institution-Based Botany in California, 1853–1906."

2.  John Muir, "Torn Notebook," 39.12, Series 5B, Related Papers, Wolfe Transcripts, JMP.

3.  John Muir, *My First Summer in the Sierra*, 211. John Muir, "For the Boston Recorder. The Calypso Borealis. Botanical Enthusiasm. From Prof. J. D. Butler," *Boston Recorder*, December 21, 1866, 1.

4.  UJJM, March 1872, 88. John Muir, "By-Ways of Yosemite Travel. Bloody Cañon," *The Overland Monthly* 13 (September 1874): 272.

Left: *Cypripedium montanum* Dougl., Mountain Lady's Slipper

5.  See Paul B. Sears, "Plant Ecology," in *A Short History of Botany in the United States,* ed. Joseph Ewan, 124–131. John Muir, "Fragment X-1," JMP. John Muir to Jeanne C. Carr, Yosemite Valley, October 7, 1874, LTAF, 168–169; K&RS, 252–253.

6.  John Muir, First Draft Autobiography, c. 1908, 245. Dictated at Pelican Bay, Klamath Lake, Oregon, at the Harriman Retreat, JMP 46:11583–12048.

7.  John Muir to Jeanne C. Carr, Near Snelling, Merced Co., California, July 26, 1868, LTAF, 36; K&RS, 71.

8.  John Muir, "A Wind Storm in the Forests of the Yuba," *Scribner's Monthly* 17 (November 1878): 57.

9.  Robert Underwood Johnson, *Remembered Yesterdays,* 281–282. See John Muir, "The Treasures of the Yosemite," *The Century Magazine* 40 (August 1890): 483–500; John Muir, "Features of the Proposed Yosemite National Park," *The Century Magazine* 40 (September 1890): 656–667. "Mr. Muir then addressed the Club as follows," Sierra Club Public Forum, "The National Parks and Forest Reservations," November 1895, *Sierra Club Bulletin* 1 (January 1896): 273.

10. Willis Linn Jepson, "The Message of John Muir by Dr. Willis Linn Jepson," John Muir Birthday, April 21, 1936, 3:15–3:45, KLX Broadcast, Tribune Tower, Oakland, Calif., Willis Jepson Collection, Box 2, Jepson Herbarium Archives, University and Jepson Herbaria, University of California, Berkeley.

11. John Muir to Robert Underwood Johnson, Martinez, September 12, 1895, JMP A8: 04989. *Sierra Club Bulletin* (1896): 273. See John Muir, "The National Parks and Forest Reservations," *Harper's Weekly* 41 (June 5, 1897): 563–567; John Muir, "The American Forests," *Atlantic Monthly* 80 (August 1897): 145–157.

12. Muir Autobiography, 305, JMP 46:11583–12048. UJJM, 90.

13. "Without photosynthesis, 99 percent of the life on Earth simply wouldn't be here...green plants give life the power to proliferate." William C. Burger, *Flowers: How They Changed the World,* 11–19, 189. See Loren Eiseley, "How Flowers Changed the World," in *The Immense Journey,* 61–77.

14. Robyn Stacey and Ashley Hay, *Herbarium,* 1. Sandra Knapp, *Plant Discoveries: A Botanist's Voyage through Plant Exploration,* 324. Bill Neal, *Gardener's Latin,* vi. See William Martin Smallwood and Mabel Sarah Coon Smallwood, *Natural History and the American Mind,* 346–353.

15. Stacey and Hay, *Herbarium,* 1, 25–26. "The Value of Herbaria," *Bulletin of the Torrey Botanical Club* 7 (December 1880): 126–128. Robert McCracken Peck, "Alcohol and Arsenic, Pepper and Pitch: Brief Histories of Preservation Techniques," in *Stuffing Birds, Pressing Plants, Shaping Knowledge: Natural History in North America, 1730–1860,* ed. Sue Ann Prince, 42. See Barbara Ertter, "Our Undiscovered Heritage: Past and Future Prospects for Species-Level Botanical Inventory," *Madroño* 47 (2000): 237–252.

## ONE: FROM SCOTLAND TO WISCONSIN

1.  John Muir. *The Story of My Boyhood and Youth,* 30.

2.  BADE, 20. John Muir, First Draft Autobiography, c. 1908, 345, JMP 46:11583–12048. Muir, *Boyhood and Youth,* 41.

3.  Muir, *Boyhood and Youth,* 45. See Erik R. Brynildson, "Restoring the Fountain of John Muir's Youth," *Wisconsin Academy Review* (December 1988): 5.

4.  Muir, *Boyhood and Youth,* 45. LJM, 29. Muir Autobiography, 346–347, JMP 46:11583–12048.

5.  Muir, *Boyhood and Youth,* 61–62.

6.  Ibid., 62.

7. Ibid., 62–63.

8. Thomas Dick, *The Christian Philosopher; or, The Connection of Science and Philosophy with Religion*, vol. 1, 13–21, 97–100.

9. Aaron Sachs, *The Humboldt Current: Nineteenth-Century Exploration and the Roots of American Environmentalism*, 2, 12, 42–43, 47. Helmut de Terra, "Alexander von Humboldt: Correspondence with Jefferson, Madison, and Gallatin," *Proceedings of the American Philosophical Society* 103 (1959): 783–806. Alexander von Humboldt, *Personal Narrative of Travels to the Equinoctial Regions of America During the Years 1799–1804*, 1–3.

10. Gerard Helferich, *Humboldt's Cosmos: Alexander von Humboldt and the Latin American Journey that Changed the Way We See the World*, xxii, xviii. Sachs, *The Humboldt Current*, 43, 47. See Stephen J. Gould, "Church, Humboldt, and Darwin: The Tension and Harmony of Art and Science," in *Frederic Edwin Church*, ed. Franklin Kelly (Washington, DC: Smithsonian Institution Press, 1989), 94–107.

11. Muir, *Boyhood and Youth*, 101. John Muir to Mrs. Pelton, n.d., SHSW.

12. *Wisconsin State Journal*, Tuesday, September 25, 1860: 1. John Muir to Sarah Muir Galloway, Madison, October 1860, JMP A1:00063. Muir, *Boyhood and Youth*, 107.

13. John Muir to Mary, Anna, and Joanna Muir, May 1861, JMP A1:00117. Jeanne C. Carr, "John Muir," *The Californian Illustrated Magazine* (June 1892): 91. Muir Autobiography, 241, JMP 46:11583–12048.

14. Ezra Slocum Carr, undated article, SHSW. Ezra Slocum Carr, "Inaugural Address to the Wisconsin University Board of Regents," January 16, 1856. John Muir to Jeanne C. Carr, Trout's Mill, near Meaford, September 13, 1865, LTAF, 8–15; K&RS, 29–32.

15. Muir Autobiography, 234–237, JMP 46:11583–12048. Muir, *Boyhood and Youth*, 109.

16. Muir Autobiography, 234–237, JMP 46:11583–12048. Muir, *Boyhood and Youth*, 110.

17. Milton S. Griswold, "Reminiscence of John Muir," SHSW. Alphonso Wood, *Class-Book of Botany: Being Outlines of the Structure, Physiology and Classification of Plants; With a Flora of the United States and Canada*. Charles J. Lyon, "Centennial of Wood's 'Class-Book of Botany,'" *Science* 101 (July 1945): 486. Charles E. Ford, "Botany Texts: A Survey of Their Development in American Higher Education, 1643–1906," *History of Education Quarterly* 4 (1964): 63–64. "A Class Book of Botany," *American Journal of Science* 49 (1845): 190.

18. Muir, *Boyhood and Youth*, 110. John Muir to Judge Milton Griswold, Martinez, California, April 3, 1901, SHSW.

19. Jeanne C. Carr, "Cultivation of Annuals," *Wisconsin Farmer* 9 (April 1857): 147–148. Jeanne C. Carr, "My Rose Garden," *Wisconsin Farmer* 9 (May 1857): 183–184. Carr, "John Muir," *The Californian*, 88. I. A. Lapham, J. G. Knapp, and H. Crocker, *Report on the Disastrous Effects of the Destruction of Forest Trees, Now Going on So Rapidly in the State of Wisconsin* (Madison: Atwood & Rublee, State Printers, Journal Office, 1867). A distinction should be drawn between the study of botany and forestry; see Char Miller, *Gifford Pinchot and the Making of Modern Environmentalism*, 131–132.

20. Muir, *Boyhood and Youth*, 109. John Muir, "Wisconsin Prairies" notebook, c. 1863, JMP 31:00117.

21. John Muir to Emily Pelton, Recess in the Bluffs, near MacGregor, Iowa, July 7, 1863, in John Muir to Emily Pelton, Fountain Lake, February 27, 1864, SHSW. Muir Autobiography, 243–244, JMP 46:11583–12048.

22. BADE, 68. Muir, *Boyhood and Youth*, 111. Muir Autobiography, 229, JMP 46:11583–12048. John Muir to M. S. Griswold, San Francisco, California, March 27, 1913, SHSW.

## TWO: CANADA AND INDIANAPOLIS

1.  Frederick Turner, *Rediscovering America: John Muir in His Times and Ours,* 111. In a letter to Mrs. Ambrose Newton, Emily Pelton's aunt and the wife of the proprietor of Mondell's Boarding House in Prairie du Chien, Wisconsin, Muir mentioned that he was about to start for Ann Arbor but that a draft was "being made" that kept him home. John Muir to Mrs. Ambrose Newton, Fountain Lake, February 16, 1864, JMP A1:00336.

2.  LJM, 91. John Muir to Emily Pelton, March 1, 1864, BADE, 69.

3.  According to Jeanne Carr, when Trout's Mill burned, Muir's money, clothes, books, and papers were destroyed in the fire. Jeanne C. Carr, "John Muir," *The Californian Illustrated Magazine* (June 1892): 91. See Millie Stanley, *The Heart of John Muir's World: Wisconsin, Family, and Wilderness Discovery,* 117. BADE, 69–70.

4.  BADE, 72–73.

5.  John Muir, First Draft Autobiography, c. 1908, 245–247, JMP 46:11583–12048. "For the Boston Recorder. The Calypso Borealis. Botanical Enthusiasm. From Prof. J. D. Butler," *Boston Recorder,* December 21, 1866, 1.

6.  Jeanne C. Carr to John Muir, Madison, Wisconsin, October 12, [1866], K&RS, 38. James D. Butler, one of Muir's professors at the University of Wisconsin, without consent took the letter from a table at the Carr home on Gilman Street and submitted it to the *Boston Recorder* for publication without mentioning the name of the author. See K&RS, 23.

7.  John Muir to Annie L. Muir, Meaford, Ontario, October 23, 1864, JMP A1:00356. This letter mentions John Muir and his brother Daniel seeing Niagara Falls for the first time. Muir Autobiography, 248, JMP 46:11583–12048. John Muir to Emily Pelton, Near Meaford, May 23, 1865, SHSW. John Muir to Emily Pelton, Trout's Mill, November 12, 1865, SHSW.

8.  John Muir to Jeanne C. Carr, Trout's Mill, near Meaford, September 13, [1865], LTAF, 8–15; K&RS, 29–32.

9.  Daniel Muir to John Muir, Buffalo, [November 1865], JMP A1:00391.

10. Muir to Pelton, November 12, 1865, SHSW. Carr, "John Muir," *The Californian,* 91. Muir Autobiography, 249, JMP 46:11583–12048. See Peter M. Rinaldo, *Nature, Nurture, and Chance: The Lives of William, Edward, and Peter Trout* (Briarcliff Manor, N.Y.: DorPete Press, 1998), 35. Asa Gray's *Botany for Young People and Common Schools: How Plants Grow, a Simple Introduction to Structural Botany,* first published in 1858, was a student guide to plant propagation and plant structure with a modest key to plant taxonomy and included engravings to assist in identification. In the absence of Wood's *Class-Book,* Hattie Trout wrote to Muir, "I am deriving a great deal of pleasure and profit from the *Structural* which I am sure you will miss very much." Hattie Trout to John Muir, Meaford, [Canada], May, 10, 1866, JMP A1:00433. It is unclear whether Hattie Trout was referring to Gray's *Botany for Young People* or Gray's *Introduction to Structural and Sytematic Botany, and Vegetable Physiology.* Muir's copy, the fifth and revised edition, published in 1866, was located in the James Eastman Shone Collection of Muiriana, Holt-Atherton Department of Special Collections, University of the Pacific Library.

11. Carr, "John Muir," *The Cailfornian,* 91. Muir Autobiography, 250–251, 255, JMP 46:11583–12048.

12. John Muir to Sarah Muir Galloway, Indianapolis, Indiana, May 1866, JMP A1:00443. James D. Butler to Catharine Merrill, Madison, Wisconsin, April 26, 1866, JMP B1: 00428.

13. Jeanne C. Carr to John Muir, Madison, October 12, [1865], K&RS, 38.

14. John Muir to Osgood & Smith, Indianapolis, Winter 1866-67, JMP A1:00510. Muir Autobiography, 251–252, JMP 46:11583–12048. John Muir to Ann G. Muir, Indianapolis, March 9, 1867, JMP A1:00493. John Muir to Sarah M.

and David M. Galloway, Indianapolis, April 12, 1867, JMP A1:00527. Jeanne C. Carr to John Muir, Madison, March 15, [1867], K&RS, 43. John Muir to Jeanne C. Carr, [Indianapolis], April 6, 1867, LTAF, 16–19; K&RS, 44–46. Jeanne C. Carr to John Muir, Madison, April 6, 1867, K&RS, 46–47. See John Muir to Trout Family, Indianapolis, April 4, 1867, *John Muir Letters to His Meaford Friends*, 18–19. Carr, "John Muir," *The Californian*, 91.

15. Ibid. John Muir to Daniel H. Muir, December 31, 1866, JMP A1:00477. Muir Autobiography, 253–255, JMP 46:11583–12048.

16. John Muir to Jeanne C. Carr, [Portage City, August 1867], LTAF, 25–31; K&RS, 53–56. John Muir to Catharine Merrill, Portage, August 12, 1867, JMP A1:00579. Carr, "John Muir," *The Californian,* 91.

17. Muir to Carr, [August 1867], LTAF, 25–31; K&RS, 53–56. See Hugh H. Iltis, "Botanizing on Muir's Lake," *Wisconsin Academy Review* (Spring 1957).

18. John Muir to Sarah M. and David M. Galloway, Madison, July [1867], JMP A1:00306. See Merrill Moores, "Reminiscence," 1919, JMP 51:00032. See John Muir to Moores Family, July 1867, JMP A1:00570.

19. Muir to Merrill, August 12, 1867, JMP A1:00579. Muir to Carr [August 1867], LTAF, 25–31; K&RS, 53–56. Muir Autobiography, 255, JMP 46:11583–12048.

20. Muir to Carr, [August 1867], LTAF, 25–31; K&RS, 55.

21. Muir to Merrill, August 12, 1867, JMP A1:00579. John Muir, "Anemone nuttalliana," August 1867, JMP B34:01961.

22. Muir, "Anemone nuttalliana," JMP B34:01961.

## Three: Kentucky to the Gulf of Mexico

1. John Muir to Jeanne C. Carr, Indianapolis, August 30, 1867, LTAF, 31–32; K&RS, 57.

2. John Muir, Journal, Florida and Cuba Trip, September 1867–February 1868, JMP A23:00021.

3. JMP A23:00022.

4. Ibid.

5. John Muir, "Recollections of the Winds," JMP B34:01978. JMP A23:00025. John Muir to Jeanne Carr, Among the Hills of Bear Creek, seven miles southeast of Burkesville, Kentucky, September 9, [1867], LTAF, 33–35; K&RS, 58.

6. JMP A23:00027-00029.

7. JMP A23:00037.

8. JMP A:23:00029-00030, 00034. Muir, "Recollections of the Winds," JMP B34:01978.

9. JMP A23:00031-00034. John Muir, *A Thousand-Mile Walk to the Gulf,* 126.

10. JMP A23:00034, 00040-00041.

11. JMP A23:00044-00047. Muir, "Recollections of the Winds," JMP B34:01978.

12. JMP A23:00048-00050.

13. JMP A23:00055, 00062-00064. John Muir to Jeanne Carr, September–October, 1867, K&RS, 59; Jeanne C. Carr, "John Muir," *The Californian Illustrated Magazine* (June 1892): 92.

14. John Muir to David Gilrye Muir, Near Fernandina, Florida, October 15, 1867, JMP A1:00595.

15. JMP A23:00070-00072.

16. John Muir to the Moores Family, Cedar Keys, January 6, 1868, JMP A1:00610. JMP A23:00072-00075.

17. JMP A23:00091, 00097, 00099. John Muir to Jeanne Carr, Cedar Keys, [Florida], November 8, [1867], LTAF, 35–36; K&RS, 60.

18. John Muir to David Gilrye Muir, Cedar Keys, Florida, December 13, 1867, JMP A1:00601. JMP A23:00128, 00131. John Muir to Moores Family, New York, March 4, 1868, JMP A1:00492.

19. John Muir to David Gilrye Muir, March 3, 1868, New York, JMP A1:00617. Sarah M. Galloway to John Muir, Mount Hill, March 17, 1868, JMP A1:00621.

20. Annie L. Muir to John Muir, Portage, Wisconsin, October 18, 1902, JMP A12:07251. John Muir to Louie Wanda Strentzel Muir, Cloudland, North Carolina, September 25, 1898, JMP. John Muir to Charles Sprague Sargent, Martinez, October 28, 1897, JMP A9:05652. See "Examining Western Forests. Work of the National Forestry Commission to the Present Time," *New York Times* (September 11, 1896): 3; Frederick Turner, *Rediscovering America: John Muir in His Times and Ours,* 300–304. John Muir to Henry F. Osborn, Martinez, California, November 1897, JMP A9:05674.

21. John Muir to Wanda Muir, October 28, 1898, JMP A10:05930. John Muir to Helen and Wanda Muir, Key West, Florida, November 17, 1898, JMP A10:05972. John Muir to Louie Strentzel Muir, Miami, Florida, November 14, 1898, JMP. John Muir, "Rambles thru the South," 1898, Notebook 40, JMP MS48, Series 5A, Related Papers, Badè Transcripts of Muir Journals, Box 5. Charles T. Mohr, initially a self-studied botanist, contributed a collection of mosses from southern Alabama to Leo Lesquereux's *Manual of the Mosses of North America* (1884). He wrote *The Forests of Alabama and Their Products* (1879), *Economic Botany of Alabama* (1900), and *Plant Life of Alabama* (1901). John Muir to Sarah Muir Galloway and Annie L. Muir, Hotel Ethel, Live Oak, Florida, November 22, 1898, JMP A10:05977. John Muir to Louie Strentzel Muir, Hotel Ethel, C. P. Willard, Proprietor, Live Oak, Florida, November 21, 1898, JMP. S. M. Dugger, *The Balsam Groves of Grandfather Mountain*, JMP.

22. John Muir to Charles S. Sargent, Martinez, December 28, 1898, JMP A10:06012.

## Four: California, the High Sierra, and Yosemite

1. John Muir, *My First Summer in the Sierra,* 248. UJJM, 439. John Muir to Jeanne Carr, New Sentinel Hotel, Yosemite Valley, [April 1872], LTAF, 159–161; K&RS, 174–175.

2. John Muir to Jeanne C. Carr, Near Snelling, Merced County, California, July 26, 1868, LTAF, 36–43; K&RS, 71–74.

3. "Mr. Muir then addressed the Club as follows," Sierra Club Public Forum, "The National Parks and Forest Reservations," November 1895, *Sierra Club Bulletin* 1 (January 1896): 281–282. John Muir to Jeanne C. Carr, Hopeton, Merced County, California, At a sheep ranch between the Tuolumne and Stanislaus rivers, November 1, [1868], LTAF, 43–48; K&RS, 78–80.

4. BADE, 101. Muir to Carr, Near Snelling, July 26, 1868, LTAF, 36–43; K&RS, 71–74.

5. John Muir to Jeanne C. Carr, Merced County, California, July 26, 1868, LTAF, 36–43; K&RS, 71–74. Muir to Carr, At a sheep ranch,... November 1, [1868], LTAF, 43–48; K&RS, 78–80. UJJM, 2, 8.

6. Robert Bauer, "How I Found Smokey Jack's Camp and Twenty-Hill Hollow, *John Muir Newsletter* 6 (Winter 1995-96): 1. Robert Bauer, "Shepherd of the Plains: John Muir at Twenty Hill Hollow," in *John Muir in Historical Perspective*, ed. Sally M. Miller, 233–247. John Muir, "Twenty Hill Hollow," *The Overland Monthly* 9 (July 1872): 81, 85. John Muir, First Draft Autobiography, c. 1908, 274–278, 281, JMP 46:11583–12048.

7. Jeanne C. Carr to John Muir, Castleton, Vermont, August 31, 1868, K&RS, 74–77.

8.  John Muir to Jeanne C. Carr, Near Snelling, Merced County, [California], February 24, 1869, LTAF, 48–52; K&RS, 80–82.

9.  Muir, "Twenty Hill Hollow": 86. John Muir to Daniel H. Muir, April 17, 1869, JMP A2:00719.

10. BADE, 105.

11. BADE, 106. Jeanne C. Carr, "Miscellaneous Notes," c. 1875–1890, CA 25, Jeanne C. Carr Papers, Huntington Library, San Marino, California. John Muir to Jeanne C. Carr, Five miles West of Yosemite, July 11, 1869, LTAF, 62; K&RS, 87–88. Jeanne C. Carr, "Biographical Notes on John Muir," c. 1892, CA 40, Carr Papers, Huntington Library.

12. Jeanne C. Carr, "John Muir," *The Californian Illustrated Magazine* 2 (June 1892): 93. Jeanne C. Carr to John Muir, Yosemite, Wednesday evening, July 30, [1869], K&RS, 89–90.

13. John Muir, "The Passes of the Sierra," *Scribner's Monthly* 17 (March 1879): 648–651

14. John Muir to David G. Muir, Near La Grange, September 24, 1869, JMP A2:00749. John Muir, "Journal, Twenty Hill Hollow," January 1, 1869–May 31, 1869, JMP 23:00174. Frederick Turner, *Rediscovering America: John Muir in His Times and Ours,* 180.

15. John Muir to Jeanne C. Carr, Two miles below La Grange, October 3, 1869, LTAF, 66–70; K&RS, 91–93. In a letter to Ralph Waldo Emerson written in 1871 (John Muir to Ralph Waldo Emerson, Yosemite, July 6, 1871, JMP A2:00940), Muir stated that in 1869, while crossing the basin of Yosemite Creek a mile or two back of the top of the falls, he "observed what appeared as indication of a glacier." Whether Muir observed evidence of glaciation this early in his Sierra studies is left for further consideration and is mentioned to provide a context in which to understand what he was exploring and examining during his first summer in the Sierra. According to Steven J. Holmes, Muir's earliest extant account of his first summer in the Sierra consists of three notebooks that he prepared in 1887. Heavily revised, they cannot be taken as a straightforward description of Muir's experience at the time, particularly with regard to his studies of the glacial origins of Yosemite Valley. See Steven J. Holmes, *The Young John Muir: An Environmental Biography*, 200. John Fiske, "Following Muir's First Summer Route," *John Muir Newsletter* 5 (Winter 1994-95): 1, 4–6.

16. John Muir, *A Thousand-Mile Walk to the Gulf* in John Muir, *The Eight Wilderness Discovery Book*, 182–183. John Muir to Sarah Muir Galloway, At camp in Spruce Grove near upper end of Yosemite two miles from the north wall, August 1, 1869, JMP A2:00742.

17. John Muir to Ralph Waldo Emerson, Yosemite Valley, Monday night, May 8, 1871, JMP A2:00924. Muir published his first statement on his glacial theory of the origin of Yosemite Valley in the *New York Daily Tribune* on December 5, 1871. See John Muir, "Yosemite Glaciers. The Ice Streams of the Great Valley. Their Progress and Present Condition. Scenes Among the Glacier Beds. (From an Occasional Correspondent of the Tribune) Yosemite Valley, California, September 28, 1871," *New York Daily Tribune* (December 5, 1871): 8, cols. 5–6. In 1874 he published his conclusive series of articles on glaciation under the general title "Studies in the Sierra" in *The Overland Monthly*.

18. John Muir to Jeanne C. Carr, Yosemite, December 11, 1871, K&RS, 152–154.

19. John Muir, "Torn Notebook," 39.12, Series 5B, Related Papers, Wolfe Transcripts, JMP. John Muir, "Yosemite National Park," *Atlantic Monthly* 84 (August 1899): 152.

20. John Muir to Jeanne C. Carr, Yosemite, April 13, 1870, LTAF; K&RS, 105–106. John Muir to David Gilrye Muir, Yosemite, May 1870, JMP A2:00828. John Muir to Jeanne C. Carr, Yosemite, May 17, [1870], LTAF, 77–80; K&RS, 106–108.

21. John Muir to Jeanne C. Carr, Yosemite, December 6, 1869, LTAF, 71–73; K&RS, 94–95. John Muir to Jeanne C. Carr, Squirrelville, Sequoia Co., Nut-Time [Autumn], K&RS, 119–121. John Muir to Jeanne C. Carr, Tuolumne

River, two miles below La Grange, November 4, [1870], LTAF, 93–96; K&RS, 121–122. See John Muir to Jeanne C. Carr, Yosemite, [Spring 1871], LTAF, 96 –101; K&RS, 133–135.

22. LJM, 144.

23. John Muir to Jeanne C. Carr, Near La Grange, California, December 22, [1870], K&RS, 123–124. John Muir to Sarah Muir Galloway, In the Sawmill, Yosemite Valley, April 5, 1871, BADE, 128–129. John Muir to Sarah Muir Galloway, April 5, 1871, JMP A2:00916. John Muir to Sarah Muir Galloway, Yosemite Valley, January 11, 1872, JMP. Sarah Muir Galloway to John Muir, Mound Hill, January 15, 1871, JMP A2:00895. John Muir to Sarah Muir Galloway, [Spring, 1871], JMP A2:00904.

24. John Muir to Jeanne C. Carr, Yosemite, September 8, [1871], LTAF, 104–111; K&RS, 147–150. John Muir, "Exploration in the Great Tuolumne Cañon," *The Overland Monthly* 11 (August 1873): 141.

25. Ann G. Muir to John Muir, November 9, 1871, JMP A2:00993.

26. John Muir to Jeanne C. Carr, New Sentinel Hotel, Yosemite Valley, July 14, 1872, LTAF, 125–127; K&RS, 181–182.

27. John Muir, "Rambles of a Botanist among the Plants and Climates of California," *Old and New* 5 (June 1872): 767–772. John Muir to Sarah Muir Galloway, Yosemite Valley, July 16, 1872, JMP A2:01131.

28. Asa Gray to John Muir, Botanic Garden, Cambridge, Massachusetts, January 4, 1872, JMP A2:01020. Jepson Field Notebook 1909, Trip to Yosemite Valley and Hetch Hetchy with the Sierra Club, Mount Dana, July 14, 1909, 55–57, Jepson Herbarium Archives, University and Jepson Herbaria, University of California, Berkeley. Redfield knew Gray from the Lyceum of Natural History in New York, where Gray had been the librarian. Both Gray and Redfield had studied with Torrey. The reason, in part, that Gray, Torrey, and Redfield were traveling was because of the annual meeting of the American Association for the Advancement of Science held in Dubuque, Iowa. Gray, who was president of the AAAS, delivered his presidential address on "Sequoia and Its History." Kellogg had sent plant specimens to Redfield from 1867 until 1870. Anderson Hunter Dupree, *Asa Gray 1810–1888* (Cambridge: Harvard University Press, 1959), 345–347.

29. Howard R. Cooley, "John Muir's Botanical Nomenclature," TMs [photocopy], revised edition of an article first published in the *John Muir Newsletter* 6 (Summer 1996): 4–6.

30. Barbara Ertter, "People, Plants, and Politics: The Development of Institution-Based Botany in California 1853–1906," 216. W. G. Farlow, "The Task of American Botanists," *Popular Science Monthly* 31 (1887): 311. Andrew Denny Rodgers, *American Botany 1873–1892: Decades of Transition*, 156–159. Barbara Ertter, "The Changing Face of California Botany," *Madroño* 42 (1995): 118–119. Joseph A. Ewan, "San Francisco as a Mecca for Nineteenth Century Naturalists," 23–24. See Barbara Ertter, "The Flowering of Natural History Institutions in California," *Proceedings of the California Academy of Sciences* 55 (suppl. 1, no. 4), 58–87; Robert V. Bruce, *The Launching of Modern American Science 1846–1876*; Nancy M. Slack, "Botanical Exploration of California from Menzies to Muir (1786–1900), 194–242.

31. Asa Gray to John Muir, Botanic Garden, Cambridge, Massachusetts, September 11, 1872, JMP A2:01154. John Muir to Asa Gray, October 10, 1872, Yosemite Valley, JMP A2:01186. John Muir, "Reminiscences of Joseph LeConte," *University of California Magazine* 7 (September 1901): 211.

32. Jeanne C. Carr to John Muir, Oakland, October 2, [1872], K&RS, 193.

33. John Muir to J. B. McChesney, Yosemite, December 10, 1872, JMP A2:01203. Ertter, "People, Plants, and Politics," 207. The first volume of the botanical component to the Geological Survey of California was not published until 1876, under the direction of Asa Gray, William H. Brewer (who had been the botanist on the State Geological Survey with Josiah D. Whitney), and Sereno Watson, curator of the Gray Herbarium at Harvard. The second volume was published by Watson in 1880. Asa Gray to John Muir, Cambridge, September 21, 1872, JMP A2:01158.

Asa Gray, *Botany for Young People: How Plants Behave: How They Move, Climb, Employ Insects to Work for Them*. Asa Gray, *Manual of the Botany of the Northern United States, Including the District East of the Mississippi and North of North Carolina and Tennessee*, 5th ed. Asa Gray, *Gray's School and Field Book of Botany*. Asa Gray, *Introduction to Structural and Systematic Botany, and Vegetable Physiology*, 5th ed. See John Muir to Asa Gray, Yosemite Valley, December 18, 1872, BADE 183–184.

34. John Muir, "A Geologist's Winter Walk," *The Overland Monthly* 10 (April 1873): 355–358. John Muir to Jeanne C. Carr, Yosemite Valley, December 25, 1872, K&RS, 199–202. Muir to Gray, December 18, 1872.

35. John Muir to Asa Gray, Yosemite Valley, February 22, 1873, BADE, 187–188.

36. Muir to Gray, February 22, 1873. Asa Gray to John Muir, Botanic Garden, Cambridge, Massachusetts, April 9, 1873, BADE, 188.

37. See Bonnie Johanna Gisel, "'Those Who Walk Apart but Ever Together Are True Companions.' Jeanne Carr and John Muir in the High Sierra," in *John Muir: Family, Friends, and Adventures*, ed. Sally M. Miller (Albuquerque: University of New Mexico Press, 2005), 215–233. John Muir, "Little Yosemite Valley 1873," 25:11, Series 5B, Related Papers, Wolfe Transcripts, JMP.

38. UJJM, 145–148. John Muir to Asa Gray, Yosemite Valley, September 10, 1873, JMP A2:01296.

39. See "Mrs. Carr's Remarks on the Big Tuolumne Cañon, Etc.," *Illustrated Press* 1 (October 1873). Jeanne C. Carr to Louie Wanda Strentzel, University of California, Oakland, California, October 29, 1873, K&RS, 227–228. John Muir to Asa Gray, Oakland, November 25, 1873, JMP A2:01322.

40. John Muir to Sarah Muir Galloway, Yosemite Valley, September 3, 1873, JMP A2:01294.

41. John Muir to Sarah Muir Galloway, Oakland, September 7, 1874, JMP. John Muir to Jeanne C. Carr, Yosemite Valley, [September 1874], K&RS, 241–250.

42. John Muir to Jeanne C. Carr, Yosemite Valley, October 7, 1874, LTAF, 168–169; K&RS, 252–253. Muir to Carr, Squirrelville [Autumn 1870], 119–121.

43. John Muir, "Torn notebook, undated notes on forests," 39.12, Series 5B, Related Papers, Wolfe Transcripts, JMP.

44. John Muir, "Wild Sheep of California," *The Overland Monthly* 12 (April 1874): 358–363. John Muir, "Wild Wool," *The Overland Monthly* 14 (April 1875): 361–366. John Muir, "God's First Temples. How Shall We Preserve Our Forests? The Question Considered by John Muir, the California Geologist—The View of a Practical Man and a Scientific Observer—A Profoundly Interesting Article. (Communicated to *The Record-Union*)," *Sacramento Daily Union*, February 5, 1876: 8, cols. 6–7. John Muir, "Great Evils from Destruction of Forests," *San Francisco Real Estate Circular* 14 (April 1879): 2. See John Muir, "The Treasures of the Yosemite," *The Century Magazine* 40 (August 1890): 483–500; John Muir, "Features of the Proposed Yosemite National Park," *The Century Magazine* 40 (September 1890): 656–667.

45. John Muir to Jeanne C. Carr, Yosemite, July 29, [1870], LTAF, 85–90; K&RS, 114–116. John Muir to Jeanne C. Carr, Black's Hotel, Yosemite, California, July 31, 1875, K&RS, 260–261.

## FIVE: ALASKA

1. John Muir, "Alaska Coast Scenery. Sailing among the Islands—Delightful Views. Wonderful Variety of Lovely Pictures. Effects of Glaciation—An Archipelago of Evergreen Isles. (Special Correspondence of the *Bulletin*.) Fort Wrangel, Alaska, September 25, 1879." SFDEB, October 29, 1879: 4, col. 1. John Muir to Louie Wanda Strentzel, Fort Wrangel, Alaska, October 9, 1879, JMP A3:01927.

2. John Muir to the Bidwell Family, 920 Valencia Street, San Francisco, June 19, 1879, JMP A3:01886. Frank E. Buske, "Book Review. John Muir, Letters from Alaska, ed. Robert Engberg and Bruce Merrell. Madison: University of

Wisconsin, 1993," *John Muir Newsletter* 4 (Spring 1994): 3. See Sheldon Jackson, *Alaska and Missions on the North Pacific Coast.* John Muir to the Bidwell Family, June 19, 1879, JMP A3:01886. John Muir to Jeanne C. Carr, San Francisco, June 19, 1879, LTAF, 193–194; K&RS, 294.

3. John Muir to Louie Wanda Strentzel, Steamship *California*, On the Columbia, a few miles below Astoria, July 9, 1879, JMP A3:01895. Louie Wanda Strentzel to John Muir, Alhambra, June 27, 1879, JMP A3:01893. John Muir to Louie Wanda Strentzel, Victoria, British Columbia, July 10, 1879, JMP A3:01899.

4. John Muir, "Notes of a Naturalist. John Muir in Alaska—Wrangel Island and Its Picturesque Attractions. Summer Days That Have No End—Pictures of Sound Life. Life among the Indians—Boat Life—Wild Berries. (Special Correspondence of the *Bulletin*.) Fort Wrangel, Alaska, August 8, 1879." SFDEB, September 6, 1879: 1, col. 4. Louie Wanda Strentzel to John Muir, Post Office, Martinez, September 9, 1879, JMP A3:01923. Louie Wanda Strentzel to John Muir, Alhambra, August 12, 1879, JMP A3:01912.

5. John Muir, "Notes of a Naturalist. John Muir on Puget Sound and Its Lovely Scenery. Forest Belts—Mount Rainier—Thriving Towns—Coal Fields. (Special Correspondence of the *Bulletin*.) Seattle, Washington Territory, June 28, 1879." SFDEB, August 29, 1879: 1, col. 3. Muir, "Alaska Coast Scenery": 4, col. 1. John Muir to the Strentzel Family, On Board the *Zephyr* between Steilacoom and Olympia, June 25, 1879, JMP A3:01890.

6. Muir, "Alaska Coast Scenery": 4, col. 1. John Muir to Annie K. Bidwell, Sitka, Alaska, July 16, 1879, JMP A3:01905. UJJM, 249, 259.

7. John Muir to the Strentzel Family, Sitka, July 15, 1879, JMP A3:01901.

8. John Muir, "Alaska Glaciers. An Ounalaska Yosemite. Glacial Theology and Sermons in Ice. The Rocks, Plants and Trees of Alaska. (Correspondence of the *Bulletin*.) Fort Wrangel, Alaska, September 5, 1879." SFDEB, September 23, 1879: 4. col. 1. Muir, "Alaska Forests."

9. Samuel Hall Young, *Alaska Days with John Muir*, 627.

10. Ibid., 627–628.

11. Ibid., 631–636.

12. John Muir, *Travels in Alaska*, 764–765. John Muir to Louie Wanda Strentzel, August 19, 1879, JMP A3:01918.

13. John Muir to Louie Wanda Strentzel, Fort Wrangel, Alaska, October 9, 1879, JMP A3:01927.

14. Young, *Alaska Days*, 639. Muir, *Travels in Alaska*, 776–777.

15. Young, *Alaska Days*, 646–650. See Muir, *Travels in Alaska*, 776–777. John Muir, "Wanderings in Alaska. A Lovely Sail—Majestic Mountain Views—More Glaciers. Visit to a Deserted Indian Village. Habitations of the Natives—Carved Images and Other Relics—Indian Rites—A Doomed Race. Fort Wrangel, October 12, 1879." SFDEB, November 1, 1879: 1, col. 4.

16. Louie Wanda Strentzel to John Muir, Alhambra, December 1, 1879, JMP A3:01934. Strentzel to Muir, August 12, 1879, JMP A3:01912. Louie Wanda Strentzel Muir to John Muir, Alhambra, August 23, 1880, JMP A4:02106.

17. Jeanne C. Carr to Louisiana E. Strentzel, Pasadena, May 1880, JMP B4:02054.

18. John Muir to Asa Gray, Martinez, Contra Costa County, June 19, 1880, JMP A4:02067. Asa Gray to John Muir, Herbarium of Harvard University, Botanic Garden, Cambridge, Massachusetts, June 28, 1880, JMP A4:02077.

19. John Muir to Louie Wanda Strentzel Muir, Off Cape Flattery, August 2, 1880, JMP A4:02094.

20. John Muir, "Alaska Land. John Muir Revisits the Scene of Last Year's Exploration. A Land of Abundance—A Canoe Voyage among the Islands and Icebergs. Magnificent Scenery—The Hoona Indians—Among the Salmon. (Special

Correspondence of the *Bulletin*.) In Camp, Near Cape Fanshaw, August 18, 1880." SFDEB, September 25, 1880: 4, cols. 6–8. See John Muir to Louie Wanda Strentzel Muir, Residence of Mr. Young, Fort Wrangel, August 14, 1880, JMP.

21. John Muir, "Alaska Land. A Canoe Voyage Among the Islands and Icebergs. Sum Dum Bay—Enormous Glaciers—Gold Mines—Products and Future Development of Alaska. (Special Correspondence of the *Bulletin*.) Sum Dum Bay, Alaska, August 22, 1880." SFDEB, October 7, 1880: 1, col. 1. Muir, *Travels in Alaska*, 823.

22. John Muir, "An Adventure with a Dog and a Glacier." *The Century Magazine* 54 (September 1897): 769–775. Frank E. Buske, "John Muir and the Alaska Gold Rush," *The Pacific Historian* 25 (Summer 1981): 44–45. "Reports of Captain L. A. Beardslee Relative to Affairs in Alaska of the U.S.S. "Jamestown" Under His Command While in the Waters of That Territory," *Senate Executive Document* 71, 47th Cong., 1 sess., 1882, 196–197. Muir, *Travels in Alaska*, 831, 841.

23. Louisiana Erwin Strentzel, Diary 1880–1881, C-F 16: 9, Bancroft Library, University of California, Berkeley.

24. John Muir to Emily O. Pelton, Martinez, March 28, 1881, SHSW. John Muir to Mary L. Swett, March 29, 1881, JMP A4:02199. Louie Wanda Strentzel Muir to John Muir, Alhambra, August 23, 1880, JMP A4:02106.

25. John Muir, "The Aleutian Islands. Geological Notes of the Group—Glaciers and Volcanoes. Fauna and Flora of the Group—Agricultural Notes—The Inhabitants. (Special Correspondence of the *Bulletin*.) (By the Alaska Commercial Company's steamer *Dora*...the following delayed letter...Came to hand:) Ounalaska, May 21, 1881," SFDEB, July 25, 1881: 1, col. 3. John Muir, "Botanical Notes on Alaska," in *Cruise of the Revenue-Steamer* Corwin *in Alaska and the N.W. Arctic Ocean in 1881. Notes and Memoranda*, 47–48. John Muir to Louie Wanda Strentzel Muir, St. Michael, Alaska, June 21, 1881, BADE, 270–271.

26. John Muir, "Return to St. Michael's. Preparing for Another Cruise—The Busy Season at St. Michael's—San Francisco Prospectors Heard From—Fauna and Flora—Volcanic Cones. St. Michael's Alaska, July 8, 1881." SFDEB, August 15, 1881: 3, col. 8. John Muir, "At East Cape. Ashore—A Siberian Village—The Arctic Hunter's Luxurious Home—Arctic Cemeteries—Botanizing on the Siberian Shore—Tracing the Ice Floods. Steamer *Corwin*, East Cape, Siberia, July 1, 1881," SFDEB, August 16, 1881: 1, col. 2. John Muir to Louie Wanda Strentzel Muir, Between Plover Bay and St. Lawrence Island, July 2, 1881, BADE, 271–273.

27. Asa Gray to John Muir, Botanic Garden, Cambridge, Massachusetts, January 4, 1872, JMP A2:01020.

28. John Muir, "The *Jeannette* Search. Exploration of Herald Island—No Signs of the Missing Ship. Dangers of Arctic Exploration—Fauna and Flora of the North. (Special Correspondence of the *Bulletin*.) Steamer *Corwin* (off Herald Island), Arctic Ocean, July 31, 1881," SFDEB, September 28, 1881: 4, col. 3.

29. Ibid. John Muir, "Wrangel Island, Conflict with the Ice—A Struggle to Reach Shore. The *Corwin* in an Arctic River—Acquisition to the National Domain. Steamer *Corwin*, Off Point Barrow, August 16, 1881," SFDEB, September 29, 1881: 1, col. 3. John Muir, "On Wrangel Land. Wreckage Found on the Beach—Condition of the Soil. Improbability of Any Landing Having Been Made by Captain DeLong. Difficulties Which Beset the *Corwin*—Narrow Escape from the Ice. (Special Correspondence of the *Bulletin*.)...Steamer *Corwin*, off Point Barrow, August 17, 1881," SFDEB, October 22, 1881: 4, col. 3. John Muir, "Botanical Notes on Alaska," 52–53. The earliest news of the landing on Wrangel Land reached the world in the letter from John Muir published in the SFDEB, September 29, 1881.

30. John Muir to Louie Wanda Strentzel Muir, Point Barrow, August 16, 1881, BADE, 276–277. John Muir, "Homeward Bound. End of the *Corwin*'s Cruise in the Arctic Ocean. Elephant Point—A Fossil Glacier and Its Exuberant Vegetation. Shipwrecked Prospectors—An Alaskan Silver Mine and Oonalaska Scenery. (Special Correspondence of the *Bulletin*.) Steamer *Corwin*, Oonalaska, October 4, 1881," SFDEB, October 31, 1881: 1, col. 1.

31. John Muir to Asa Gray, Martinez, Contra Costa County, California, October 31, 1881, JMP A4:02321.

32. See Ted C. Hinckley, "The Inside Passage: A Popular Gilded Age Tour," *Pacific Northwest Quarterly* 56 (April 1965): 67–74. Roderick Frazier Nash, *Wilderness and the American Mind*, 4th ed., 282–283. John Muir, "Wild Parks and Forest Reservations of the West," *The Atlantic Monthly* 81 (January 1898): 17.

## APPENDIX

1. Daniel H. Muir, Jr., "In the Trunk," c. 1867, Huntington Library. BADE, 69.

2. Annie L. Muir, Portage, Wisconsin, to John Muir, October 8, 1902, JMP A12:07251.

3. John Muir to Jeanne Carr, Tuolumne River, two miles below La Grange, November 4, [1870], LTAF, 93–96; K&RS, 121–122. Louie Wanda Strentzel to John Muir, Alhambra, June 27, 1879, JMP A3:01893.

4. Wanda Muir Hanna to William Trout, Martinez, California, January 31, 1915, in William Henry Trout, *Trout Family History* (Milwaukee: W. H. Trout, 1916), 133–134.

5. The other plants Muir collected in July 1873 were *Arabis lyallii, Saxifraga virginiensis, Ivesia lycopodioides, Draba stenoloba, Erigeron pygmaeum, Poa alpina,* and *Sibbaldia procumbens.*

6. See Asa Gray to John Muir, Botanic Garden, Cambridge, Massachusetts, January 4, 1872, JMP A2: 01020.

7. John Muir to John H. Redfield, 1419 Taylor Street, San Francisco, California, May 15, 1875, Academy of Natural Sciences of Philadelphia Archives, Philadelphia, Pennsylvania. John Muir to John H. Redfield, 1419 Taylor Street, San Francisco, California, April 24, 1876, Academy of Natural Sciences of Philadelphia Archives, Philadelphia. John H. Redfield to Asa Gray, Philadelphia, February 28, 1876, Gray Herbarium Archives, Harvard University Herbaria, Cambridge, Massachusetts.

8. John W. Harshberger, *The Botanists of Philadelphia and Their Work*, 211–217. *Missouri Botanical Garden Ninth Annual Report* (St. Louis: Board of Trustees of the Missouri Botanical Garden, 1897), 15. *Missouri Botanical Garden Eleventh Annual Report* (1900), 15. *Missouri Botanical Garden Twelfth Annual Report* (1901), 14–15. See Andrew Denny Rodgers III, "Engelmann and Parry in Oregon and California," in *American Botany 1873–1892: Decades of Transition*, 131–143.

9. See George Engelmann to John Strentzel, San Francisco, November 15, 1880, JMP B4:02138. George Engelmann to John Muir, St. Louis, Missouri, April 11, 1881, JMP A4:02214. John Muir to George Engelmann, Martinez, April 28, 1881, JMP A4:02219.

10. See John Muir to Asa Gray, Martinez, Contra Costa County, California, October 31, 1881, JMP A4:02321. See John Muir, "Botanical Notes on Alaska," in *Cruise of the Revenue-Steamer* Corwin *in Alaska and the N.W. Arctic Ocean in 1881. Notes and Memoranda*, 47–53.

11. See Allison Kyle Leopold, *The Victorian Garden*, 42–45.

12. According to a letter from Hattie Trout to John Muir, Meaford, [Canada], May 10, 1866, JMP A1:00433, Hattie Trout kept Muir's copy of Asa Gray's *Structural*. This was either Gray's *Botany for Young People* or more likely Gray's *Introduction to Structural and Systematic Botany*, which means he had access to another taxonomical resource while he was in Canada. See Howard R. Cooley, "John Muir's Botanical Nomenclature," TMs [photocopy], revised version of an article first published in the *John Muir Newsletter* 6 (Summer 1996): 4–6.

# JOHN MUIR'S
# BOTANICAL BIBLIOGRAPHY

The following is a bibliography of botanical works that comprise a part of John Muir's personal library located in the Holt-Atherton Department of Special Collections at the University of the Pacific and at the Huntington Library. It also includes other botanical works to which it is either known or assumed that Muir had access.

Agassiz, Louis. *Methods of Study in Natural History*. Boston: Ticknor and Fields, 1863.

Ahern, George P. *Compilation of Notes on the Most Important Timber Tree Species of the Philippine Islands*. Manila: Forestry Bureau, 1901.

Allen, Richard Lamb. *A Brief Compend of American Agriculture*. 4th ed. New York: C. M. Saxton, 1847.

Apgar, Austin C. *Trees of the Northern United States: Their Study, Description and Determination, for the use of schools and private students*. New York: American Book Co., 1892.

Badlam, Alexander. *The Wonders of Alaska*. San Francisco: The Bancroft Co., 1890.

Bailey, Frederick Manson. *The Queensland Flora*. 5 vols. Queensland: H. J. Diddams & Co., 1899–1902.

Bates, Henry Walter. *The Naturalist on the River Amazon*. London: John Murray, 1910.

"The Battle of the Forest." *National Geographic*. (June 1894).

Bigelow, Jacob. *American Medical Botany, Being a Collection of the Native Medicinal Plants of the United States, containing their botanical history and chemical analysis, and properties and uses in medicine, diet and the arts, with coloured engravings*. Boston: Cummings and Hilliard, 1817–1820.

Bolander, H. N. "A Catalogue of the Plants Growing in the Vicinity of San Francisco." *California Medical Gazette* (January 1870): 83–93. JMP, Scrapbook, annexed between 12–13.

———. "A Catalogue of the Plants Growing in the Vicinity of San Francisco." *California Medical Gazette* (February 1870): 111–118. JMP, Scrapbook, annexed between 14–15.

Brewer, William H., Sereno Watson, and Asa Gray. *Botany*, 2 Vols. 2d ed. Geological Survey of California. Cambridge, Mass.: John Wilson and Son, 1880.

Brisbin, James S. *Trees and Tree Planting.* New York: Harper, 1888.

Brongniart, Adolphe. *Histoire des Végétaux Fossiles, ou Recherches Botaniqueset Géologiques sur les Végétaux Renfermés dans les Diverses Couches du Globe.* Paris: G. Dufour et E. d'Ocagne, 1828.

Burroughs, John, John Muir, and George Bird Grinnell. *Harriman Alaska Expedition Series. Alaska. Narrative, Glaciers, Natives.* Vol. 1. New York: Doubleday, Page & Co., 1901.

California State Agricultural Society. *Transactions of the California State Agricultural Society during the Year 1863.* Sacramento: O. M. Clayes, State Printer, 1864.

Candolle, Alphonse de. *Géographie Botanique Raisonnée; Géou, Exposition des faits principaux et des lois concernant la distribution geographique des plantes de l'époque actuelle.* 2 Vols. Paris: V. Masson, 1855.

Clark, Galen. *The Big Trees of California, Their History and Characteristics.* Yosemite Valley, Calif.: Galen Clark, c. 1902.

Comstock, J. L. *A System of Natural Philosophy.* New York: Pratt, Woodford and Co., 1845.

Creevey, Caroline A. *Recreations in Botany.* New York: Harper & Brothers, 1893.

Darwin, Charles. *On the Origin of Species by means of natural selection.* Reprinted from 6th London ed. New York: A. L. Burt, 1880.

———. *On the Origin of Species by means of natural selection, or, the preservation of favored races in the struggle for life.* New York: D. Appleton and Co., 1897.

———. *The Life and Letters of Charles Darwin.* Edited by Francis Darwin. 2 Vols. New York: D. Appleton and Co., 1911.

Davidson, Alice Merritt. *California Plants in Their Homes: A Botanical Reader for Children.* Los Angeles: B. R. Baumgardt & Co., 1898.

Davidson, James Wood. *The Florida of To-Day.* New York: D. Appleton and Co., 1889.

Downing, A. J. *The Fruits and Fruit Trees of America.* 14th ed. New York: John Wiley, 1853.

Dugger, S. M. *The Balsam Groves of Grandfather Mountain.* Banner Elk, N.C.: Shepherd M.Dugger, 1892.

Dutton, Clarence E. *Tertiary History of the Grand Cañon District.* Vol. 2. U.S. Geological Survey. Washington, D.C.: Government Printing Office, 1881 (1882).

Eastwood Alice. *A Handbook of the Trees of California.* San Francisco: California Academy of Sciences, 1905.

Emerson, George B. *A Report on the Trees and Shrubs Growing Naturally in the Forests of Massachusetts: Published Agreeably to an Order of the Legislature, by the Commissioners on the Zoological and Botanical Survey of the State.* Boston: Dutton and Wentworth, 1846.

Figuier, Louis. *The Vegetable World: Being a History of Plants, with Their Botanical Descriptions and Peculiar Properties.* New York: D. Appleton and Co., 1867.

Finck, Henry T. *The Pacific Coast Scenic Tour.* New York: Charles Scribner's Sons, 1891.

*First, Second, and Third Annual Reports of the United States Geological Survey of the Territories for the Years 1867, 1868, and 1869.* Washington, D.C.: Government Printing Office, 1873.

Flagg, Wilson. *Year among the Trees; or the Woods and Byways of New England.* Boston: Educational Publishing Co., 1890.

Fletcher, Stevenson W. *Soils: How to Handle and Improve Them.* New York: Doubleday, Page & Co., 1908.

Flint, Charles L., ed. *The American Farmer: A Complete Agricultural Library....* 2 vols. Hartford: Ralph H. Park & Co., 1881.

Fuller, Andrew S. *The Forest Tree Culturist: A Treatise on the Cultivation of American Forest Trees with Notes on the Most Valuable Foreign Species.* New York: American News Co., 1866.

———. *The Grape Culturalist: A Treatise on the Cultivation of the Native Grape.* New York: O. Judd and Co., 1867.

Gordon, George. *The Pinetum: Being a Synopsis of All the Coniferous Plants at Present Known.* 2d ed. London: Henry G. Bohn, 1875.

Gray, Asa. *The Botanical Text Book: An Introduction to Scientific Botany, Both Structural and Systematic, for Colleges, Schools and Private Students.* 3d ed. New York: George P. Putnam, 1850.

———. *Botany for Young People and Common Schools: How Plants Grow, with a Simple Introduction to Structural Botany with a Popular Flora, or an Arrangement and Description of Common Plants Both Wild and Cultivated.* 5th ed. New York: Ivison, Phinney & Co., 1860.

———. *Introduction to Structural and Systematic Botany, and Vegetable Physiology.* 5th ed. New York: Ivison, Phinney, Blakeman & Co., 1866.

———. *Manual of the Botany of the Northern United States.* 5th ed. New York: Ivison, Blakeman, Taylor & Co., 1870.

———. *Gray's School and Field Book of Botany, Consisting of "Lessons in Botany" and "Field, Forest, and Garden Botany."* New York: Ivison, Blakeman, Taylor & Co., 1870.

———. *Sequoia and Its History: An Address Delivered at the Meeting Held at Dubuque, Iowa, August, 1872.* Salem, Mass.: Salem Press, 1872.

———. *Botany for Young People: How Plants Behave. How They Move, Climb, Employ Insects to Work for Them.* New York: American Book Company, 1872.

———. *Darwiniana: Essays and Reviews Pertaining to Darwinism.* New York: D. Appleton and Co., 1876.

———. *Manual of the Botany of the Northern United States.* New York: Ivison, Blakeman & Co., 1889.

———. *Scientific Papers of Asa Gray.* Edited by Charles Sprague Sargent. 2 vols. Boston: Houghton Mifflin and Co., 1889.

———. *Letters of Asa Gray.* Edited by Jane Loring Gray. 2 vols. Cambridge, Mass.: The Riverside Press, 1893.

Greely, Major General. *Handbook of Alaska.* New York: Charles Scribner's Sons, 1905.

Greene, Edward Lee. *Illustrations of West American Oaks from Drawings by the Late Albert Kellogg.* San Francisco: Bosqui Engraving & Printing Co., 1889.

———. *Manual of the Botany of the Region of the San Francisco Bay.* San Francisco: Cubery & Co., 1894.

Grund, Francis J. *Elements of Natural Philosophy.* 2d ed. Boston: Carter, Hendee, and Co., 1835.

Hancock, Joseph Lane. *Nature Sketches in Temperate America.* Chicago: A. C. McClure & Co., 1911.

*Harriman Alaska Expedition with Cooperation of Washington Academy of Science.* 3 vols. New York: Doubleday, Page and Co., 1901, 1904.

Hartwig, G. H. Guernsey. *The Polar and Tropical Worlds.* New ed. Springfield, Mass.: C. A. Nichols & Co., 1878.

Harwood, W. S. *New Creations in Plant Life: An Authoritative Account of the Life and Work of Luther Burbank.* New York: The Macmillan Co., 1906.

Hayden, F. V. *Preliminary Report of the United States Geological Survey of Wyoming and Portions of Contiguous Territories.* Washington, D.C.: Government Printing Office, 1872.

———. *Annual Report of the United States Geological and Geographical Survey of the Territories, Embracing Colorado, Being a Report of Progress of the Exploration of the Year 1873.* Washington, D.C.: Government Printing Office, 1874.

———. *Annual Report of the United States Geological and Geographical Survey of the Territories, Embracing Colorado and Parts of Adjacent Territories.* Washington, D.C.: Government Printing Office, 1876.

———. *Eleventh Annual Report of the United States Geological and Geographical Survey of the Territories, Embracing Idaho and Wyoming, Being a Report of Progress of the Exploration for the Year 1877*. Washington, D.C.: Government Printing Office, 1879.

Hooker, Joseph Dalton. *Himalayan Journals; or Notes of a Naturalist in Bengal, the Sikkim and Nepal Himalayas, the Khasia Mountains, etc.* London: Ward, Lock, Bowden & Co., 1891.

Hooper, Calvin L. *Report of the Cruise of the Revenue-Steamer* Corwin *in Alaska and the N.W. Arctic Ocean in 1881*. Washington, D.C.: Government Printing Office, 1883.

Hooper, Edward J. *Western Fruit Book: A Compendious Collection of Facts from the Notes and Experiences of Successful Fruit Culturists, Arranged for Practical Use in the Orchard and Garden*. Cincinnati, 1857.

Humboldt, Alexander von. *Cosmos: A Sketch of a Physical Description of the Universe*. 2 vols. Translated by E. C. Otte. London: George Bell & Sons, 1878.

———. *Views of Nature, or, Contemplations on the Sublime Phenomena of Creation*. London: George Bell & Sons, 1896.

Humboldt, Alexander von, and Aime Bonpland. *Personal Narrative of Travels to the Equinoctial Regions of America during the Years 1799–1804*. 3 vols. London: George Bell & Sons, 1907.

Husman, George. *American Grape Growing and Wine Making*. New York: Orange Judd Co., 1881.

———. *Grape Culture and Wine Making in California*. San Francisco: Payot, Upham & Co., 1888.

Hutchings, J. M. *Scenes of Wonder and Curiosity in California*. New York: A. Roman and Co., 1876.

———. *Hutchings Tourist's Guide to the Yosemite Valley and the Big Tree Groves for the Spring and Summer of 1877*. San Francisco: A. Roman and Co., 1877.

Lamson-Scribner, F. *American Grasses*. Washington, D.C.: Government Printing Office, 1900.

Lemmon, J. G. *Handbook of West-American Cone-Bearers*. 3d ed. Oakland: California Board of Forestry, 1895.

———. *Handbook of West-American Cone-Bearers*. 4th ed. Oakland: California Board of Forestry, 1900.

Lesquereux, Leo. *United States Geological Survey of the Territories. Contributions to the Fossil Flora of the Western Territories. Part I. The Cretaceous Flora*. Washington, D.C.: Government Printing Office, 1874.

———. *The Flora of the Dakota Group: A Posthumous Work*. Edited by F. H. Knowlton. Washington, D.C.: Government Printing Office, 1891.

Lindley, John, and William Hutton. *The Fossil Flora of Great Britain; or, Figures and Descriptions of the Vegetable Remains Found in a Fossil State in This Country*. 3 vols. London: James Ridgway, 1831–1833, 1837.

Lukens, Theodore P. "Why Forests Are Needed: They Would Hold Back Half the Rain and Prevent Disastrous Floods." *Water and Forest* I (1902): 13

———. "The Relation of Forestry to Agriculture." *Pacific Rural Press* (October 4, 1902).

———. "Effects of Forests on Water Supply." *Forestry and Irrigation* 10 (1904): 465–469.

Magee, Thomas. "Plant Life above the Clouds: Remarkable Californian Flowers on Mt. Whitney, 1,500 Feet above the Timberline, 13,500 Feet above the Sea—A Life of Daily Alternating Sunshine and Frost...." *San Francisco Daily Evening Bulletin* (September 15, 1885). JMP, Scrapbook, 26.

———. *The Alphabet and Language; Immortality of the Big Trees; Wealth and Poverty of the Chicago Exposition. Three Essays*. San Francisco: William Doxey, 1895.

Maiden, J. M. "Where Are the Largest Trees in the World?" JMP, Box 5, MS 48, Series 7, Memorabilia 64:20.

Marsh, George Perkins. *Man and Nature, or, Physical Geography as Modified by Human Action.* New York: C. Scribner, 1864.

Marshall, Nina L. *The Mushroom Book: A Popular Guide to the Identification and Study of Our Common Fungi, with Special Emphasis on the Edible Varieties.* New York: Doubleday, Page and Co., (1901), 1902.

Mathews, F. Schuyler. *Familiar Flowers of Field and Garden.* New York: D. Appleton, 1895.

———. *Familiar Trees and Their Leaves, Described and Illustrated.* New York: D. Appleton, (c. 1896), 1908.

Merriam, C. Hart. *Life Zones and Crop Zones of the United States.* Washington, D.C.: U.S. Department of Agriculture, 1898.

Miller, Hugh. *The Cruise of the Betsey, or, A Summer Ramble among the Fossiliferous Deposits of the Hebrides, with Rambles of a Geologist, or, Ten Thousand Miles over the Fossiliferous Deposits of Scotland.* New York: Hurst and Co., 1858.

———. *Popular Geology.* New York: Hurst and Co., 1859.

———. *The Life and Letters of Hugh Miller.* 2 vols. Edited by Peter Bayne. Boston: Gould and Lincoln, 1871.

*Missouri Botanical Garden. Twenty-Second Annual Report.* St. Louis: Board of Trustees of the Missouri Botanical Garden, 1911.

Mohr, Charles Theodore. *The Timber Pines of the Southern United States.* Washington, D.C.: Government Printing Office, 1896.

Mueller, Ferd[inand] von. *Select Extra-Tropical Plants, Readily Eligible for Industrial Culture or Naturalisation, with Indications of Their Native Countries and Some of Their Uses.* 7th ed. Melbourne: Robert S. Brain, 1888.

Newhall, Charles S. *The Trees of North-Eastern America.* New York: G. P. Putnam's Sons, 1898.

Newman, John B. *Botany Illustrated.* New York: Fowler & Wells, 1856.

Osterhout, W. J. V. *Experiments with Plants.* 4th ed. New York: The Macmillan Co., 1908.

Parker, Richard Green. *A School Compendium of Natural and Experimental Philosophy.* New York: A. S. Barnes and Co., 1856.

Parsons, Mary Elizabeth. *The Wild Flowers of California.* San Francisco: Cunningham, Curtiss & Welch, 1907.

Philippines Bureau of Forestry. *Report of the Chief of the Bureau of Forestry of the Philippine Islands for the Period from September 1, 1903, to August 31, 1904.* Manila: Bureau of Public Printing, 1905.

Pinchot, Gifford. *Primer of Forestry.* 2d ed. Washington, D.C.: Government Printing Office, 1900.

Pinchot, Gifford, and Henry S. Graves. *The White Pine.* New York: The Century Co., 1896.

Rattan, Volney. *A Popular California Flora.* San Francisco: A. L. Bancroft & Co., 1879.

Reemelin, Charles. *The Vine-Dresser's Manual: An Illustrated Treatise on Vineyards and Wine-Making.* New York: C. M. Saxton, 1856.

Sargent, Charles Sprague. *The Silva of North America: A Description of the Trees Which Grow Naturally in North America, Exclusive of Mexico.* Boston: Houghton, Mifflin and Co., 1902.

———. *Manual of the Trees of North America.* Boston: Houghton, Mifflin and Co., 1905.

Schimper, Wilhelm Philipp. *Traité de Paléontologie Végétale, ou, La Flore du Monde Primitif dans ses Rapports avec les Formations Géologiques et la Flore du Monde Actuel.* Paris: J. B. Baillière et fils, 1869.

Schroter, Ludwig, and Carl Schroter. *Taschenflora des Alpen-Wanderers.* Zurich: A. Raustein, 1904.

Schwarz, George Frederick. *Forest Trees and Forest Scenery.* New York: Grafton Press, 1901.

Scott, Dukinfield Henry. *Studies in Fossil Botany.* London: Adam and Charles Black, 1900.

Seward, Albert Charles. *Fossil Plants: A Text-Book for Students of Botany and Geology.* Cambridge: Cambridge Univ. Press, 1898.

Sharp, Katharine Dooris. *Summer in a Bog.* Cincinnati: Stewart & Kibb Co., 1913.

Smiles, Samuel. *Robert Dick: Baker, of Thurso, Geologist and Botanist.* New York: Harper & Brothers, 1879.

Solms-Laubach, Hermann. *Fossil Botany: Being an Introduction to Paleophytology from the Standpoint of the Botanist.* Translated by Henry E. F. Garnsey. Rev. ed. Oxford: Clarendon Press, 1891.

Spencer, Herbert. *The Principles of Biology.* 2 vols. New York: D. Appleton and Co., 1866–1867.

Stearns, Robert E. C. *Forest Tree Culture in California: Read before the American Forestry Association, Cincinnati Meeting, April 1882.* Berkeley: s.n., 1882.

Thoreau, Henry David. *Walden.* Boston: Ticknor and Fields, 1862.

———. *A Week on the Concord and Merrimack Rivers.* Boston: Ticknor and Fields, 1868.

Thoreau, Henry David, John Burroughs, and John Muir. *In American Fields and Forests.* Boston: Riverside Press, 1909.

Torrey, Bradford. *A Florida Sketch-Book.* Cambridge, Mass.: Riverside Press, 1895.

Trelease, William. *Views of Nature: Or Contemplations on the Sublime Phenomena of Creation.* London: George Bell & Sons, 1896.

———. "Alvin Wentworth Chapman." *The American Naturalist* 33 (August 1899): 643–646.

———. *The Yucceae.* Thirteenth Annual Report of the Missouri Botanical Garden. St. Louis: Missouri Botanical Garden, July 30, 1902.

U.S. Dept. of Agriculture. *Report of the Commissioner of Agriculture for the Year 1862.* Isaac Newton, Commissioner of Agriculture. Washington, D.C.: Government Printing Office, 1863.

U.S. Dept. of Agriculture. *Report of the Commissioner of Agriculture for the Year 1863.* Isaac Newton, Commissioner of Agriculture. Washington, D.C.: U.S. House of Representatives, 1863.

U.S. Dept. of Agriculture. *Report of the Commissioner of Agriculture for the Year 1866.* Isaac Newton, Commissioner of Agriculture. Washington, D.C.: Government Printing Office, 1867.

U.S. Dept. of Agriculture. *Report of the Commissioner of Agriculture for the Year 1868.* Horace Capron, Commissioner of Agriculture. Washington, D.C.: Government Printing Office, 1869.

U.S. Dept. of Agriculture. *Report of the Commissioner of Agriculture for the Year 1874.* Fred. K. Watts, Commissioner of Agriculture. Washington, D.C.: Government Printing Office, 1875.

U.S. Dept. of Agriculture. *Report of the Commissioner of Agriculture for the Year 1879.* Wm. G. Le Duc, Commissioner of Agriculture. Washington, D.C.: Government Printing Office, 1880.

U.S. Geological Survey. *Report of the Petrified Forests of Arizona,* by Lester F. Ward. Washington, D.C.: Government Printing Office, 1900.

U.S. Geological Survey of the Territories. *The Cretaceous Flora: Contributions to the Fossil Flora of the Western Territories.* Part I. Washington, D.C.: Government Printing Office, 1874.

U.S. Patent Office. *Report of the Commissioner of Patents for the Year 1853: Agriculture.* Charles Mason, Commissioner of Patents. Washington, D.C.: Government Printing Office, 1854.

U.S. Patent Office. *Report of the Commissioner of Patents for the Year 1854: Agriculture.* Charles Mason, Commissioner of Patents. Washington, D.C.: A. O. P. Nicholson, 1855.

U.S. Patent Office. *Report of the Commissioner of Patents for the Year 1855: Agriculture.* Charles Mason, Commissioner of Patents. Washington, D.C.: A. O. P. Nicholson, 1856.

U.S. Patent Office. *Report of the Commissioner of Patents for the Year 1856: Agriculture.* Charles Mason, Commissioner of Patents. Washington, D.C.: Government Printing Office, 1857.

U.S. Patent Office. *Report of the Commissioner of Patents for the Year 1859. Agriculture*. William D. Bishop, United States Commissioner of Patents. Washington, D.C.: Government Printing Office, 1860.

U.S. Treasury Dept. *Report of the Cruise of the Revenue-Steamer* Corwin *in Alaska and the N.W. Arctic Ocean in 1881* by Calvin L. Hooper, U.S.R.M. Washington, D.C.: Government Printing Office, 1883.

Wallace, Alfred Russel. *Island Life or, The Phenomena and Causes of Insular Faunas and Floras*. New York: Harper & Brothers, 1881.

———. *The World of Life*. New York: Moffat, Yard & Co., 1911.

Whitford, H. N. *The Forests of the Philippines. Part II: The Principal Forest Trees*. Manila: Bureau of Printing, 1911.

Wilcox, Walter Dwight. *The Rockies of Canada*. New York: G. P. Putnam's Sons, 1900.

Wisconsin State Agricultural Society. *Transactions of the Wisconsin State Agricultural Society, 1861–68*. Vol. 7. Madison, Wisc.: Atwood & Rublee, 1868.

Wisconsin State Agricultural Society. *Transactions of the Wisconsin State Agricultural Society, 1869*. Vol. 8. Madison, Wisc.: Atwood & Culver, 1870.

Wood, Alphonso. *Class-Book of Botany: Being Outlines of the Structure, Physiology, and Classification of Plants; with a flora of the United States and Canada*. New York: A. S. Barnes & Burr, 1862.

Wright, Ellen. *Elizur Wright's Appeals for the Middlesex Fells and the Forests with a Sketch of What He Did for Both*. Boston: George H. Ellis, 1893.

## KNOWN OR ASSUMED

Carr, Jeanne C. "Cultivation of Annuals." *Wisconsin Farmer* 9 (April 1857): 147–148.

———. "My Rose Garden." *Wisconsin Farmer* 9 (May 1857): 183–184.

———. "The Rural Homes of California." *California Horticulturist* 3 (February 1873): 39–41.

———. "Flower Studies." *Illustrated Press* 1 (February 1873).

———. "Flower Studies.—No. 2." *Illustrated Press* 1 (March 1873).

———. "The Rural Homes of California." *California Horticulturist* 3 (March 1873): 69–72.

———. "Flower Studies.—No. 3." *Illustrated Press* 1 (April 1873).

———. "California Flower Studies.—No. 4." *Illustrated Press* 1 (May 1873).

———. "Nursery and Residence of W. F. Kelsey, Oakland, Cal.," *California Horticulturalist* 3 (May 1873): 147–148.

———. "California Flower Studies.—No. 5." *Illustrated Press* 1 (July 1873).

———. "The Flowers of California." *California Farmer*, c. 1875, Jeanne C. Carr Papers, Scrapbook I, 16, Huntington Library, San Marino, California.

———. "Fruit and Vine." August 24, 1882. Jeanne C. Carr Papers, Scrapbook I, 71. Huntington Library, San Marino, California.

———. "What Shall We Do with Our Fruit!" *Pasadena & Valley Union*, February 23, 1884.

———. "John Muir." *The Californian Illustrated Magazine* 2 (September 1892): 565–578.

Coville, Frederick V. "The Willows of Alaska." *Proceedings of the Washington Academy of Sciences: Papers from the Harriman Alaska Expedition*, 297–362. Vol. 3. August 31, 1901.

Dick, Thomas. *The Christian Philosopher, or, The Connection of Science and Philosophy with Religion.* 2 vols. Glasgow: William Collins, 1846.

Eaton, Daniel Cody. *The Ferns of North America.* 2 vols. Salem, Mass.: S. E. Cassino, 1879.

Jepson, Willis Linn. *The Trees of California.* San Francisco: Cunningham, Curtiss & Welch, 1909.

Lesquereux, Leo, and Thomas P. James. *Manual of the Mosses of North America.* Boston: S. E. Cassino and Co., 1884.

Marshall, Humphrey. *Arbustum Americanum: The American Grove, or, An Alphabetical Catalogue of Forest Trees and Shrubs.* Philadelphia: Joseph Crukshank, 1785.

Michaux, Francois Andre. *The North American Sylva, or, A Description of the Forest Trees of the United States, Canada, and Nova Scotia.* Philadelphia: D. Rice and A. D. Hart, 1859.

Nuttall, Thomas. *The Genera of North American Plants, and a Catalogue of the Species, to the Year 1817.* Philadelphia: Printed for the author by D. Heartt, 1818.

———. *An Introduction to Systematic and Physiological Botany.* Boston: Hilliard, Gray, Little, and Wilkins, and Richardson and Lord, 1827.

Parsons, Frances Theodora. *How to Know the Ferns: A Guide to the Names, Haunts, and Habits of Our Common Ferns.* New York: Charles Scribner's Sons, 1899.

Pursh, Frederick. *Flora Americae Septentrionalis, or, A Systematic Arrangement and Description of the Plants of North America.* 2 vols. London: White, Cochrane, 1814.

Rexford, Eben Eugene. *Home Floriculture: A Practical Guide to the Treatment of Flowering and Other Ornamental Plants in the House and Garden.* New York: Orange Judd Co., 1890.

Sargent, Charles Sprague. *Garden and Forest: A Journal of Horticulture, Landscape Art and Forestry.* New York: Garden and Forest Publishing Co., 1887–1897.

# BIBLIOGRAPHY

Adas, Michael. *Machines as the Measure of Men: Science, Technology, and Ideologies of Western Dominance.* Ithaca: Cornell Univ. Press, 1989.

Agassiz, Louis. *Contributions to the Natural History of the United States.* Boston: Little, Brown, 1857.

Apgar, Austin C. *Trees of the Northern United States.* New York: American Book Co., 1892.

Arber, E. A. N., and J. Parkin. "On the Origin of Angiosperms." *Journal of the Linnaean Society* 38 (1907): 29–80.

Arno, Stephen F. *Discovering Sierra Trees.* Yosemite National Park: Yosemite Association, 1973.

Badè, William Frederic, ed. *The Life and Letters of John Muir.* 2 Vols. Boston: Houghton Mifflin, 1924. (See also Gifford, *John Muir: His Life and Letters and Other Writings.*)

Bailey, I. W. "Origins of the Angiosperms: Need for a Broader Outlook." *Journal of the Arnold Arboretum* 30 (1949): 64–70.

Bailey, Liberty Hyde. *Cyclopedia of American Horticulture.* New York: Macmillan, 1902–1903.

———. *How Plants Get Their Names.* New York: Macmillan Co., 1933.

———. *Manual of Cultivated Plants: Most Commonly Grown in the Continental United States and Canada.* Rev. ed. New York: Macmillan Co., 1949.

Bailey, William Whitman. *Botanizing: A Guide to Field Collecting and Herbarium Work.* Providence, R.I.: Preston and Rounds, 1899.

Barnhart, John H. *Biographical Notes on Botanists.* 3 Vols. Boston: G. K. Hall, 1965.

Bartlett, W. C. *A Breeze from the Woods.* Oakland: Oakland Evening Tribune, 1880.

Barton, Benjamin Smith. *Elements of Botany, or, Outlines of the Natural History of Vegetables.* Philadelphia: R. Desilver, 1836.

Bartram, John. *Travels in Pensilvania and Canada.* London: J. Whiston and B. White, 1751.

———. *A Description of East Florida, with a Journal Kept by John Bartram, of Philadelphia, Botanist to His Majesty for the Floridas.* 3d ed. London, 1769.

Bartram, William. *Travels through North and South Carolina, Georgia, East and West Florida.* Philadelphia: James & Johnson, 1791.

———. *Travels of William Bartram.* Edited by Mark Van Doren. New York: Dover Press, 1928.

Bate, Jonathan. *Romantic Ecology: Wordsworth and the Environmental Tradition.* New York: Routledge, 1991.

Bates, Marston. *The Nature of Natural History.* New York: Scribner, 1950.

Behr, Hans Herman. *Synopsis of the Genera of Vascular Plants in the Vicinity of San Francisco: with an Attempt to Arrange Them According to Evolutionary Principles.* San Francisco: Payot, Upham & Company, 1884.

———. *Flora of the Vicinity of San Francisco.* San Francisco: 1888.

———. *Changes in Fauna and Flora of California.* San Francisco: California Academy of Sciences, 1888.

Beidleman, Richard G. "Douglas in Pursuit of Plants." *Horticulture* 47 (1969): 30–31, 49, 59.

———. "Botany Man Jepson, Naturalist Muir, and the Sierra Club Outing of 1909." *Fremontia* 34 (July 2006): 3–8.

———. *California's Frontier Naturalists.* Berkeley: Univ. of California Press, 2006.

Benedict, Barbara M. *Curiosity: A Cultural History of Early Modern Inquiry.* Chicago: Univ. of Chicago Press, 2001.

Berliocchi, Luigi. *The Orchid in Lore and Legend.* Portland: Timber Press, [1996] 2000.

Bishop, G. Norman. *Native Trees of Georgia.* Athens, Ga.: Georgia Agricultural Extension Service, 1940.

Blackwell, Laird R. *Wildflowers of the Sierra Nevada and the Central Valley.* Edmonton: Lone Pine, 1999.

Bledstein, Burton J. *The Culture of Professionalism: The Middle Class and the Development of Higher Education in America.* New York: W. W. Norton, 1976.

Blunt, Wilfrid. *The Complete Naturalist: A Life of Linnaeus.* New York: Viking Press, 1971.

Bolander, Henry N. *A Catalogue of the Plants Growing in the Vicinity of San Francisco.* San Francisco: A. Roman & Co., 1870.

Bonta, Marcia Myers. *Women in the Field: America's Pioneering Women Naturalists.* College Station: Texas A & M Univ. Press, 1991.

Botti, Stephen J. *An Illustrated Flora of Yosemite National Park.* Yosemite National Park: Yosemite Association, 2001.

Bowen, Margarita. *Empiricism and Geographical Thought: From Francis Bacon to Alexander von Humboldt.* Cambridge: Cambridge Univ. Press, 1981.

Boyle, Robert. *General Heads for the Natural History of a Country.* London, 1692.

Bozeman, Theodore Dwight. *Protestants in the Age of Science: The Baconian Ideal and Antebellum American Thought.* Chapel Hill: Univ. of North Carolina Press, 1977.

Bradley, Ian. *The Call to Seriousness: The Evangelical Impact on the Victorians.* New York: Macmillan Publishing Co., 1976.

Bradley, James. *A Western Journey with Mr. Emerson.* Boston: Little, Brown and Co., 1884.

Branch, Michael, ed. *John Muir's Last Journey: South to the Amazon and East to Africa.* Washington, D.C.: Island Press, 2001.

Brandegee Katharine. "The Flora of Yo Semite." *Zoe* 2 (1891): 155–167.

———. "Dr. Albert Kellogg." *Zoe* 4 (1893): 1–2.

———. "The Size of Herbarium Sheets." *Zoe* 5 (1901): 138–139.

Brendel, Frederick. "Historical Sketch of the Science of Botany in North America From 1635–1840." *American Naturalist* 13 (1879): 754–771 and 14 (1880): 25–38.

Brentano, Carroll. "'Passionate Lovers of Nature.' The University of the High Sierra" *Chronicle of the University of California* (Spring 2000): 77–84.

Brewer, William H. *Up and Down California in 1860–1864. The Journal of William H. Brewer.* Edited by Francis P. Farquhar. New Haven: Yale Univ. Press, 1930.

Brewer, William H., Sereno Watson, and Asa Gray. *Botany [of California].* Vol. 1. Cambridge, Mass.: Welch, Bigelow, & Co., University Press, 1876.

Brewster, Edwin T. *Life and Letters of Josiah Dwight Whitney.* Boston: Houghton Mifflin, 1909.

Brooke, John Hedley. *Science and Religion: Some Historical Perspectives.* Cambridge: Cambridge Univ. Press, 1991.

Brooks, Paul. *Speaking for Nature: How Literary Naturalists from Henry Thoreau to Rachael Carson Have Shaped America.* San Francisco: Sierra Club, 1980.

Brooks, Walter R. *God in Nature and Life. Selections from the Sermons and Writings of Walter R. Brooks.* New York: Anson D. F. Randolph, 1889.

Brown, Chandos Michael. *Benjamin Silliman: A Life in the Young Republic.* Princeton: Princeton Univ. Press, 1989.

Browning, Peter. *Place Names of the Sierra Nevada: From Abbot to Zumwalt.* Berkeley: Wilderness Press, 1986.

Bruce, Robert V. *The Launching of Modern American Science, 1846–1876.* New York: Knopf, 1987.

Brummitt, R. K. *Vascular Plant Families and Genera.* Kew: Royal Botanic Gardens, 1992.

Brynildson, Erik B. "Restoring the Fountain of John Muir's Youth." *Wisconsin Academy Review* (December 1988): 4–10

Burger, William C. *Flowers: How They Changed the World.* Amherst, N.Y.: Prometheus Books, 2006.

Burroughs, John. *Far and Near.* New York: Houghton Mifflin, 1904.

Burroughs, John, John Muir, and George Bird Grinnell. *Narrative, Glaciers, Natives.* Vol. I. Harriman Alaska Expedition Series. New York: Doubleday, Page and Co., 1901.

Buske, Frank. "John Muir. Go to Alaska. Go and See." *The Alaska Journal* 9 (Summer 1979): 32–37.

———. "John Muir and the Alaska Gold Rush." *The Pacific Historian* 25 (Summer 1981): 37–49.

———. "John Muir's Alaska Experience." *The Pacific Historian: John Muir: Life and Legacy* 29 (Summer/Fall 1985): 113–123.

Butler, Joseph. *The Analogy of Religion, Natural and Revealed, To the Constitution and Course of Nature.* New York: John W. Lovell, 1890.

Butterfield, C. W. *History of the University of Wisconsin, from Its First Organization to 1879.* Madison: Univ. of Wisconsin Press, 1879.

Caddy, Florence. *Through the Fields with Linnaeus: A Chapter in Swedish History.* 2 Vols. London: Longmans, Green, and Co., 1887.

Callicott, J. Baird. "Genesis and John Muir." *ReVision* 12 (Winter 1990): 31–47.

Candolle, Augustin Pyramus de. *Théorie Elémentaire de la Botanique.* Paris: Deterville, 1813; 3d ed., Paris: Roret, 1844.

Cannon, Susan Faye. *Science in Culture: The Early Victorian Period.* New York: Science History Publications, 1978.

Cardot, J., and I. Theriot. *The Mosses of Alaska.* Harriman Alaska Expedition Series, 293–372. Vol. 4. Washington, D.C.: The Academy, 1902.

Carr, Ezra S. *The Patrons of Husbandry on the Pacific Coast.* San Francisco: A. L. Bancroft, 1875.

Carr, Jeanne C. "John Muir." *The California Illustrated Magazine* 2 (September 1892): 565–578.

Cash, Catherine. *The Slipper Orchid.* Portland: Timber Press, 1991.

Cassino, Samuel E., ed. *The Naturalist's Directory.* Boston, 1886.

Castner, James L. *Photographic Atlas of Botany and Guide to Plant Identification.* Gainesville, Fla.: Feline Press, 2004.

Catesby, Mark. *The Natural History of Carolina, Florida and the Bahama Islands.* 2 Vols. London: Mark Catesby, 1731–43, 1754, 1771.

Channing, Walter. "A Survey of the Botany of the United States." *North American Review* 13 (1821): 100–134.

Chapman, A. W. *Flora of the Southern United States.* New York: Ivison, Phinney & Co., 1860.

Chickering, Sherman. "Growing Herbaria at the California Academy of Sciences." *Fremontia* 17 (1989): 3–10.

Christensen, Carl. *Index Filicum.* Hafniae (Copenhagen): H. Hagerup, 1906.

Cittadino, Eugene. "Ecology and the Professionalization of Botany in America, 1890–1905." *Studies in History of Biology* 4 (1980): 171–198.

Coats, A. M. *The Plant Hunters.* New York: McGraw-Hill, 1969.

Cockerell, T. D. A. "With John Muir in the Land of Flowers and Ice." *Dial* 60 (1916): 17–18.

Codman, John. *The Round Trip: By Way of Panama through California, Oregon, Nevada, Utah, Idaho, and Colorado.* 3d ed. New York: G. P. Putnam's Sons, 1882.

Coffey, Timothy. *The History and Folklore of North American Wildflowers.* Boston: Houghton Mifflin, 1993.

Cohen, Michael P. *The Pathless Way: John Muir and American Wilderness.* Madison: Univ. of Wisconsin Press, 1984.

Constance, Lincoln. "The Systematics of the Angiosperms." In *A Century of Progress in the Natural Sciences, 1853–1953,* 405–483. San Francisco: California Academy of Sciences, 1955.

——— . *Botany at Berkeley: The First Hundred Years.* Berkeley: Univ. of California Press, 1978.

Cooley, Howard. "The Botanical Nomenclature of John Muir." *The John Muir Newsletter* 6 (Summer 1996):4–6.

Coolidge, Susan [Sarah C. Woolsey]. "A Few Hints on a California Journey." *Scribner's Monthly* 6 (May 1873): 25–31.

Correll, Donovan Stewart. *Native Orchids of North America: North of Mexico.* Waltham Mass.: Chronica Botanica, 1950.

Cruickshank, Helen Gere, ed. *John and William Bartram's America.* Garden City: Doubleday & Co., 1957.

Cummings, Constance F. Gordon. *Granite Crags.* Edinburgh: W. Blackwood and Sons, 1884.

Curti, Merle Eugene. *The Growth of American Thought.* New Brunswick, N.J.: Transition Books, 1982.

Curti, Merle, and Vernon Carstensen. *The University of Wisconsin: A History, 1845–1925.* Madison: Univ. of Wisconsin Press, 1949.

Dale, Peter Allan. *In Pursuit of a Scientific Culture: Science, Art, and Society in the Victorian Age.* Madison: Univ. of Wisconsin Press, 1989.

Dall, William H. *Alaska and Its Resources.* Boston: Lee and Shepard, 1870.

Dana, Edward S. *A Century of Science in America.* New Haven: Yale Univ. Press, 1918.

Dance, S. Peter. *The Art of Natural History.* Woodstock, N.Y.: Overlook Press, 1978.

Daniels, George H. "The Process of Professionalism in American Science: The Emergent Period, 1820–1860." *Isis* 58 (1967): 151–166.

——— . *American Science in the Age of Jackson.* New York: Columbia Univ. Press, 1968.

——— . *Science in American Society: A Social History.* New York: Knopf, 1971.

——— . *Nineteenth-Century American Science: A Reappraisal.* Evanston: Northwestern Univ. Press, 1972.

Darby, John. *A Manual of Botany Adapted to the Productions of the Southern States.* Macon, Ga.: Benjamin F. Griffin, 1841.

——— . *Botany of the Southern States.* New York: A. S. Barnes and Co., 1860.

Darwin, Charles. *The Life and Letters of Charles Darwin.* 2 Vols. Edited by Francis Darwin. New York: D. Appleton and Co., 1911.

Davenport, George E. "A Bit of Fern History." *Botanical Gazette* 7 (May 1882).

Davies, John. *Douglas of the Forests: The North American Journals of David Douglas*. Seattle: Univ. of Washington Press, 1980.

Davis, Liam H. "Sereno Watson: Early California Botanist." *Fremontia* 22 (1994): 20–23.

De Long, George Washington. *The Voyage of the Jeannette: The Ship and Ice Journals of George W. De Long, Lieutenant-Commander U.S.N., and Commander of the Polar Expedition of 1879–1881*. 2 Vols. Boston: Houghton Mifflin, 1883.

Demars, Stanford E. *The Tourist in Yosemite, 1855–1985*. Salt Lake City: Univ. of Utah Press, 1991.

Dick, Thomas. *The Christian Philosopher; or, The Connection of Science and Philosophy with Religion*. 2 Vols. Glasgow: William Collins, Sons, & Co., 1865.

Donovan, Edward. *Instructions for Collecting and Preserving Various Subjects of Natural History*. London: privately printed, 1794.

Duncan, Wilbur H. *Guide to Georgia Trees*. Athens: Univ. of Georgia Press, 1941.

Duncan, Wilbur H., and Leonard E. Foote. *Wildflowers of the Southeastern United States*. Athens: Univ. of Georgia Press, 1975.

Dupree, Anderson Hunter. *Asa Gray, 1810–1888*. Cambridge: Harvard Univ. Press, 1959; New York: Atheneum, 1968.

Earl, John. *John Muir's Longest Walk*. Garden City, N.Y.: Doubleday & Co., 1975.

Earnest, Ernest. *John and William Bartram: Botanists and Explorers*. Philadelphia: Univ. of Pennsylvania Press, 1940.

Eastwood, Alice. "Early Botanical Explorers on the Pacific Coast and the Trees They Found There." *California Historical Society Quarterly* 18 (1939): 335–346.

Eaton, Amos. *Manual of Botany, for North America*. 5th ed. Albany: Websters & Skinners, 1829.

Eaton, Amos, and John Wright. *North American Botany: Comprising the Native and Common Cultivated Plants*. Troy, N.Y.: E. Gates, (1840), 1887.

Eaton, Daniel Cady. *The Ferns of North America*. 2 Vols. Salem, Mass.: S. E. Cassino, 1879–1880.

Egerton, Frank N. *History of American Ecology*, 311–351. New York: Arno Press, 1977.

Eifert, Virginia L. S. *Tall Trees and Far Horizon; Adventures and Discoveries of Early Botanists in America*. New York: Dodd, Mead and Co., 1965.

Eiseley, Loren C. *The Immense Journey*, 61–77. New York: Random House, 1957.

Eisner, Thomas, and Mary M. Woodsen. "The Science of Wonder." *Wild Earth* (Spring/Summer 2004): 10–13.

Elliott, Clark A. *Biographical Dictionary of American Science: The Seventeenth through the Nineteenth Centuries*. Westport, Conn.: Greenwood Press, 1979.

Elliott, Stephen. *A Sketch of the Botany of South Carolina and Georgia*. 2 Vols. Charleston, S.C.: J. R. Schenck, 1821.

Emerson, Ralph Waldo. *Nature*. Boston: J. Munroe and Co., 1836.

Engberg, Robert. "John Muir: From Poetry to Politics, 1871–1876." In *The World of John Muir*, ed. Lawrence R. Murphy and Dan Collins, 11–19. Stockton, Calif.: Univ. of the Pacific, 1981.

Engelmann, George. *The Oaks of the United States*. St. Louis: R. P. Studley, 1876.

——— . *The Botanical Works of the Late George Engelmann*. Edited by William Trelease and Asa Gray. Cambridge, Mass.: J. Wilson and Son, 1887.

Ertter, Barbara. "The Changing Face of California Botany." *Madroño* 42 (1995): 114–122.

——— . "People, Plants, and Politics: The Development of Institution-Based Botany in California, 1853–1906." In *Cultures and Institutions of Natural History: Essays in the History and Philosophy of Science*, ed. Michael T. Ghiselin and Alan E. Leviton, 203–248. San Francisco: California Academy of Sciences, 2000.

——— . "Our Undiscovered Heritage: Past and Future Prospects for Species-Level Botanical Inventory." *Madroño* 47 (2000): 237–252.

————. "A Mulwrangler, a Lawyer, and a Lone Woman: The Continuing Legacy of Jepson's Collecting Network." *The Jepson Globe* 11 (August 2000): 3.

————. "The Flowering of Natural History Institutions in California." *Proceedings of the California Academy of Sciences* 55 (Suppl. 1, No. 4): 58–87.

————. "Botany: A Woman's Place in Science? A View from the West." TMs [photocopy]. University and Jepson Herbaria, University of California, Berkeley, California.

Ewan, Joseph A. "San Francisco as a Mecca for Nineteenth Century Naturalists." In *A Century of Progress in the Natural Sciences, 1853–1953*, 1–63. San Francisco: California Academy of Sciences, 1955.

————. *A Short History of Botany in the United States*. New York: Hafner Publishing Co., 1969.

————. "Roots of the California Botanical Society." *Madroño* 24 (1987): 1–17.

Farber, Paul L. "The Transformation of Natural History in the Nineteenth Century." *Journal of the History of Biology* 15 (1982): 145–152.

Farlow, W. G. "The Task of American Botanists." *Popular Science Monthly* 31 (1887): 305–314.

Farquhar, Francis P. *Yosemite, the Big Trees and the High Sierra: A Selective Bibliography*. Berkeley: Univ. of California Press, 1948.

————. *History of the Sierra Nevada*. Berkeley: Univ. of California Press, 1965.

Fernow, B. E. *Forests of Alaska*. Harriman Alaska Expedition Series, 235–256. Vol. 2. New York: Doubleday, Page and Co., 1901.

Ferris, G. F. "The Contribution of Natural History to Human Progress." In *A Century of Progress in the Natural Sciences, 1853–1953*, 75–87. San Francisco: California Academy of Sciences, 1955.

Fisher, George P. *Life of Benjamin Silliman*. New York: C. Scribner and Co., 1866.

Ford, Charles E. "Botany Texts: A Survey of Their Development in American Higher Education, 1643–1906." *History of Education Quarterly* 4 (1964): 59–71.

Fox, Stephen. *The American Conservation Movement: John Muir and His Legacy*. Boston: Little, Brown and Co., 1981.

Frankiel, Sandra Sizer. *California's Spiritual Frontiers: Religious Alternatives in Anglo-Protestantism, 1850–1910*. Berkeley: Univ. of California Press, 1988.

Freidson, Eliot. *Professional Powers: A Study of the Institutionalization of Formal Knowledge*. Chicago: Univ. of Chicago Press, 1986.

Geiser, Samuel Wood. *Naturalists on the Frontier*. Dallas: Southern Methodist Univ. Press, 1937.

Geison, Gerald L. *Professions and Professional Ideologies in America*. Chapel Hill: Univ. of North Carolina Press, 1983.

Gifford, Terry, ed. *John Muir: His Life and Letters and Other Writings*. London: Baton Wicks, 1996.

Gilman, Henry. "Our Northern Orchids." *Appleton's Journal* 9 (1873): 431.

Gisel, Bonnie. *Kindred & Related Spirits: The Letters of John Muir and Jeanne C. Carr*. Salt Lake City: Univ. of Utah Press, 2001.

————. "'Those Who Walk Apart but Ever Together Are True Companions': Jeanne Carr and John Muir in the High Sierra." In *John Muir: Family, Friends, and Adventures*, ed. Sally M. Miller. Albuquerque: Univ. of New Mexico Press, 2005.

Gleason, Henry A., and Arthur Cronquist. *Manual of Vascular Plants of North-Eastern United States and Adjacent Canada*. 2d ed. New York: New York Botanical Garden, 1991.

Goetzmann, William H. *Explorations and Empire: The Explorer and the Scientist in the Winning of the American West*. New York: Random House, 1966.

————. *New Lands, New Men: America and the Second Great Age of Discovery*. New York: Viking Press, 1986.

Goetzmann, William H., and Kay Sloan. *Looking Far North: The Harriman Expedition to Alaska, 1899.* New York: Viking Press, 1982.

Good, John Mason. *The Book of Nature.* Hartford: Belknap & Hamersley, 1842.

Good, Ronald. "Plant Geography." In *A Century of Progress in the Natural Sciences 1853–1953,* 747–765. San Francisco: California Academy of Sciences, 1955.

Goody, Jack. *The Culture of Flowers.* Cambridge: Cambridge Univ. Press, 1993.

Gray, Asa. *Manual of the Botany of the Northern United States: Including the District East of the Mississippi and North of North Carolina and Tennessee.* 5th ed. New York: Ivison, Blackman, Taylor & Co., 1867.

——— . *Gray's School and Field Book of Botany.* New York: Ivison, Blakeman, Taylor & Co., 1868.

——— . *Botany for Young People: How Plants Grow. Popular Flora of Common Plants.* New York: Ivison, Blakeman, Taylor & Co., 1874.

——— . *Synoptical Flora of North America.* New York: Ivison, Blakeman, Taylor & Co., 1886.

——— . *Letters of Asa Gray.* 2 Vols. Edited by Jane Lathrop Loring Gray. Boston: Houghton Mifflin, 1893.

——— . *Field, Forest, and Garden Botany: A Simple Introduction to the Common Plants of the United States East of the 100th Meridian, both Wild and Cultivated.* New York: America Book Co., 1895.

Gray, F. C. "American Forest Trees." *North American Review* 44 (1837): 361.

Green, M. L. "History of Plant Nomenclature." Royal Botanic Gardens, Kew, *Bulletin of Miscellaneous Information* 10 (1927): 403–415.

Greene, Edward Lee. "Studies in the Botany of California and Parts Adjacent." *Bulletin of the California Academy of Sciences* 1 (1885): 66–127.

——— . "Biographical Notice of Dr. Albert Kellogg." *Pittonia* 1 (1887): 145–151.

——— . *Illustrations of West American Oaks: From Drawings by the Late Albert Kellogg.* San Francisco: Bosqui Engraving & Printing Co., 1889–1890.

——— . *Flora Franciscana. An Attempt to Classify and Describe the Vascular Plants of Middle California.* San Francisco: Cubery & Company, 1891.

——— . *Manual of the Botany of the Region of San Francisco Bay.* San Francisco: Cubery & Company, 1894.

——— . *Landmarks of Botanical History: A Study of Certain Epochs in the Development of the Science of Botany.* Washington, D.C.: Smithsonian Institution, 1909.

Greene, John C. "Science and the Public in the Age of Jefferson." *Isis* 49 (1958): 13–25.

——— . *American Science in the Age of Jefferson.* Ames: Iowa State Press, 1984.

Greenwood, Grace. *New Life in New Lands.* New York: J. B. Ford and Co., 1873.

Griffiths, Mark. *Index of Garden Plants.* London: Royal Horticultural Society, 1994.

Gudde, Erwin G. *California Place Names.* Edited by William Bright. Berkeley: Univ. of California Press, 1998.

Hall, Harvey Monroe, and Carlotta Case Hall. *A Yosemite Flora.* San Francisco: Paul Elder & Co., 1912.

Harshberger, John W. *The Botanists of Philadelphia and Their Work.* Philadelphia: T. C. Davis & Son, 1899.

Harvey, Athelstan G. *Douglas of the Fir: A Biography of David Douglas, Botanist.* Cambridge: Harvard Univ. Press, 1947.

Haulenbeek, Rod. *Tree Adventures in Yosemite Valley.* Carnelian Bay, Calif.: Wide-Eyed Publications, 1994.

Hays, Samuel P. *Conservation and the Gospel of Efficiency: The Progressive Conservation Movement, 1890–1920*. Cambridge: Harvard Univ. Press, 1959.

Helferich, Gerard. *Humboldt's Cosmos: Alexander von Humboldt and the Latin American Journey That Changed the Way We See the World*. New York: Gotham Books, 2004.

Henderson, Andrew, Gloria Galeano, and Rodrigo Bernal. *Field Guide to the Palms of the Americas*. Princeton: Princeton Univ. Press, 1995.

Hensley, Carl Wayne. "Rhetorical Visions and the Persuasion of a Historical Moment: The Disciples of Christ in Nineteenth-Century American Culture." *Quarterly Journal of Speech* 61 (October 1975): 250–264.

Hickman, James C., ed. *The Jepson Manual: Higher Plants of California*. Berkeley: Univ. of California Press, 1993.

Hinckley, Ted C. "The Inside Passage: A Popular Gilded Age Tour." *Pacific Northwest Quarterly* 56 (April 1965): 67–74.

———. *The Americanization of Alaska, 1867–1897*. Palo Alto: Pacific Books, 1972.

Hitchcock, A. S. *Manual of the Grasses of the United States*. 2d ed. 2 Vols. New York: Dover Publications, 1993.

Holmes, Steven J. *The Young John Muir: An Environmental Biography*. Madison: Univ. of Wisconsin Press, 1999.

Holton, Gerald, and William A. Blanpied. *Science and Its Public: The Changing Relationship*. Dordrecht: D. Reidel Co., 1976.

Hooker, Joseph Dalton. *Outlines of the Distribution of Arctic Plants*. London: Linnean Society of London, 1861.

———. *Botany*. New York: D. Appleton and Company, 1877.

Horn, Elizabeth L. *Sierra Nevada Wildflowers*. Missoula, Mont.: Mountain Press Publishing, 1998.

Humboldt, Alexander von. *Cosmos: A Sketch of the Physical Description of the Universe*. Translated by E. C. Otte. 2 Vols. New York: Harper, 1850.

———. *Personal Narrative of Travels to the Equinoctial Regions of America, during the Years 1799–1804*. Vol. 1. Translated by Thomasina Ross. London: Henry G. Bohn, 1852.

Humphrey, Harry Baker. *Makers of North American Botany*. New York: Ronald Press Co., 1961.

Huxley, Leonard. *Life and Letters of Sir Joseph Dalton Hooker*. 2 Vols. London: John Murray, 1918.

Hyde, Anne Farrar. *An American Vision: Far Western Landscape and National Culture, 1820–1920*. New York: New York Univ. Press, 1990.

Jackson, Sheldon. *Alaska and Missions on the North Pacific Coast*. New York: Dodd, Mead, 1880.

Jacob, Margaret C. *Scientific Culture and the Making of the Industrial West*. New York: Oxford Univ. Press, 1997.

Janzen, Daniel. "How to Grow a Wildland: The Gardenification of Nature." In *The Biodiversity Crisis*, ed. Michael J. Novacek, 156–162. New York: New Press, 2001.

Jepson, Willis Linn. *A Flora of Western Middle California*. Berkeley: Encina Publishing Company, 1901.

———. *The Trees of California*. San Francisco: Cunningham, Curtiss & Welch, 1909.

———. *A Flora of California*. San Francisco: Cunningham, Curtiss & Welch, 1909.

———. *Sequoia Sempervirens and Gigantea*. Berkeley: The University Press, 1910.

———. *A Manual of the Flowering Plants of California*. Berkeley: Associated Students Store, University of California, 1925.

———. *General Key to the Families of Flowering Plants of California*. Berkeley: Associated Students Store, University of California, 1928.

———. "The Botanical Explorers of California XI," *Madroño* 2 (1934): 156–157.

Johnson, Robert Underwood. *Remembered Yesterdays*, 281–282. Boston: Little, Brown, and Co., 1923.

Johnston, Hank. *The Yosemite Grant, 1864–1906: A Pictorial History.* Yosemite National Park: Yosemite Association, 1995.

Jones, Holway. *John Muir and the Sierra Club: The Battle for Yosemite.* San Francisco: Sierra Club, 1965.

Kartesz, John T. *A Synonymized Checklist of the Vascular Flora of the United States, Canada, and Greenland. The Biota of North America.* Vol. 2. 2d ed. Portland, Ore.: Timber Press, 1994.

Keator, Glenn. *Complete Garden Guide to the Native Shrubs of California.* San Francisco: Chronicle Books, 1994.

Keeney, Elizabeth B. *The Botanizers: Amateur Scientists in Nineteenth-Century America.* Chapel Hill: Univ. of North Carolina Press, 1992.

Kellogg, Albert. *Forest Trees of California.* Sacramento: State Mining Bureau, 1882.

Kimes, William F., and Maymie B. Kimes. *John Muir: A Reading Bibliography.* Fresno: Panorama West Books, 1986.

Knapp, Sandra. *Plant Discoveries: A Botanist's Voyage through Plant Exploration.* London: Firefly Books, 2003.

Koerner, Lisbet. *Linnaeus: Nature and Nation.* Cambridge: Harvard Univ. Press, 1999.

Lamartine, Alphonse de. *The Stone-Mason of Saint Point: A Village Tale.* New York: Harper and Brothers, 1851.

Lawson, G. *The Royal Water-lily of South America and the Water-lilies of Our Own Land: Their History and Cultivation.* Edinburgh: James Hogg, 1851.

Leavitt, Robert Greenleaf. *Outlines of Botany.* New York: American Book Co., 1901.

LeConte, Joseph. *A Journal of Ramblings through the High Sierra of California by the University Excursion Party.* 6th ed. San Francisco: Sierra Club (1875), 1960.

Lemmon, John Gill. "Conifers of the Pacific Slope: How to Distinguish Them." *Sierra Club Bulletin* 2 (1897): 61–78; 156–173.

———. *Handbook of West-American Cone-Bearers.* Oakland, Calif.: 1900.

———. "Notes by a Pioneer Botanist—I." *Muhlenbergia* 4 (1908): 17–21.

Leopold, Allison Kyle. *The Victorian Garden.* New York: Clarkson Potter, 1995.

Lesquereux, Leo, and Thomas Potts James. *Manual of the Mosses of North America.* Boston: S. E. Cassino, 1884.

Limbaugh, Ronald H. "The Nature of Muir's Religion." *Pacific Historian* 29 (Summer-Fall 1985): 16–29.

Lincoln, Almira H. *Familiar Lectures on Botany.* New York: F. J. Huntington & Co., 1841.

Lindley, J. *An Introduction to the Natural System of Botany.* London: Longman, Rees, Orme, Brown, and Green, 1830.

———. *Folia Orchidacea. An Enumeration of the Known Species of Orchids.* London: J. Matthews, 1852–1859.

Linne, Carl von. *Systema Naturae: Sistens Regna Tria Naturae in Classes et Ordines, Genera et Species Redacta Tabulisque aeneis illustrata.* Lugduni Batavorum (Leiden): Theodorum Haak, (1735), 1756.

———. *Species Plantarum.* Facsimile of the 1st ed. [1753]. London: Ray Society, 1957–1959.

———. *Philosophia Botanica, in qua Explicantur Fundamenta Botanica cum Definitionibus partium, Exemplis Terminorum, Observationibus Rariorum, Adjectis Figuris Aeneis.* Viennae: J. T. Trattner, 1763.

Linton, M. Albert. *The Academy of Natural Sciences of Philadelphia: 150 Years of Distinguished Service.* New York: Newcomen Society of North America, 1962.

Lockman, Ronald F. "Forests and Watershed in the Environmental Philosophy of Theodore P. Lukens." *Journal of Forest History* 23 (April 1979): 82–91.

Looby, Christopher. "The Constitution of Nature: Taxonomy as Politics in Jefferson, Peale, and Bartram." *Early American Literature* 22 (1987): 252–273.

Lukens, Theodore P. "Why Forests Are Needed: They Would Hold Back the Rain and Prevent Disastrous Floods." *Water and Forest* 1 (1902): 13.

———. "Effects of Forests on Water Supply." *Forestry and Irrigation* 10 (1904): 465–469.

Lyon, Charles J. "Centennial of Wood's 'Class-Book of Botany.'" *Science* 101 (1945): 484–486.

Lyon, William S. *Gardening in California.* Los Angeles: George Rice & Sons, 1904.

Mabberley, D. J. *The Plant-Book: A Portable Dictionary of the Higher Plants.* 2d ed. Cambridge: Cambridge Univ. Press, 1997.

Macklin, J. A., J. B. Phipps, and D. E. Bufford. "Charles Sargent's Type Concept: A Guide to Interpreting His Names in Crataegus (Rosaceae)." *Harvard Papers in Botany* 5 (2000): 123–128.

Marsden, George M. *Fundamentalism and American Culture: The Shaping of Twentieth-Century Evangelicalism: 1870–1925.* New York: Oxford Univ. Press, 1980.

Marsh, George Perkins. *Man and Nature; or, Physical Geography as Modified by Human Action.* New York: Charles Scribner, 1864.

Marx, Leo. *The Machine in the Garden: Technology and the Pastoral Ideal in America.* London: Oxford Univ. Press, 1964.

Mathias, Mildred E. "The Fascinating History of the Early Botanical Exploration and Investigations in Southern California." *Aliso* 12 (1989): 407–433.

Mattoon, Wilbur R., and Thomas D. Burleigh. *Common Forest Trees of Georgia: How to Know Them.* Athens, Ga.: 1923.

McKibben, Bill. "The Walk That Changed America." *Conde Nast Traveler* (September 1995): 132–145, 186–188.

McKnight, Kent H., and Vera B. McKnight. *A Field Guide to Mushrooms: North America.* Boston: Houghton Mifflin, 1987.

McMinn, Howard E. *An Illustrated Manual of California Shrubs.* San Francisco: J. W. Stacey, 1939.

Melham, Tom. *John Muir's Wild America.* Washington, D.C.: National Geographic Society, 1976.

Merrell, Bruce. "A Wild Discouraging Mess: John Muir Reports on the Klondike Gold Rush." *Alaska History* 7 (Fall 1992): 30–39.

Merriam, C. Hart. *Results of a Biological Survey of Mount Shasta, California.* Washington, D.C.: U.S. Department of Agriculture, Division of Biological Survey, 1899.

Meyers, Amy R. W., and Margaret Beck Pritchard. *Empire's Nature: Mark Catesby's New World Vision.* Chapel Hill: Univ. of North Carolina Press, 1998.

Michaux, Andre. *Flora Boreali-Americana.* Paris [1803]; New York: Hafner Press, 1974.

Miller, Char. *Gifford Pinchot and the Making of Modern Environmentalism.* Washington, D.C.: Island Press, 2001.

Miller, David C. *Dark Eden: The Swamp in Nineteenth-Century American Culture.* New York: Cambridge Univ. Press, 1989.

Miller, Sally M., ed. *John Muir in Historical Perspective.* New York: Peter Lang, 1999.

Mitchell, Ann Lindsay, and Syd House. *David Douglas: Explorer and Botanist.* London: Aurum Press, 1999.

Moran, Robbin. *The Natural History of Ferns.* Portland, Ore.: Timber Press, 2004.

Morris, Frank, and Edward A. Eames. *Our Wild Orchids: Trails and Portraits.* New York: Charles Scribner's Sons, 1929.

Morwood, William. *Traveler in a Vanished Landscape: The Life and Times of David Douglas.* London: Gentry Books, 1973.

Muir, John. "Botanical Notes on Alaska." In *Cruise of the Revenue-Steamer* Corwin *in Alaska and the N.W. Arctic Ocean in 1881,* 45–53. Washington, D.C.: Government Printing Office, 1883.

———. *The Mountains of California*. New York: The Century Company, 1894. (See also: Muir, *The Eight Wilderness Discovery Books*, 1991.)

———. *Our National Parks*. Boston: Houghton Mifflin, 1901. (See also: Muir, *The Eight Wilderness Discovery Books*, 1991.)

———. "Sargent's Silva." *Atlantic Monthly* 92 (July 1903): 9–22.

———. *Edward Henry Harriman*. New York: Doubleday, Page and Co., 1911.

———. *My First Summer in the Sierra*. Boston: Houghton Mifflin, 1911. (See also: Muir, *The Eight Wilderness Discovery Books*, 1991.)

———. *The Yosemite*. New York: The Century Co., 1912. (See also: Muir, *The Eight Wilderness Discovery Books*, 1991.)

———. *The Story of My Boyhood and Youth*. Boston: Houghton Mifflin, 1913. (See also: Muir, *The Eight Wilderness Discovery Books*, 1991.)

———. *Letters to a Friend: Written to Mrs. Ezra Carr, 1866–1879*. Boston: Houghton Mifflin, 1915; reprint, Dunwoody, Ga.: Norman Berg, 1973.

———. *Travels in Alaska*. Boston: Houghton Mifflin, 1915. (See also: Muir, *The Eight Wilderness Discovery Books*, 1991.)

———. *A Thousand Mile Walk to the Gulf*. Boston: Houghton Mifflin, 1916. (See also: Muir, *The Eight Wilderness Discovery Books*, 1991.)

———. *The Cruise of the* Corwin. Boston: Houghton Mifflin, 1917.

———. *The Life and Letters of John Muir*. Ed. William Frederic Badè. 2 Vols. Boston: Houghton Mifflin, 1924.

———. *John of the Mountains: The Unpublished Journals of John Muir*. Edited by Linnie Marsh Wolfe. Boston: Houghton Mifflin, 1938; reprint, Madison: Univ. of Wisconsin Press, 1979

———. *To Yosemite and Beyond: Writings from the Years 1863 to 1875*. Edited by Robert Engberg and Donald Wesling. Madison: Univ. of Wisconsin Press, 1980.

———. *John Muir: The Eight Wilderness Discovery Books*. Introduction by Terry Gifford. London: Diadem Books, 1991 (includes *The Story of My Boyhood and Youth; A Thousand Mile Walk to the Gulf; My First Summer in the Sierra; The Mountains of California; Our National Parks; The Yosemite; Travels in Alaska;* and *Steep Trails*).

———. *John Muir: His Life and Letters and Other Writings*, ed. Terry Gifford. London: Baton Wicks, 1996.

Munz, Philip A. *A California Flora*. Berkeley: Univ. of California Press, 1959; 1968; 1973.

———. *Introduction to California Mountain Wildflowers*. Rev. ed. Phyllis M. Faber and Diane Lake. Berkeley: Univ. of California Press, 2003.

Munz, Philip A., and David D. Keck. *A California Flora*. Berkeley: Univ. of California Press, 1959.

Musgrave, Toby. *The Plant Hunters: Two Hundred Years of Adventure and Discovery around the World*. London: Ward Lock, 1998.

Nash, Gerald D. "The Conflict between Pure and Applied Science in Nineteenth Century Public Policy: The California State Geological Survey, 1860–1874." *Isis* 55 (1963): 217–228.

Nash, Roderick Frazier. *Wilderness and the American Mind*. 4th ed. New Haven: Yale Univ. Press, 2001.

Neal, Bill. *Gardener's Latin*. Chapel Hill: Algonquin Books, 2003.

Newcomb, Lawrence. *Newcomb's Wildflower Guide*. Boston: Little, Brown and Co., 1977.

Newcomb, Raymond L., and Richard W. Bliss. *Our Lost Explorers: The Narrative of the* Jeannette *Arctic Expedition*. Hartford: American Publishing, 1882.

Niklas, Karl J. *Plant Biomechanics: An Engineering Approach to Plant Form and Function.* Chicago: Univ. of Chicago Press, 1992.

Nilsson, Karen B. *A Wild Flower by Any Other Name: Sketches of Pioneer Naturalists Who Named Our Western Plants.* Yosemite National Park: Yosemite Association, 1994.

Noll, Mark A. "Common Sense Traditions and American Evangelical Thought." *American Quarterly* 37 (Spring 1985): 216–238.

Novak, Barbara. *Nature and Culture: American Landscape and Painting, 1825–1875.* New York: Oxford Univ. Press, 1980.

Nuttall, Thomas. *The North American Sylva.* 3 Vols. Philadelphia: Robert Smith, 1854.

Oelschlaeger, Max. *The Idea of Wilderness.* New Haven: Yale Univ. Press, 1991.

———. *The Wilderness Condition: Essays on Environment and Civilization,* 271–308. San Francisco: Sierra Club Books, 1992.

Oleson, Alexandra, and Sanborn C. Brown, eds. *The Pursuit of Knowledge in the Early American Republic: American Scientific and Learned Societies from Colonial Times to the Civil War.* Baltimore: Johns Hopkins Univ. Press, 1976.

Oleson, Alexandra, and John Voss, eds. *The Organization of Knowledge in Modern America, 1860–1920.* Baltimore: Johns Hopkins Univ. Press, 1979.

Olmsted, Frederick Law. *A Journey in the Back Country.* New York: Mason Brothers, 1860.

———. *The Cotton Kingdom: A Traveler's Observations on Cotton and Slavery in the American Slave States.* New York: Mason Brothers, 1861.

———. *Yosemite and the Mariposa Grove: A Preliminary Report, 1865.* Yosemite National Park: Yosemite Association (1865), 1995.

Ornduff, Robert. "Piss and Vinegar: Skeletons in Our Botanical Closet." *Fremontia* 28 (2000): 18–20.

Orr, Robert T., and Margaret C. Orr. *Wildflowers of Western America.* New York: Knopf, 1974.

Orth, Donald J. *Dictionary of Alaska Place Names.* Washington, D.C.: U.S. Government Printing Office, 1967.

Paley, William. *A View of the Evidences of Christianity.* New York: Griffin and Rudd, 1814.

———. *Natural Theology; or, Evidences of the Existence and Attributes of the Deity, Collected from the Appearances of Nature.* Boston: Gould and Lincoln, 1863.

Park, Mungo. *Travels in the Interior Districts of Africa.* Hertfordshire: Wordsworth Editions Limited, [1860], 2002.

Parry. C. C. "Herbarium Cases." *American Naturalist* 8 (1873): 471–473.

Parry, Joan. "Who First Discovered These Western Flowers?" *Pacific Discovery* 9 (1956): 12–20.

Parsons, Frances Theodora. *How to Know the Ferns: A Guide to the Names, Haunts, and Habits of Our Common Ferns.* New York: Charles Scribner's Sons, 1899.

———. *How to Know the Wild Flowers.* New York: Charles Scribner's Sons, 1928.

Parsons, Mary Elizabeth. *The Wildflowers of California: Their Names, Haunts, and Habits.* San Francisco: William Dexey, 1897.

Paruk, Jim. *Sierra Nevada Tree Identifier.* Yosemite National Park: Yosemite Association, 1997.

Peattie, Donald. *A Natural History of Western Trees.* Boston: Houghton Mifflin, 1950.

Penhallow, David P. *A Review of Canadian Botany from 1800 to 1895.* Ottawa: Royal Society of Canada, 1897.

Perry, Lewis. *Intellectual Life in America: A History.* New York: Franklin Watts, 1984.

Phillips, Venia T., and Maurice E. Phillips. *Guide to the Manuscript Collections in the Academy of Natural Sciences of Philadelphia.* Philadelphia: The Academy, 1963.

Pollan, Michael. *The Botany of Desire: A Plant's-Eye View of the World.* New York: Random House, 2001.

Pomeroy, Elizabeth. *John Muir: A Naturalist in Southern California*. Pasadena: Many Moons Press, 2001.

Prince, Sue Ann, ed. *Stuffing Birds, Pressing Plants, Shaping Knowledge: Natural History in North America, 1730–1860*. Philadelphia: American Philosophical Society, 2003.

Proctor, Samuel, ed. "Leaves From a Travel Diary: A Visit to Augusta and Savannah, 1882." *Georgia Historical Quarterly* 41 (1957): 309–315.

Pursh, Frederick. *Flora Americae Septentrionalis: or, A Systematic Arrangement and Description of the Plants of North America*. London: Printed for White, Cochrane and Co., 1814.

Quinn, D. Michael. "Religion in the American West." In *Under an Open Sky: Rethinking America's Western Past*, ed. William Cronon, George Miles, and Jay Gitlin, 145–166. New York: W. W. Norton & Co., 1992.

Reingold, Nathan. "Definitions and Speculations: The Professionalization of Science in America in the Nineteenth Century." In *The Pursuit of Knowledge in the Early American Republic: American Scientific and Learned Societies from Colonial Times to the Civil War*, ed. Alexandra Oleson and Sanborn C. Brown, 33–69. Baltimore: Johns Hopkins Univ. Press, 1976.

Reingold, Nathan, ed. *Science in Nineteenth-Century America: A Documentary History*. New York: Hill and Wang, 1964.

Rigal, Laura. *The American Manufactory: Art, Labor, and the World of Things in the Early Republic.* Princeton: Princeton Univ. Press, 1998.

Ritterbush, Philip C. *Overtures to Biology: The Speculations of Eighteenth-Century Naturalists*. New Haven: Yale Univ. Press, 1964.

Roberts, Patricia. "Reading the Writing on Nature's Wall." *Essays in Reader-Oriented Theory, Criticism, and Pedagogy* 18 (Fall 1987): 31–44.

Roberts, William. "The Campus Conservatory." *Chronicle of the University of California* 3 (2000): 27–28.

Rocco, Fiammetta. *The Miraculous Fever-Tree: Malaria and the Quest for a Cure that Changed the World*. New York: HarperCollins, 2003.

Roderick, Wayne. "Early Plant Explorers of the Pacific Coast." *Manzanita* 5 (2001): 1–7.

Rodgers, Andrew Denny III. *John Torrey: A Story of North American Botany*. Princeton: Princeton Univ. Press, 1942.

——— . *American Botany, 1873–1892: Decades of Transition*. Princeton: Princeton Univ. Press, 1944.

Rodgers, Daniel T. *The Work Ethic in Industrial America, 1850–1920*. Chicago: Univ. of Chicago Press, 1978.

Rossiter, Margaret W. *Women Scientists in America: Struggles and Strategies to 1948*. Baltimore: Johns Hopkins Univ. Press, 1982.

Rudolph, Emanuel D. "How It Developed That Botany Was the Science Thought Most Suitable for Victorian Young Ladies." In *Children's Literature*, ed. Francelia Butler, 92–97. Vol. 2. Philadelphia: Temple Univ. Press, 1975.

——— . "Women in Nineteenth Century American Botany: A Generally Unrecognized Constituency." *American Journal of Botany* 69 (September 1982): 1346–1355.

Runte, Alfred. *Yosemite: The Embattled Wilderness*. Lincoln: Univ. of Nebraska Press, 1990.

Sachs, Aaron. *The Humboldt Current. Nineteenth-Century Exploration and the Roots of American Environmentalism*. New York: Viking, 2006.

Sargent, Charles Sprague. *Report on the Forests of North America*. Washington, D.C.: Government Printing Office, 1884.

——— . *Garden and Forest. A Journal of Horticulture, Landscape Art and Forestry*. New York: The Garden and Forest Publishing Co., 1887–1897.

——— . *The Silva of North America: A Description of the Trees Which Grow Naturally in North America Exclusive of Mexico*. 14 Vols. Boston: Houghton Mifflin, 1891–1902.

———. *Manual of Trees of North America.* 2 Vols. 2d ed. New York: Houghton Mifflin, 1922.

Saunders, Charles F. *Western Wild Flowers and Their Stories.* Garden City: Doubleday, Doran and Co., 1933.

Saunders, Gill. *Picturing Plants: An Analytical History of Botanical Illustration.* Los Angeles: Univ. of California Press, 1995.

Schiebinger, Londa. *Nature's Body: Sexual Politics and the Making of Modern Science.* Cambridge: Harvard Univ. Press, 1994.

Schofield, Edmund A. "John Muir's Yankee Friends and Mentors: The New England Connection." *Pacific Historian* 29 (Summer-Fall 1985): 65–89.

Schuster, Rudolf Mathias. *The Hepaticae and Anthocerotae of North America East of the Hundredth Meridian.* 6 Vols. New York: Columbia Univ. Press, 1966–1992.

Seltzer, Leon E. *The Columbia Lippincott Gazetteer of the World.* Morningside Heights, N.Y.: Columbia Univ. Press, 1952.

Shi, David E. *The Simple Life: Plain Living and High Thinking in American Culture.* New York: Oxford Univ. Press, 1985.

———. *Facing Facts: Realism in American Thought and Culture, 1850–1920.* New York: Oxford Univ. Press, 1995.

Shteir, Ann B. *Cultivating Women, Cultivating Science: Flora's Daughters and Botany in England, 1760 to 1860.* Baltimore: Johns Hopkins Univ. Press, 1996.

Simpson, John Warfield. *Yearning for the Land: A Search for the Importance of Place.* New York: Pantheon Books, 2002.

Slack, Nancy M. "Botanical Explorations of California: From Menzies to Muir." In *John Muir: Life and Work,* ed. Sally M. Miller, 194–242. Albuquerque: Univ. of New Mexico Press, 1993.

Small, John Kunkel. *Flora of the Southeastern United States.* New York: John Kunkel Small, 1903.

Smallwood, William Martin, and Mabel Sarah Coon Smallwood. *Natural History and the American Mind.* New York: Columbia Univ. Press, 1941.

Smith, J. E. *A Selection of the Correspondence of Linnaeus, and Other Naturalists, from the Original Manuscripts.* 2 Vols. London: Longman, Hurst, Rees, Orme, and Brown, 1821.

Smith, Michael L. *Pacific Visions: California Scientists and the Environment, 1850–1915.* New Haven: Yale Univ. Press, 1987.

Stacey, Robyn, and Ashley Hay. *Herbarium.* Cambridge: Cambridge Univ. Press, 2004.

Stadtman, Verne A. *The University of California, 1868–1968.* New York: McGraw Hill, 1970.

Stanley, Millie. *The Heart of John Muir's World: Wisconsin, Family and Wilderness Discovery.* Madison, Wisc.: Prairie Oak Press, 1995.

Starr, Kevin. *Americans and the California Dream, 1850–1915.* New York: Oxford Univ. Press, 1973.

Stephens, Lester D. *Joseph LeConte: Gentle Prophet of Evolution.* Baton Rouge: Louisiana State Univ. Press, 1982.

Stevenson, George B. *Palms of South Florida.* N.p.: George B. Stevenson, 1974.

Stock, Eleanor B. "Trees Came First." *The Christian Home* (May 1967): 32–35, 63–64.

Stoddard, Richard Henry. *The Life, Travels, and Books of Alexander von Humboldt.* New York: Rudd and Carleton, 1859.

Stoll, Mark. "God and John Muir: A Psychological Interpretation of John Muir's Journey from the Campbellites to the 'Range of Light.'" In *John Muir: Life and Works,* ed. Sally M. Miller, 65–81. Albuquerque: Univ. of New Mexico Press, 1993.

———. *Protestantism, Capitalism, and Nature in America.* Albuquerque: Univ. of New Mexico Press, 1997.

Stuckey, Ronald L., ed. *Development of Botany in Selected Regions of North America Before 1900.* New York: Arno Press, 1978.

Taylor, Judith M., and Harry Morton Butterfield. *Tangible Memories: Californians and Their Gardens, 1800–1950*. Philadelphia: Xlibris, 2003.

Teute, Fredrika J. "The Loves of the Plants; or, the Cross-Fertilization of Science and Desire at the End of the Eighteenth Century." *The Huntington Library Quarterly* 63 (2000): 319–345.

Thoreau, Henry David. *The Succession of Forest Trees and Wild Apples. With a Biographical Sketch by Ralph Waldo Emerson*. Boston: Houghton Mifflin, 1863.

———. *Excursions*. Boston: Ticknor and Fields, 1863.

———. *The Maine Woods*. Princeton: Princeton Univ. Press, 1972.

———. *A Week on the Concord and Merrimack Rivers*. Edited by Carl F. Hovde, William L. Howarth, and Elizabeth Hall Witherell. Princeton: Princeton Univ. Press, 2004.

Thwaites, Reuben Gold, ed. *The University of Wisconsin: Its History and Its Alumni*. Madison: J. N. Purcell, 1900.

Torrey, John, and Asa Gray. *A Flora of North America*. 2 Vols. New York: Hafner Publishing Co., (1838–1843), 1969.

Trelease, William, et al. *Alaska: Cryptogamic Botany*. Harriman Alaska Expedition Series, 375–397. Vol. 5. New York: Doubleday, Page and Co., 1904.

Tresidder, Mary Curry. *The Trees of Yosemite*. Stanford: Stanford Univ. Press, 1932.

Turner, Frederick. *Rediscovering America: John Muir in His Times and Ours*. New York: Viking Press, 1985.

Turner, Tom. *Sierra Club: 100 Years of Protecting Nature*. New York: Harry N. Abrams, Inc., 1991.

Turrill, W. B. *Joseph Dalton Hooker: Botanist, Explorer, and Administrator*. London: Thomas Nelson and Sons, 1963.

Uhl, Natalie W., and John Dransfield, Jr. *Genera Palmarum: A Classification of Palms Based on the Work of Harold E. Moore, Jr.* Lawrence, Kan.: Allen Press, 1987.

Vale, Thomas R., and Geraldine R. Vale. *Walking with Muir across Yosemite*. Madison: Univ. of Wisconsin Press, 1998.

Vines, Robert A. *Trees, Shrubs and Woody Vines of the Southwest*. Austin: Univ. of Texas Press, 1960.

Vitt, Dale H., Janet E. Marsh, and Robin B. Bovey. *Mosses, Lichens and Ferns of Northwest North America*. Seattle: Univ. of Washington Press, 1988.

Wadden, Kathleen Anne. "John Muir and the Community of Nature." *Pacific Historian* 29 (Summer-Fall 1985): 94–102.

Wallace, Alfred Russel. *Palm Trees of the Amazon and Their Uses*. London: John Van Voorst, 1853.

Walls, Laura Dassow. *Seeing New Worlds: Henry David Thoreau and Nineteenth-Century Natural Sciences*. Madison: Univ. of Wisconsin Press, 1995.

Walter, Thomas. *Flora Caroliniana*. London: J. Fraser, 1788.

Watson, Sereno. *Botany of California*. Vol. 2. Boston: Little, Brown, and Co., 1880.

White, Richard. "Discovering Nature in North America." *Journal of American History* 79 (December 1992): 874–891.

Wiebe, Robert H. *The Search for Order, 1877–1920*. New York: Hill & Wang, 1967.

Wieland, George R. "Origin of Angiosperms." *Nature* 131 (1933): 360–361.

Williams, Dennis C. "John Muir, Christian Mysticism, and the Spiritual Value of Nature." In *John Muir: Life and Works*, ed. Sally M. Miller, 83–99. Albuquerque: Univ. of New Mexico Press, 1993.

———. *God's Wilds: John Muir's Vision of Nature*. College Station: Texas A & M Univ. Press, 2002.

Williams, John G., and Andrew E. Williams. *Field Guide to Orchids of North America*. New York: Universe Books, 1983.

Williams, Michael. *Deforesting the Earth: From Prehistory to Global Crisis*. Chicago: Univ. of Chicago Press, 2003.

Wilson, Amie Marie, and Mandi Dale Johnson. *Images of America. Historic Bonaventure Cemetery: Photographs from the Collection of the Georgia Historical Society*. Charleston, S.C.: Arcadia Publishing, 1998.

Wilson, Leonard G. "The Emergence of Geology as a Science in the United States." *Journal of World History* 10 (1967): 416–437.

Wilson, Lynn, Jim Wilson, and Jeff Nicholas. *Wildflowers of Yosemite*. El Portal: Sierra Press, (1987), 1998.

Wolfe, Linnie Marsh. *Son of the Wilderness: The Life of John Muir*. Madison: Univ. of Wisconsin Press, 1945.

Wood, Alphonso. *First Lessons in Botany*. Boston: Crocker and Brewster, 1843.

———. *Leaves and Flowers: or, Object Lessons in Botany*. A. S. Barnes and Co., 1860.

———. *Class-Book of Botany: Being Outlines of the Structure, Physiology, and Classification of Plants; with a Flora of the United States and Canada*. New York: A. S. Barnes and Burr, 1861.

Worsdell, W. C. "The Origin of the 'Flower.'" *Science Progress* 2 (1907): 255–262.

Worster, Donald. *Nature's Economy: A History of Ecological Ideas*. New York: Cambridge Univ. Press, 1977.

Wright, Ellen. *Elizur Wright's Appeals for the Middlesex Fells and the Forests with a Sketch of What He Did for Both*. Boston: George H. Ellis, 1893.

Young, Samuel Hall. *Alaska Days with John Muir*. New York: Fleming H. Revell, 1915; reprint, Salt Lake City: Peregrine Smith, 1990.

———. *Hall Young of Alaska, "The Mushing Parson": The Autobiography of S. Hall Young*. New York: Fleming H. Revell, 1927.

# INDEX

# ABOUT THE AUTHORS

BONNIE JOHANNA GISEL is an environmental historian and the curator at the Sierra Club's LeConte Memorial Lodge in Yosemite National Park. She is the editor of *Kindred & Related Spirits: The Letters of John Muir and Jeanne C. Carr* (University of Utah Press, 2001) and *Nature Journaling with John Muir* (Poetic Matrix Press, 2006), and she has published articles and lectured extensively on John Muir as well as published articles about her personal journey in wilderness, and lectured on issues of environmental awareness and environmental literacy. Gisel taught in the Caspersen School of Graduate Studies at Drew University and at Green Mountain College, and she was the interim director of the John Muir Center for Environmental Studies at the University of the Pacific. The recipient of the 2006 John Muir Conservation Award from the John Muir Association at the John Muir National Historic Site, Gisel received a Master of Divinity degree from Harvard University and a PhD from Drew University, and also earned two degrees in fine art.

STEPHEN J. JOSEPH has been a photographer for over forty years. His diverse skills range from creating daguerreotypes to modern digital photography. His subject matter includes twenty-five years of photographing Mount Diablo and the surrounding Bay Area, his California Artist Studio Series, his historical photographic essay of Oneonta, New York, and his work supporting open space. After receiving his MFA from the California College of Arts and Crafts, he taught there and at Hartwick College. Joseph has had numerous exhibits of his work, including at the Oakland Museum of California, the Fine Arts Museums of San Francisco Legion of Honor, the Ansel Adams Gallery, and the LeConte Memorial Lodge in Yosemite National Park. His work has been widely collected, most notably by the Achenbach Foundation, the East Bay Regional Park District, numerous California environmental organizations, the Save Mount Diablo land trust, and various private collections. Joseph has also been honored as the Centennial Photographer for the Muir Woods National Monument, Artist in Residence for Yosemite's LeConte Memorial Lodge, scenic set designer for the George Coates Performance Works in San Francisco, and as a member of the board of directors for Save Mount Diablo. He currently lives in the Bay Area with his wife and son.